Textbook of Fish Production and Hygiene

The Authors

Dr. Ashwani Kumar, M.V.Sc., Ph.D., FIAVPHS is Professor, Veterinary Public Health at College of Veterinary Medicine and Agriculture, Addis Ababa University, Bishoftu, Ethiopia. He has earlier worked as Professor at College of Veterinary Medicine, Mekelle University, Mekelle, Ethiopia and as Professor and Head of Department of Veterinary Public Health, College of Veterinary Sciences, LUVAS, Hisar, India. He has a vast experience of teaching and research in various capacities in India and Ethiopia.

Dr. Niraj Kumar is Associate Professor in Animal Production Team in College of Veterinary Medicine, Mekelle University, Mekelle since 2010. He has worked as Veterinary Doctor in quarantine sector for six years in several Middle East and African countries.

Dr. Etsay Kebede Assefa is Associate Professor in Parasitology and Animal Production and is former Department Head of Livestock Resources and Fishery and Regional Veterinary Laboratory in Tigray Bureau of Agriculture and Natural Resource; Department Head of Pathobiology and Infectious Diseases and Veterinary Medicine and Team Leader in Training and Education in Center of Extension and Consultancy in College of Veterinary Medicine, Mekelle University, Ethiopia. He is engaged in teaching fishery and aquaculture at Ayder subcity, Mekelle, Ethiopia.

Dr. S. R. Garg, M.V.Sc., Ph.D., FIAVPHS is Professor in the Department of Veterinary Public Health and Epidemiology and Director, Institute of Para Veterinary Sciences in the Lala Lajpat Rai University of Veterinary and Animal Sciences, Hisar (India). He has 35 years experience of teaching, research and extension education in the field of Veterinary Sciences. He has published 10 books from various internationally acclaimed publishing houses.

Textbook of Fish Production and Hygiene

Ashwani Kumar

Niraj Kumar

Etsay Kebede Assefa

Sudhi Ranjan Garg

2018

Daya Publishing House®

A Division of

Astral International Pvt. Ltd.

New Delhi - 110 002

ISBN: 9789387057289 (Int. Edition)

Published by : **Daya Publishing House®**
A Division of
Astral International Pvt. Ltd.
– ISO 9001:2015 Certified Company –
4736/23, Ansari Road, Darya Ganj
New Delhi-110 002
Ph. 011-43549197, 23278134
E-mail: info@astralint.com
Website: www.astralint.com

Preface

Food security and nutrition represent a global challenge. Despite vigorous efforts to alleviate hunger and malnutrition, the situation in many parts of the world is gloomy. According to the State of Food Insecurity in the World 2015, almost 780 million people still remain undernourished. Fisheries and aquaculture constitute important sources of food and nutrition. Dramatic growth in aquaculture production during the last two decades has boosted average consumption of fish and fishery products across the countries. According to the FAO's report 'The State of World Fisheries and Aquaculture 2016: Contributing to food security and nutrition for all', the global per capita annual fish consumption increased from 9.9 kg in the 1960s to 14.4 kg in the 1990s and 19.7 kg in 2013. Fish accounted for about 17% of the global population's intake of animal protein and 6.7% of all protein consumed in 2013. Due to vigorous growth in aquaculture, per capita fish supply in the world attained a new record high of 20 kg in 2014. It provided more than 3.1 billion people with almost 20% of their average per capita intake of animal protein. Though there has been a steady rise in annual per capita consumption of fish in developing countries from 5.2 kg in 1961 to 18.8 kg in 2013 and in low income food-deficit countries from 3.5 to 7.6 kg, it is far behind the industrialized nations which recorded the annual per capita fish consumption as 26.8 kg in 2013.

The share of aquaculture in total fishery production has shown substantial growth. Recent developments indicate that aquaculture will increasingly be the main driver of change in the fisheries and aquaculture sector. In 2010, global production of farmed food fish was 59.9 million tonnes (mt) which surged to 73.8 mt in the year 2014 with an estimated first sale value of US$160.2 bn. It surpassed the quantum of wild-caught fish for the first time. Consequently, aquaculture now provides half of all fish for human consumption and it is expected to reach 102 mt by 2025.

Besides contributing to the global food and nutritional security, fisheries and aquaculture provide a source of income and livelihoods to millions of people round the globe. According to the FAO's report, an estimated 56.6 million people were engaged in the primary sector of fish production in 2014. Of these, an estimated 18 million (33%) were involved in fish farming, the highest number being primarily in Asia (94%), followed by Latin America and the Caribbean (1.9%, 3.5 million people) and Africa (1.4%, 2.6 million people). Fish is among the most traded food commodities worldwide. Its trade creates huge avenues for employment, income generation, economic growth and development. Developing countries are indeed the most potential gainers from fish trade and exports. The exports from developing economies represented just 37% of world trade in 1976, which in 2014 increased to 54% of total fishery export value and 60% of the quantity (live weight).

It is anticipated that in future almost all of the increase in aquaculture production will originate from developing countries. However, the task is quite challenging for such largely resource constrained regions. Highly perishable nature of fish makes it quite vulnerable to rapid spoilage and becoming unsafe for human consumption resulting in wastage and loss.

To face the challenges of the competitive environment in trade, strict national and international regulations for food safety and the unprecedented consumers' demand for quality assurance, it is imperative that the students of veterinary, fishery and agricultural sciences and the professionals engaged in fish production are thoroughly acquainted with the modern techniques of hygienic fish production, post-harvest handling, processing, preservation, packaging and storage. They also need to have excellent knowledge of the health hazards associated with substandard products and the advanced methods of quality control and quality assurance of foods.

This book represents a humble effort in this direction. Written in simple language, it deals with the basic principles of establishment of a new fish farm, its management, good practices and ideal conditions for optimum production of fish. Important infectious and non-infectious diseases of fish have been amply elaborated along with methods of their diagnosis, prevention and control. Great emphasis has been given to the hygienic aspects in fish production and quality assurance of fish as food. The diseases transmissible to consumers through unhygienic fish and fish products are also highlighted. The authors earnestly believe that this book will provide a unique resource for the students, educators and the professionals.

Ashwani Kumar

Niraj Kumar

Etsay Kebede Assefa

Sudhi Ranjan Garg

Contents

1

Fish Versus Higher Vertebrates

Fish is a red blooded, back boned animal which lives in water throughout its life. Its body is typically covered with scales. It breathes by means of gills and propels itself by sinuous movement of its body, and by fins, which are the balancing organs. However, the word fish has been associated with quite a few unrelated animals that from zoological point of view are not fishes at all *e.g.* jelly fishes, cray fishes, star fishes, cuttle fishes. Five vertebrate classes have species which could be called fish, but only two of these groups, namely, the sharks and rays, and the bony fish are generally important and widely distributed in the aquatic environment.

Fish are the most numerous of the vertebrates, with at least 20,000 known species, and more than half (58%) are found in the marine environment. They are most common in the warm and temperate waters of the continental shelves (some 8,000 species). About 1,100 species are found in the cold polar waters. In the oceanic pelagic environment, well away from the effect of land, only about 225 species occur. Surprisingly, the number of species increases in the deeper mesopelagic zone of the pelagic environment (between 100 and 1,000 m depth). There are about 1,000 species of the so called mid-water fish (Thurman and Webber, 1984).

Classification

Phylum: Chordata

Subphylum I: Protochordata

Class 1: Hemichordata

Class 2: Urochordata

Class 3: Cephalochordata

Subphylum II: Vertebrata

Class I: Pisces including Cyclostomata (Fishes come under it.)

Class II: Amphibia (Frogs and toads)

Class III: Reptilia (Reptiles)

Class IV: Aves (birds)

Class V: Mammalia (Mammals)

Fish is the lowest class of vertebrates belonging to the subkingdom Chordate, distinguished by three half-marks as (i) presence of a series of disc- like bones, supporting the back column or its precursor, the notochord; (ii) presence of a dorsal, tubular nerve cord, ending in a complex brain; and (iii) the mouth passage perforated by clefts; the gill slits at some stage or other in the life of the individual.

Fishes of the Present Day World

These may be broadly grouped into three important subclasses:

1. **Cyclostomes/Agnathan:** These are cup-shape (round) mouthed fishes which lack true jaws and the paired fins. They also lack the internal skeleton system. They have a circular toothed mouth (cyclostomic) by which they bore the body of their victim and suck their blood. These have 7-14 pairs of gills. These are classified into two major types, Lampreys and Hag fishes which are found in deep seas.
2. **Chondrichthyes/Cartilaginous fishes:** These comprise sharks, skate, rays and allied fishes. Internal skeleton in these remains cartilaginous throughout their life, bone being absent. Peculiar features in their anatomy are: body is covered by microscopic, teeth like scales, and the gill slit opens directly outside i.e. gills are not covered with gill cover. They have high urea content in their muscles. Most of them are carnivorous and ferocious creatures armed with large cutting teeth.
3. **Osteichthyes/Teleostei:** These are called bony fishes because bone is the chief tissue of skeleton with numerous vertebrae. Mucous glands and embedded dermal scales are present in the skin. These fishes have paired fins; jaws are present; gill arches support the gills; and these are protected by the operculum. They comprise a higher group and have three subdivisions listed below.
   i. **Lobe fins (Crossopterygia):** In these, there is presence of a prominent muscular basal lobe in the pectoral and pelvic fins; tailfin is trilobed.
   ii. **Lungfishes (Dipnoi):** Few fishes have developed lung-like structures which enable them to take in oxygen from atmosphere or air when

they come to surface for breathing. They are valuable food fishes. Being sluggish they are easily captured.

iii. **Modern teleostei (teleostei):** The modern bony fishes are grouped under Teleostei which means that their endoskeleton is totally bony without any trace of cartilage. They have their origin about 60-120 million years ago. They are thin and have round and overlapping scales. Fan shaped fins supported by segmented fin-rays, equally lobed and tail fins are the characteristic features.

Teleostei is a very diverse group inhabiting rivers, lakes, estuaries and seas. Ninety percent of fishes belong to this group. These are divided into 40 or more orders but 4 of them listed below embrace most of the familiar fishes.

Order I: Isopondyli (Clupiformis): They are highly esteemed as food and are commercially important in Europe, America and Japan. Examples include Sardines, Herring, Salmon, Hilsa and Chano.

Order II: Osteriophysi (Cypriniformis): These are scaleless fresh water fishes of rivers and lakes. Very few are found in seas. The unique feature is the presence of the Westerian apparatus which consists of chain of four small bones connecting the front portion of the swim bladder to the back of inner ear. They are considered to have a sense of hearing. Examples are carps, loaches. In India, Rohu, Mrigal, Mahasar, Catfishes are common.

Order III: Acanthopterigii (Perciformis): Prominent needle like spines in the fins are characteristic of these fishes and that is why these are known as spiny-finned fishes. They dominate the shallow and deep columns of the sea. Examples are Pearches and their allies.

Order IV: Heterrosomata (Pleuronectiformes): It is a highly specialized group of 60 or odd species, commonly called flat fishes or tongue fishes. They are sluggish and become adapted to living at the bottom. Examples are Flounders, Soles and Halibut.

Characteristic features of fish

- Purely aquatic, cold blooded creatures
- Breathing oxygen dissolved in water through gills
- Devoid of typical lungs (exception)
- Skin covered with protective scales and abundantly coated with mucus
- Organs of smell, sight and hearing found in head
- Eyes devoid of eyelids
- Ears without external or middle parts and sunken within the skull bones.
- Most fish lays eggs which hatch directly into larvae. Few bring forth alive their young ones, which develop for a period in the uterus of the mother.

Table 1.1 Fish versus mammals

Fish	Mammals
Fishes constitute the first evolved vertebrates. The number of fish species is comparatively higher (many groups with about 32,000 extant species) to mammals	Mammals evolved with birds, from the reptiles and more evolved than the fish. The most evolved group of animals is the mammals with more than 5650 extant species.
The fish live totally in water.	Mammals are mostly terrestrial.
They are cold-blooded i.e. change the body temperature with the environmental temperature.	They are warm-blooded, that means body temperature of mammals is maintained at a constant level without changing according to the environmental temperature.
All types of fish are not bony.	There is a bony skeleton in all mammals, and sometimes there are cartilaginous structures present within bones.
Fish has scaly body, laterally flattened body and fins. The fins are the structures for their locomotion.	The mammals have hairy body, not flattened, and mostly four-legged in the body forms.
Usually, the oxygen intake occurs through gills which are present throughout the lifespan.	The oxygen intake is through lungs. Although the gills are present during the foetal stage yet after birth the lungs become functional until the death.
The skin of fish is covered with scales and there is a lateral line present on a series of scales. The lateral line is sensitive for the water movements which is useful for their lifestyle.	The skin of mammals is covered with hairs and the skin has sweat glands.
Some fish species demonstrate parental care which is otherwise a feature associated with higher vertebrates. Scientists have discovered that some fish species communicate via sounds which cannot be heard by humans.	Mammals have mammary glands that function to feed the newborns. Due to the presence of mammary glands and some other characteristic behavioural features mammals care for their young ones with great courage and love.

Reference

Thurman H. V. and Webber H. H. (1984). Marine Biology. Scott, Foresman and Company, pp. 446.

2
Fish Anatomy

The shape and structure of the fish body have evolved through the stress and strain of the watery environment. The body is bilaterally symmetrical which is pointed at both ends. The head end is thicker, while the middle part gradually tapers to a thin caudal end. The anatomy of fish can be described as external structure and internal structure.

External structures

Although the fish of various types have their own characteristics of identification, yet some of them are common. All species have crania, back bone (both as a prerequisite of vertebrate animals), and possess gills and fins. The fish body comprises head, trunk and tail. In the head region, there is a snout, mouth, operculum to cover gills, eyes and in some cases barbells (sensory structures). Basic structures on the trunk part are lateral line, vent (anus), urogenital opening and a group of fins, notably the dorsal, pelvic and pectoral fins. The predominant components of tail region are the caudal fins and propulsive musculature (Fig. 2.1).

Skin: The external surface of fish is covered with a waterproof skin, which consists of two layers, viz., outer epidermis, inner dermis followed by muscles. The epidermis is usually extremely thin comprising up to 30 layers of cells with an average thickness of 250 µm. Some of the epidermal cells function as unicellular mucoid glands that secrete glycoproteins rich in mucus (slime). One of the mucus's major functions is its protective role to prevent bacteria from gaining an intimate contact with the living epidermal cells. Mucus glands constantly pour their secretions making the skin shiny. The dermis is significantly thicker than the epidermis and consists of connective tissues with few cells. It contains pigment cells, blood vessels, nerves and the derma; skeleton comprising scales/ plates.

Scales: Fishes, with the notable exception of catfish, are covered with scales that are located on whole or some parts of the surface. If scales are damaged or lost, organisms invade the underlying tissues.

Lateral line: The lateral line, found alongside a fish's body from the operculum to the tail (caudal fin), senses vibrations or movements in the water. It allows fish to locate predators and find prey. This system is made up of a series of fluid-filled canals just below the skin of the fish's head and alongside the body. The canals are filled with tiny hair-like structures that detect changes in the water pressure via tiny pores connected to the system.

Eyes: Eyes are the most noticeable sense organs in a fish. They are prominent, round/oval/elliptical structures situated on either side of the head. The fish eye comprises an anterior chamber with iris, and a spherical lens and a posterior chamber containing the vitreous humour lined by retina. The eye is flattened anteriorly so that the lens is almost in contact with cornea. Fish eyes differ from that of other vertebrates because it has to see under the water. Lens is round instead of flat or concave. Iris and diaphragm have little power of contraction. Eye lid, eye lashes and tear glands are absent. Vision of fish eye is monocular instead of binocular as in higher vertebrates. Main difference lies in mechanism of focusing. Mammalian eye changes the curvature of the lens, the fish eye changes the distance between lens and retina, like an adjustable camera.

Ears: There is no external and middle ear. Fish have internal ears with pairs of inner ear bones called otoliths that allow fish to sense sounds in the water.

Operculum: The operculum is the bony flap that protects the gills from harm. It opens and closes to allow water to pass over the gills.

Fins: They are meant for balancing in water. They are pectoral, dorsal, pelvic and anal fins. In some fishes, fins are enormously expanded and act as wings like in flying fishes. These types of fishes are commonly found in open oceans and can fly and span a distance of 200-400 meters at a speed of 10-20 meters/second.

Barbels: They are the "whiskers" found on the head area of fish such as catfish or bullheads. On the catfish and bullheads, barbels are thought to be a sensory organ to help track down prey or food. Sturgeon also has barbels.

Vent: The vent removes waste and extra water. It is also the outlet for eggs or milt (sperm) during spawning.

Internal structures

The skeleton

Being vertebrates, fish have a vertebral column and a cranium covering the brain. The backbone runs from the head to the tail fin and is composed of segments (vertebrae). These vertebrae are extended dorsally to form neural spines, and in the trunk region they have lateral processes that bear ribs. The ribs are cartilaginous or bony structures in the connective tissue (myocommata) between the muscle segments (myotomes). Usually, there are also a corresponding number of false ribs or "pin bones" extending more or less horizontally into the muscle tissue. These bones cause a great deal of trouble when fish are being filleted or otherwise prepared for food.

Muscle

Muscle anatomy in fish is different from that of terrestrial mammals. There is no tendinous system. Instead the muscle fibers run parallel and are connected to sheaths of connective tissue which in turn are anchored to the skeleton and the skin of fish. The bundles of muscle cells are called myotomes while sheaths of connective tissue as myocommata. All muscle cells run parallel with the longitudinal direction of the fish. The muscle mass on each side of the fish makes up the fillet, of which the upper part is termed the dorsal muscle and the lower part the ventral muscle.

As in mammals, fish has striated muscles. Each cell consists of sarcoplasma containing nuclei and other cellular structures including a number of myofibrils which in turn contain contractile proteins, actin and myosin. The muscle cell is surrounded by sheath of connective tissue called as sarcolemma.

Color of muscle tissue in most of the fish is white but many of them have dark tissue of a brown or reddish colour. The reddish meat coloration in fish is due to myoglobin but in some fish due to the red carotenoid, astaxanthin. The dark muscle has higher levels of lipids and myoglobin and more likely to cause technical problem of rancidity.

Alimentary tract: It starts from the mouth and ends at the anus. The size of the mouth varies from species to species of fish. The esophagus is short and allows the passage of large particles of food into the stomach. The stomach joins through a one way valve (pylorus) into the intestine with its pyloric caeca and thence to the anus (Fig. 2.2).

Gills: Gills are the feathery tissue structure that allows fish to breathe in water. Water flows in through their mouth and over their gills where oxygen is extracted and passed into the bloodstream.

Breathing structures: The breathing apparatus of a bony fish consists of the mouth cavity, throat or pharynx with its gills and the gill covering or operculum. One of the distinguishing features of fishes is their ability to breathe oxygen dissolved in water. Gills are the main breathing organs in most of the fishes and are feather like organs, richly supplied with blood capillaries for the exchange of oxygen and carbon dioxide. They are found in the pharyngeal region of the gut and are protected externally by the operculum and internally by the gill rakers. These structures direct the food particles down the throat rather than on the gills. Gills are breathed by water currents drawn through the mouth and blood exchanges its $CO2$ for oxygen contained in the water. In bony fish, there are usually four gills on each side of the pharynx or throat.

Fishes with lungs: Lung fishes belong to the class Dipnoi. The so called lung is a single spacious sac, which extends from one end of the abdomen cavity to the other. On its inner surface, run two longitudinal fibrous bands which project slightly into the lung cavity. The longitudinal bands give rise to transverse bands or septa on either side, thus subdividing the cavity into a series of alveoli. The lungs, through a pneumatic duct, open into the ventral side of the esophagus by a small glottis.

Brain: It lies in the cavity of the neurocranium and is protected by bone or cartilage, surrounding meninges and cerebral fluid and by fat that fills most of the cranial cavity. A spinal cord leaves the brain, progressing through the vertebrae.

Organs of hearing: Only internal ear is fully developed. Fishes are able to recognize sound waves conducted through water more sharply than through air.

Organs of smell: The olfactory organs of fishes are paired cup-like organs which have no connection with mouth as in higher animals. The organ may consist of a single chamber (sharks and rays) or double chamber separated by a septum (bony fishes).

Organ of taste: Fishes have no tongue in true sense. Some fish have taste buds; however, these taste buds are located on the outside of the fish's head and fins in small pores. Some fish like catfish have a very developed sense of taste.

Air bladder/Swim bladder: A large majority of fishes have devices to float which is hidden within the top of the body cavity between the backbone on one side and the gut and other organs on the side. The float is a silver white bladder- like structure filled with air and therefore popularly referred to as air bladder or swim bladder. It serves for hydrostatic balancing, sound production and reception (Fig. 2.2).

Heart: In fish, the heart has one atrium and one ventricle. The oxygen-depleted blood that returns from the body enters the atrium, and then the ventricle, and is then pumped out to the gills where the blood is oxygenated, and then it continues through the rest of the body.

Liver: It is a large, caramel-brown coloured gland, comprising up to 20% of body weight of some of the fishes like sharks. The liver is usually bi-lobed and located in intimate contact with stomach. In most fishes a gall bladder is also present.

Spleen: It is a dark brown red structure that is positioned behind the stomach or adjacent to the intestine.

Kidneys: Kidney is usually a long, slender dark brown-red organ which extends along the dorsal part of the body, just behind the vertebrae. The kidneys are paired, head kidney and posterior kidney, but are very close together and may be fused along the middle line. The head kidney is found just above the gills as a homogenous organ and is the site of antibody production and the parasites are seldom if ever found. The posterior kidney is located just below the spinal column. Swim bladder must be removed to expose it. Hematopoietic, renal and endocrine tissues are found in the kidney. Divalent ions are excreted principally from the kidney and monovalent ions and nitrogenous excretions from the gills. Accordingly lesions of kidneys and gills seriously interfere with respiration, excretion and fluid balance.

Gonads: The paired ovaries or testes are usually elongated structures suspended from the dorsal part of the abdominal cavity. At sexual maturity, they extend along the entire length of the abdomen. Roe is the mass of eggs contained in the ovaries of a female fish or shellfish, especially when ripe and used as food; the full ovaries themselves.

Other structures: Fishes lack organized lymph nodes and Kuppfer cells. Phagocytic tissue is located in the atrium of heart and hematopoietic tissue of spleen and kidney.

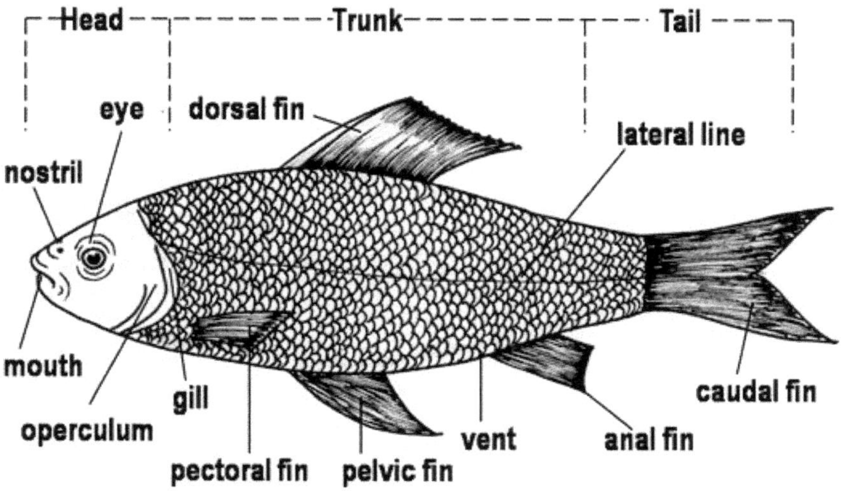

Fig. 2.1. External anatomy of fish

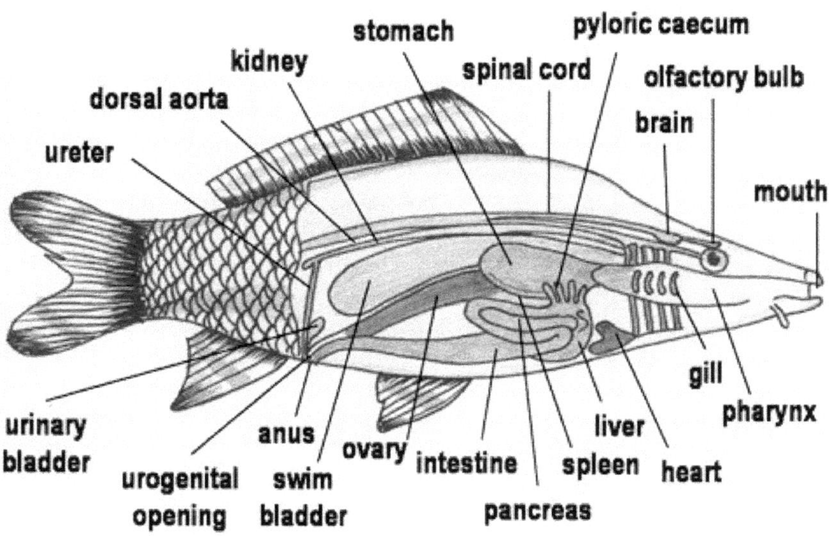

Fig. 2.2. Internal anatomy of fish

3

Fresh Water Fishes

The fresh water fishes are of two different types: 1) The fish having scales on the body, called Cyprinids; and 2) the fish having no scale on body, called Silurids. The latter type of fish differs from the former in also having second dorsal fin on the body just behind the main dorsal fin in the form of small muscular structure.

On the basis of water temperature, fresh water fishes are broadly grouped into two: a) Cold water fishes; and b) Warm Water Fishes

A. Cold Water Fishes: The fishes which prefer to live in lower water temperature are called cold water fishes. Among their many varieties, *Schizothorax* spp., locally known as Sawati, and *Tor* spp., locally called Mahaseer, are very popular and are distributed in the cold waters (Fig. 3.1). The former species is very famous for its taste while the later one is known for angling than for its taste.

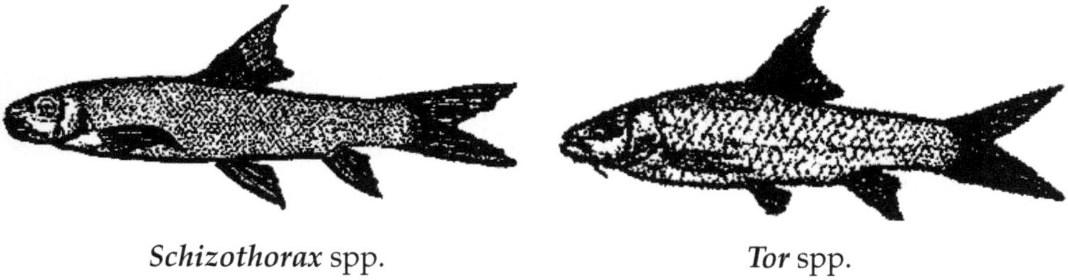

Schizothorax spp. *Tor* spp.

Fig. 3.1. Cold water fishes

B. Warm Water Fishes: The fishes preferring to live in warm waters of the warmer climatic regions are called warm water fishes. Among these, Rohu, Mori and Thaila are abundantly distributed in the rivers, streams and reservoirs (Fig. 3.2, 3.3, 3.4). All these species are famous for their taste. Besides these, many other fishes like Wallgoo attu, *Mystus singhala*, locally known as Molli and Singhada respectively, are available in the warm waters.

Cultivable Fish Species

There are 40 different species of fresh water fishes. All these different kinds of fish are not useful to culture in the pond. The cold water fishes grow very slow. Thus they turn out very expensive to the mass of the people. Therefore, certain species of fish having different cultivable characters are selected for culture to increase fish production.

The cultivable fish species may be carnivorous, herbivorous or omnivorous. The production of carnivorous fish turns out expensive but the herbivorous and omnivorous fishes are easily cultured together and these fishes are mostly of Carp family and are called Cyprinids. In culture practice mostly fishes of Carp family are cultured around the world as they do not disturb the others, grow fast and give good production. Therefore, they are called cultivable fishes. The fishes of Carp family are mostly big in size. The body is covered with small or big scales. They are either herbivorous which feeds on phytoplankton, algae, grasses and zooplankton and the omnivorous fish feeds on anything like decomposed materials, insects and its larvae as well as any supplementary feed made available in the pond.

Amongst the Carps, there are two groups of fishes: i) indigenous fishes like Rohu, Mori and Thaila that are widely distributed in the Indian Subcontinent including India, Nepal, Bangladesh, Bhutan and Pakistan; and ii) exotic fishes such as Common Carp, Silver Carp, Grass Carp and Bighead Carp. The indigenous fishes are called Indian Major Carps while those belonging to the exotic group are from China and are called Chinese Carps. These two groups of fish are cultured together in a pond and give high production per water unit areas.

Rohu

Its body is elongated and cylindrical. The big fishes may attain 2'-3' length. Compared to its body size the head is small. At the anterior end of the head, there is mouth which is characterised by thick and fringed lip. The fish has big reddish eyes on both sides of the head. The whole body is covered with big sized scales. The upper side of the body is brownish while the ventral or abdomen portion is whitish (Fig. 3.2).

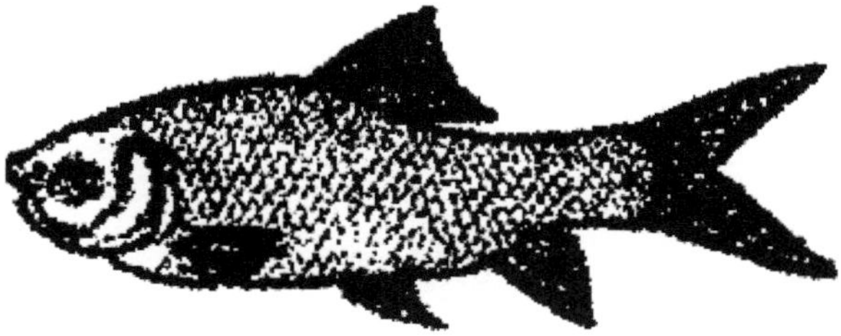

Fig. 3.2. Rohu

Rohu feeds on small plants and decomposed material in the pond and grows to a large size. A large fish may weigh even 20-30 kg. It is very popular for its taste. Rohu is still wild in nature but easy to culture in pond. In the stagnant water of the pond, the fish grows and gets sexually mature in second or third year depending on the climatic condition of a place; however, it does not breed in confined water. Therefore, induced breeding technique is applied to breed this fish. It is not difficult to breed it in hatchery.

Mori

Its body is elongated and slightly laterally compressed. The fish attains 2'-3' length. It has two big eyes on both sides of the head. This fish is easily identified by its golden coloured big eyes. The mouth lies below the head. The body is covered by medium sized scales. The dorsal part of the body is greyish while the ventral part is whitish (Fig. 3.3).

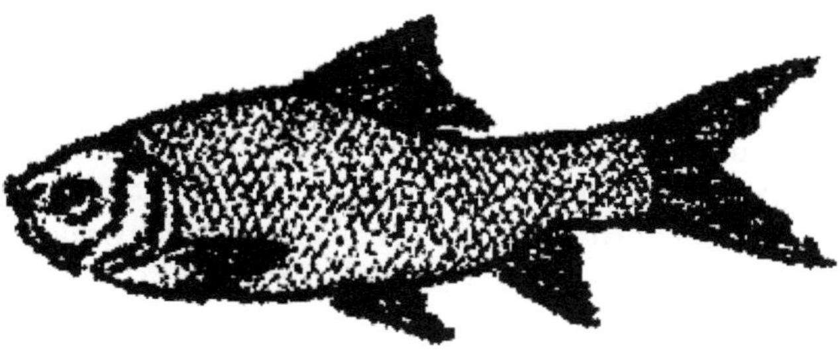

Fig. 3.3. Mori

It feeds on bigger plant cells, insects and decomposed material at the bottom and grows faster. The fish is 15-20 kg in weight. The fish is tasty. It is easily grown in pond. It matures sexually in two or three years depending on the climatic condition; however, like Rohu, it also does not breed in stagnant water of the pond. Therefore, induced breeding technique is applied to breed it. Its breeding in hatchery is not so difficult.

Thaila

The body of Thaila is laterally compressed. The front portion is much wider than the hind portion. The fish is easily recognised by its big sized head and thick lips.

The mouth lies at the anterior portion of the head. The body is covered with large sized scales. The dorsal portion of the body is greyish - black while the abdominal portion is whitish (Fig. 3.4).

Fig. 3.4. Thalia

It feeds on zooplankton and grows very fast. It grows faster than Rohu and Mori in stagnant water of pond; therefore, fish growers prefer this fish more. Thaila is considered as one of the fast growing fishes and is tasty. Though it grows faster and sexually matures in the fourth year in the stagnant water of pond, it does not breed in pond water. Hence, induced breeding technique is applied. Among the Indian Major Carps, Thaila is the most difficult to breed in confined water.

Common Carp

Common Carp is the most cultured and most domesticated fish around the world. It is laterally compressed. In proportion to its body, the head is small. The anterior portion of the body slopes down to head and it ends with mouth. The mouth has thick lips and is protractible. On the both side of the mouth, a pair of sensory organs in the form of barbell is found. There are two small eyes on the sides of the head. The posterior portion of the head has a big sized bone, called operculum that covers the gills. The anterior portion of the body is wider than the other parts. There are many varieties of Common Carp. The Scaly Common Carp has big scales on whole body (Fig. 3.5). The Mirror type of Common Carp has a row of big shining scales along the dorsal ridge of the body while the rest of the body remains naked (Fig. 3.6). The fish grows faster in the stagnant water of the pond. It grows to 2'-3' length and weighs upto 20-25 kg. Common Carp feeds on any available food such as plants, animals and decomposed material, hence called omnivorous. The Common Carp grows very fast and sexually matures within a year in the stagnant water of the pond. Unlike other Indian Major Carps, the Common Carp easily breeds even in confined water. Hence, while culturing this fish, selection of parental stock is very important and its breeding needs to be carried out in controlled conditions to maintain a good stock of fish; otherwise, the haphazard breeding is sure to degenerate the stock exhibiting poor growth. The fish is very popular for its taste.

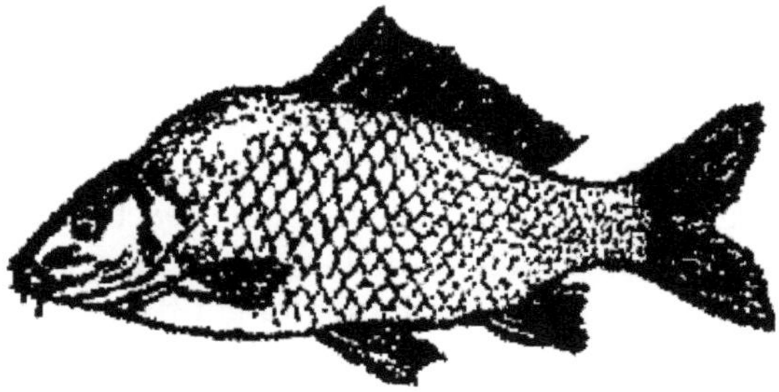

Fig. 3.5. Common Carp - Scaly

Fig. 3.6. Common Carp – Mirror

Silver Carp

Its body is laterally compressed and the abdominal region turns into a sharp edge like a knife. It grows to 2'-3' size. In proportion to its body size, the head is small but it is larger in comparison to other fishes. At the anterior end of the head, it has mouth. The mouth is large and its lower lip is slightly longer than the upper one. The eyes are small and located at the lower portion of the head. The whole body is covered with small silver white scales and it shines as silver, hence called Silver Carp (Fig. 3.7).

Fig. 3.7. Silver Carp

It feeds on small phytoplankton in the pond water. The big mouth swallows good quantity of pond water and filters the phytoplankton through the gills. Feeding on the phytoplankton it grows very fast. It sexually matures within 2-3 years of culture period depending on the climatic condition of a place but do not breed in stagnant water. Induced breeding technique is applied. This fish species is most delicate amongst the Chinese Carps; therefore, careful handling is essential. It is very tasty when it is fried.

Grass Carp

Its body is elongated and cylindrical. The fish may reach even a meter in length. Relative to the body size, the head is small. It has two big eyes. The anterior part of the head has mouth. The upper lip is slightly longer than the lower. Both the lips arc hard and strong. The whole body is covered with large dull- greenish large sized scales, while the abdomen portion remains whitish in colour (Fig. 3.8).

Fig. 3.8. Grass Carp

The fish feeds on any type of grass *e.g.* aquatic as well as terrestrial; therefore, it is called Grass Carp. As it feeds on the grasses, it is being used for biological control of the aquatic weeds of water bodies. The fish has been found feeding grasses forty times of its body weight and grows very fast in warm water. In stagnant water, the fish sexually matures in 2-3 years of culture depending on the climatic condition of a place; however, it does not breed in confined water. Induced breeding technique is applied. Though the adult fish feeds on grasses but their fingerlings feed on zooplankton. When they grow to about 3"-4", they start feeding on grass. The fish is known for its taste.

Bighead Carp

Like Silver Carp, the Bighead Carp is also laterally compressed and its abdomen is also like knife edge (Fig. 3.9). It grows to 2'-3' size. The fish is easily identified by its big head. The mouth lies at the anterior portion of the head. The eyes are small and located at the lower side of the head. The whole body is covered with small scales. The dorsal side of the body is dull white in colour while the scales in the abdomen portion shine like silver.

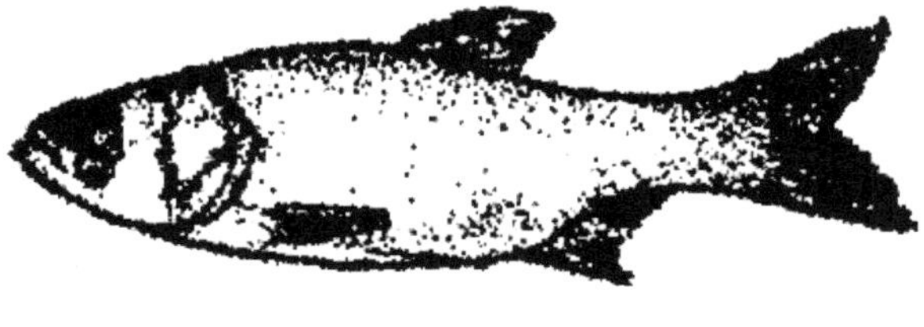

Fig. 3.9. Bighead Carp

The fish feeds on zooplankton and grows very fast. It sexually matures within 2-3 years depending on the climate of the place but like other Chinese Carp, it does not breed in confined water. It needs breeding artificially. This fish is also tasty.

Common fish species of Ethiopia

Fish provide a cheap source of protein. Although Ethiopia is a land-locked country, it is necessary to assess the potential of inland waters in order to develop a realistic view of protein production from fish. Water bodies cover only 0.7 percent of the area of Ethiopia and comprise 10 lakes located in the Central Highlands, mostly in the Rift Valley, with a total surface area of 7,500 square km. The largest lake is Lake Tana, located outside the Rift Valley on the North-western plateau, with a surface area of 3,200 km^2. Minor water bodies such as crater lakes and dam reservoirs occupy a total area of about 400 km^2. The main rivers cover together approximately 7000 km.

There are 175 species of fish in Ethiopia, forty of which are found only in Ethiopia. The most important ones are described below.

1. Nile Tilapia *(Oreochromis niloticus)*

Oreochromis niloticus (Nile tilapia) is a highly invasive fish that is present in a variety of ecosystems, particularly those located in the tropics (Fig. 3.10). Its effective mouth-brooding reproductive strategy allows it to increase in numbers at a rate which, not only crowds native species, but pollutes and unbalances the water column. It is a frequently farmed aquatic species, due to its relative ease of culture and rapid reproduction rates. It is also commercially known as mango fish, nilotica, or boulti. The first name leads to easy confusion with another tilapia traded commercially, the mango tilapia (*Sarotherodon galilaeus*).

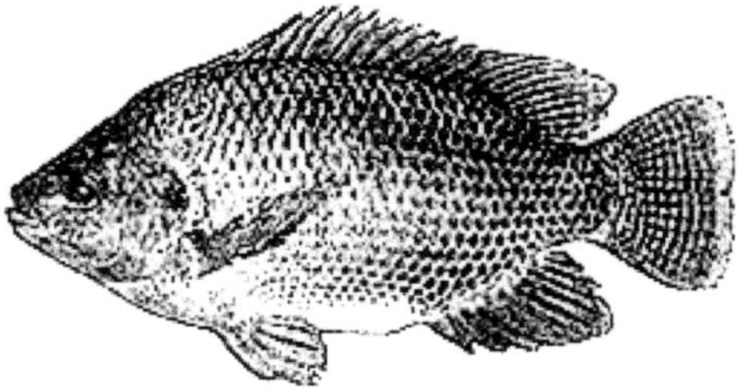

Fig. 3.10. *Oreochromis niloticus*

Biological features: Nile tilapia is large scaled bronze to black body with vertical stripes on caudal fin. Body of fish is compressed and the caudal peduncle depth is equal to length. Sexual dimorphism is not displayed by the upper jaw length. Knob like protuberance is not present on the dorsal surface of snout. Spinous and soft ray parts of dorsal fin are continuous. Dorsal fins are having 16-17 spines and 11-15 soft rays. Anal fin are having 3 spines and 10-11 rays. Caudal fin is truncated with numerous black bars. First gill arch has 27 to 33 gillrakers. During spawning season, pectoral, dorsal and caudal fins become reddish in colour.

Nutrition: Nile tilapia is omnivorous. It feeds on phytoplankton, periphyton, aquatic plants, small invertebrates, benthic fauna, and detritus. It generally feeds in shallow waters. It can filter feed by entrapping suspended particles, including phytoplankton and bacteria, on mucous in the buccal cavity, although its main source of nutrition is obtained by surface grazing on periphyton mats. The Nile tilapia typically feeds during daytime hours.

Habitat and biology: Nile tilapia is a tropical species that prefers to live in shallow water. The range for lethal temperatures for Nile tilapia are 11-12°C and 42°C, respectively, while the preferred temperature ranges from 31 to 36°C. Sexual maturity begins at 5-6 months. Spawning begins at 24 degrees. *O. niloticus* establishes a territory and digs a nest and then the females deposit eggs in the nest. After fertilization by the male, the female collects eggs in her mouth and incubates the eggs in her mouth until hatching, approximately 1-2 weeks later. Because of mouth-brooding techniques, the number of eggs per spawn is smaller than other pond species, but survival rates of young are comparatively higher. Males can fertilize eggs from a succession of females, and if there is no drop in temperature females can spawn continuously. In large scale aquaculture settings, reproduction takes place in a series of tanks and incubation spaces. Between 21-28 days of age, fish are given a food containing a male hormone that changes the sex of female members. Male specimens of *O. niloticus* grow twice as fast, and maintaining a mono-sex population and avoids stunted growth of individuals due to overcrowding. Other farming techniques include pond culture, floating cage culture and recirculation tank methods. Nile tilapia can live up to 10 years and reach weights of 5kg.

Uses: Nile tilapia is a hugely important fish in aquaculture. The development of sex-reversal procedures in the mid 1970s allowed farmers to maintain high density all male populations, thus avoiding stunted and unmarketable fish that often resulted from crowded mixed-sex tanks. The tilapia family (of which *O. niloticus* is a member) is the second most intensively farmed species in the world. China produces almost half of the world's tilapia crop, usually in the form of frozen whole fish. Tilapia is packaged in a variety of ways depending on the country of origin, including fresh or frozen fillets in "skin-on, skin-off, deep skinned, individually quick frozen, smoked forms.

2. Nile Perch *(Lates niloticus)*

The Nile perch (*Lates niloticus*) is a species of freshwater fish (Fig. 3.11). It is a fierce predator that dominates its surroundings, the Nile perch feeds on fish (including its own species), crustaceans, and insects; the juveniles also feed on zooplankton. The species is of great commercial importance as a food fish. The Nile perch is also popular with sport anglers as it attacks artificial fishing lures and is also raised in aquaculture. *Lates niloticus* (Nile perch) is widespread throughout the Ethiopian Region of Africa, occurring commonly in all major river basins including Nile, Chad, Niger, Senegal and Volta. The Nilotic population penetrates northwards well into the geographical limits of the Mediterranean Region and is present in the waters of Lake Mariout situated in the Nile Delta. Southwards the distribution includes parts of the Congo Basin.

Fig. 3.11. Nile perch *(Lates niloticus)*

Biological features: The Nile perch is a large freshwater fish. Fish is silver in colour with a blue tinge. They have a distinctive dark black eye with a bright yellow outer ring. Dorsal fin deeply notched, giving the appearance of two separate fins; the first part completely spinous; third dorsal spine enlarged. Lateral lines are continuous and caudal fin is rounded. The pre-opercle and pre-orbital bones are armed with spines, with a large spine on the free edge of the operculum.

Nile perch is a large perch-like predator. It was introduced to Lake Victoria in 1962 where it has contributed to the extinction of more than 200 endemic fish species through predation and competition for food. Nile perch are usually seen around 2-4 kg, but have been caught and seen at sizes up to 200 kg (the largest at 232 kg). They average around 85-100 cm but can grow to 193 cm. Maturity sizes strongly decreasing in recent years. The females are generally larger than males.

Nutrition: Nile perch feeds on fishes, insects, crustacea and mollusks. The type of prey ingested by the predator depends on the predator size, prey availability and abundance within a given habitat. Juvenile Nile perch feed on copepods, prawns, fish fry, small gastropods, and bivalves. As the fish matures and moves to greater depths haplochromine cichlids constitute over 95% of their food consumption. Besides crustacean zooplankton, invertebrate prey includes snails, clams, and insects. As Nile perch grow larger, they take larger prey. Nile perch less than 80 cm tend to feed on smaller fishes than those greater than 80 cm. This demonstrates that the predator is capable of shifting to other sizes of prey when more suitable sizes become scarce.

Habitat and biology: Nile perch are found in many different types of fresh water. They prefer warm, tropical waters where they grow to large sizes and occur in high densities. This species is demersal and potamodromous, and inhabits channels, lakes and irrigation canals. It prefers sandy bottoms but also found in rocky to muddy bottoms. Adult Nile perch occupy all habitats in lakes and rivers (10-60 m in depth) where there is enough oxygen with the exception of rocks, swamps, and the pelagic zone. They are voracious predator which predominantly feeds on *Tilapia* spp. and *Alestes* spp. etc. and shrimps, although the juveniles feed on larger crustaceans and insects and are planktivorous. They have long spawning season i.e. from February to August. It reproduces around the year, with peaks in the rainy season. It probably spawns in shallow sheltered areas. Juveniles occur over wide depth range but the highest concentrations of small juveniles are found in littoral and sub-littoral zones. Nile perch lives up to the age of 16 years. The growth of the Nile perch is very fast during the first year. The rate then decreases during the second, third, fourth and fifth years. There is a higher mortality rate for males than females.

The females Nile perch are generally larger than males. They are sexually dimorphic. The male has only anal and urogential openings just anterior to the anal fin, whereas the female has a genital orifice separate from the urinary opening. They become sexually mature at the age of 3 years. Ovulation takes place in the spring with the rising water temperature. Spawning is usually done in sheltered areas, but can also occur in open waters. The peak breeding season is from March to June. The range of number of offspring produced is 3,000,000 to 15,000,000 with an average of 9,000,000. The average gestation period is 20 hours. Average age at sexual or reproductive maturity in female is 3 years while that in males is 3 years.

Uses: Highly commercial, aquaculture and game fish. Caught mainly with bottom trawls, hand lines, seines, gill-nets, and traps. Fish is sold fresh and frozen (marketed mostly fresh); consumed steamed, pan-fried, broiled and baked.

3. African Sharptooth Catfish *(Clarias gariepinus)*

Clarias gariepinus or African sharp-tooth catfish is a large eel like fish with slender body, flat and broad bony head, and terminal mouth with four pairs of barbells (Fig. 3.12). These are found throughout Africa and live in lakes, rivers, human made ponds or even urban sewage system. The usual colour is dark gray or black colouration on the back, fading to white belly. The fish grow up to 3 ft to 5 ft. Sometimes length may be more than 5 ft. and weight ranges between 30-60 kg. African catfish sometimes produce loud croaking sounds. They are nocturnal and feed on living and dead animal matter. They are also able to crawl on dry ground to escape drying pools and able to survive in shallow mud for long periods of time, between rainy seasons. Courtship is preceded by highly aggressive encounters between males and mating takes place in shallow waters between isolated pairs of males and females. Spawning mostly takes place at night in the shallow, inundated areas of the rivers lakes and streams. Development of eggs and larvae is rapid, and the larvae are capable of swimming within 48–72 hours after fertilization. It was realized to be a very suitable species for aquaculture because it grows fast and feeds on a large variety of agriculture byproducts. It is hardy and tolerates adverse water quality conditions and can be raised in high densities, resulting in high net yields (6–16 t/ha/year). In most countries, it fetches a higher price than tilapia, as it can be sold live at the market. It matures and relatively easily reproduces in captivity.

Fig. 3.12. *Clarias gariepinus* (African sharptooth catfish)

4. Cornish Jack *(Mormyrops anguilloides)*

It is weakly electric fish and native to quiet waters in much of Sub-Saharan Africa. It has an electric organ and generates weak pulses of electricity for navigation, finding food, and communication. Electroceptive cells allow it to detect distortions in the electric field surrounding its body, and determine the size, distance, and properties of the causative object. It is a commercial game fish valued for its size and taste and found in the White Nile, the Lake Albert drainage basin, inland waters from Senegal to Chad, rivers in Cameroon, and small coastal basins in the Guinean zone. Fish body is elongated, snout is rounded, upper jaw slightly longer than the lower, both bearing a single row of small, pointed teeth and head is nearly twice as long as high, smooth and depressed in front. The eyes and gill openings are very small. The dorsal and anal fins are set well back on the body; the caudal fin is relatively small and forked with rounded lobes (Fig. 3.13). There are 21–30 fin rays in the dorsal and 38–51 rays in the anal fin. The colouration is gray above, lighter silvery white below, often with a bronze or yellow sheen. The juveniles are darker in colour, being grayish blue or brown. Adult are primarily piscivorous with significant seasonal variation in diet, whereas fish in river environments take both fish and crustaceans. The juveniles feed mostly on shrimps and aquatic insect larvae. Adult may reach up to 5 ft. in length and weigh up to 15 kg. They are oviparous and spawn in summer during the rainy season.

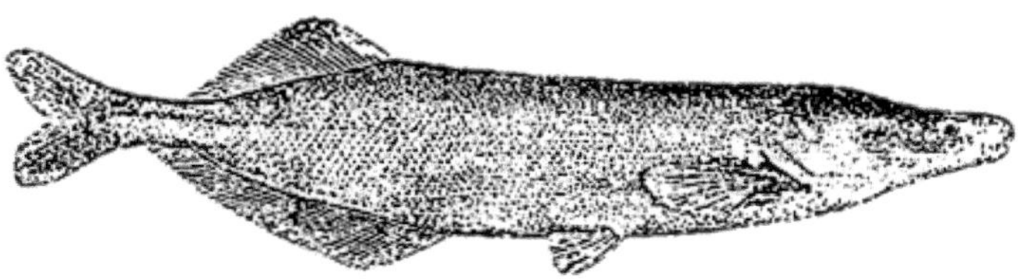

Fig. 3.13. *Mormyrops anguilloides*

5. *Garra geba*

It is a fresh water species of ray-finned fish. It lives only in tropical climate and endemic to Ethiopia. The body of fish is slender and elongated with two pairs of barbels. The first pair are called the maxillary barbels which are usually slightly longer than the other rostral pair. The Garra geba's dorsal-fin membrane is a pale cream colour with a faint band of black between the rays. It also has around 4 or 5 black spots between the rays with its anal, pelvic, and pectoral fins usually being a pale creamy brown. The caudal fin on the Garra geba is a pale brown and its median rays are dark brown. It has a total of 11 dorsal soft rays and 9 anal soft rays. Their head is depressed and they can reach up to 9 cm in length.

Garra aethiopica, Garra duobarbis, Garra makiensis, Garra quadrimaculata, Garra regressus, Garra regressus and *Garra tana* are the other species of ray-finned fish in the genus *Garra*. They are endemic to Ethiopia. *Gerra tana* reaches a maximum length of around 10.5 cm, and can be found close to shore. It is listed as vulnerable under the IUCN red list status.

6. Gymnarchus *(Gymnarchus niloticus)*

Commonly known as *Aba, aba aba,* frank fish, freshwater rat-tail, poisson-cheval, or African knife fish, it is an electric fish, and is found in swamps, lakes and rivers in the Nile, Turkana, Chad, Niger, Volta, Senegal, and Gambia basins. This is nocturnal fish with poor vision and hunts smaller fish using a weak electric field similar to that of the related elephant fish. It has a long and slender body with unusual large brain which is believed to help it interpret the electrical signals. It can make its tail negatively charged with respect to its head (Fig. 3.14). This produces a symmetrical electric field around its body. Nearby objects distort this field, and it can sense the distortion on its skin. It has no caudal, pelvic or anal fins. The dorsal fin is elongated, running along the back of the fish towards the blunt, finless tail, and is the main source of propulsion. It grows up to 5 ft in length and 20 kg in weight.

Fig. 3.14. *Gymnarchus niloticus*

7. African arowana *(Heterotis niloticus)*

Heterotis niloticus, also known as *Clupisudis niloticus,* is a species of bony tongue found throughout Africa. It is native to all the watersheds in Sahelo-Sudanese region, Senegal, and Gambia as well as parts of eastern Africa also includes the basins of Nile Rivers. They have air-breathing organs on its branchiae, enabling them to survive in oxygen-depleted water. A suprabranchial organ allows it to concentrate small planktonic food particles and also has a sensory function. This fish is gray, brown, or bronze in colour. Colouration is uniform in adults, but juveniles often have dark longitudinal bands. It is a long-bodied fish with large scales, long dorsal and anal fins set far back on the body, and a rounded caudal fin and feed extensively on planktons (Fig. 3.15). Adult mature body length may reach up to 1 m with mature body weigh ranges between 5-10 kg.

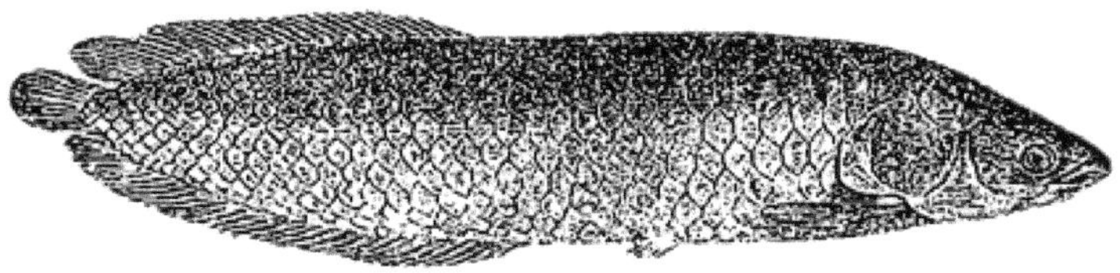

Fig. 3.15. *Heterotis niloticus*

8. African tiger fish *(Hydrocynus vittatus)*

It is a predatory freshwater fish distributed throughout much of Africa. Fishes are silver in colour, with thin black stripes running horizontally. Body is elongated and a red, forked caudal fin with a black edge. Its head is large, as well as its teeth, of which there are eight per jaw. The teeth are sharp and conical which are used to grasp and chop prey. They are able to replace their teeth simultaneously on the upper and lower jaws. These fish are fierce hunters and are mostly piscivorous and tend to eat whatever fish is most available. Insects and zooplankton may also be part of diet, especially during juvenile stages of life. It is an important food and income source for locals and promotes tourism through recreational and sport fishing. Males are larger and more full-bodied than females. Adult grows up to three to three and half ft in length.

Fish lives near the bottom of the large freshwater rivers and lakes. They tend to be found closer to the surface during day and then move towards the bottom at night. The breeding habits of this fish may take place over a couple days during December or January. The timing depends on when the rivers and streams begin to swell due to the start of the rainy season. Females will lay their eggs in submerged vegetation in shallow water close to the shore. Hatchling will remain in the safety of the vegetation until the water levels become low enough to force them further into the water. These fish may migrate up to 100 km within the stream or river they inhabit.

9. Tiger fish, Nile tiger fish or Sahelian tiger fish *(Hydrocynus brevis)*

It is a predatory freshwater fish widely distributed in Africa from Senegal to Ethiopia throughout the Nile. Fish is of silver colour during early age, with thin black horizontal stripes and an elongated body that tapers at both ends (Fig. 3.16). When matures, it will develop a bronze colouration and the stripes will fade. The ventral and caudal fins have a slight red-orange tint, and the adipose fin is grey to black. A demersal, potamodromous freshwater species feeds mainly on fish and shrimps, with smaller individuals consuming aquatic insects. Adult fish grow up to 3 ft in length.

Fig. 3.16. *Hydrocynus brevis*

10. Redeye labeo *(Labeo cylindricus)*

It is freshwater fish endemic to the rivers of East Africa prefers clear, running waters in rocky habitats of small and large rivers, and is also found in lakes and dams over rocky areas. Fish has cylindrical body, large mouth, fleshy lips, protruded snout, usually with star shaped tubercles on it. The eyes are typically red (Fig. 3.17). Young fishes are usually yellow-green colour with a darker band stretching horizontal over the body while older fish is a darker olive grey. Adult fish reaches up to 9-10 inches in length. It feeds on diatoms and other small algae from the rocks. It migrates upstream in masses to breed, using the mouth and broad pectoral fins to climb damp surfaces of barrier rocks and weirs in the river.

Fig. 3.17. *Labeo cylindricus*

11. Bayad *(Bagrus bajad)*

The bayad avoids salt water and is found in lakes, swamps and rivers and lakes of Africa like Lake Chad, Lake Mobutu, and Lake Turkana and Nile, Niger and Senegal rivers. This fish is somewhat elongated and blackish or yellow-greenish colour with a white belly. The dorsal fin has a smooth spine, and the pectoral fins have spines with serrations on the inside. The fins are darker, sometimes reddish purple. It may grow up to three to three and half feet and weight ranges between 10–100 kg. Males are usually smaller in size and weight than females. They stay in crevices of rocks and is therefore seldom seen during daylight and feed on small fishes, insects, crustaceans, mollusks and vegetable matter. There is some indication that the species comes to shallower water to breed. The parents build and guard the nest, which is like a flat disc with a central hole where the eggs are dropped; the size of the nest and the central hole depend on the fish size. The bayad is an important food fish of economic importance, commonly sold as food.

12. Banded jewelfish *(Hemichromis fasciatus)*

Also known as five-spot cichlid, it is yellow-green with a bronze iridescence and has five large, black, glossy oval patches on the side of the body (Fig. 3.18). Older specimens have a brick-red dot on each scale. It is a very aggressive and territorial species. The adult fish length reaches up to 10-11 inches. The mouth is large and white. It is distributed throughout West Africa. It can also be found in the Nile Basin and Lake Chad. Breeding is relatively easy, especially in brackish water. Up to 1000 eggs are laid on a stone. Both parents protect and accompany their offspring until the latter have reached a size of 2-3 cm (1 inch).

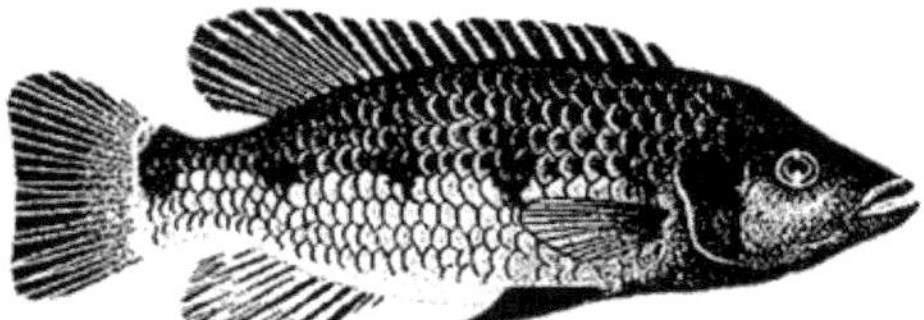

Fig. 3.18. *Hemichromis fasciatus*

13. Vundu *(Heterobranchus longifilis)*

The other synonyms for it are the Solomon fish, Tsuni, Mazunda, Sampa, Cur, Lenda and Certa. It is a large size fish of freshwater widely found in river and other freshwater habitat of Sub-Saharan Africa as well as Nile (Fig. 3.19). The fish is most active during night. Colour is light to dark olive brown on its dorsal surface and getting lighter over the mid-body to a light brown. Its belly is off-white. Fins are usually light brown. The adult fish length reaches up to 5 ft and mature body weight ranges between 25-55 kg. Due to serpent-like body, it can charge with powerful bursts of speed, and is strong enough to pull a man down to the bottom of the river. Its feed includes insects and other invertebrates when they are small. Adults are commonly fed on small vertebrates and fishes. It can survive out of water for extensive period of time.

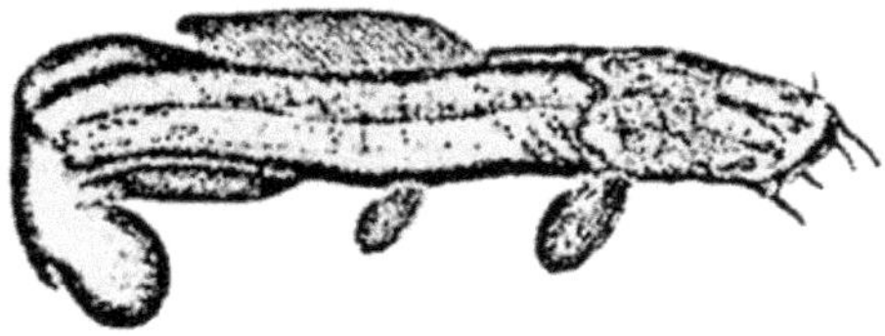

Fig. 3.19. *Heterobranchus longifilis*

14. *Malapterurus electricus*

It is a species of electric catfish that occurs widely in Africa and important for subsistence fisheries and as a game fish. Adult fish may reach up to 1 ft. in aquarium and 3-4 ft. in wild (Fig. 3.20). It is quite hardy and greedily accepts most foods. They are active burrowers and will often remove the gravel from under their favourite hiding spot.

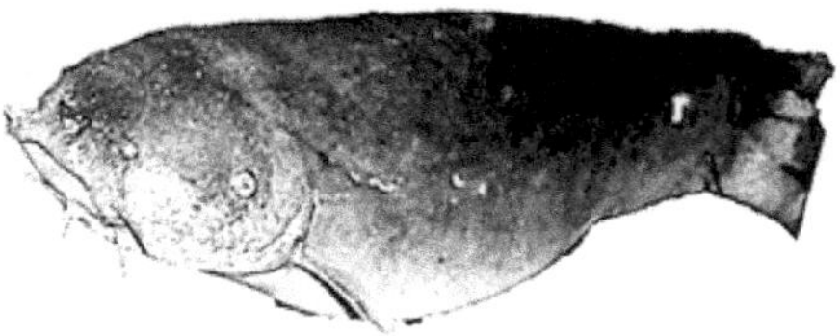

Fig. 3.20. *Malapterurus electricus*

15. Nile catfish *(Synodontis batensoda)*

This omnivore fish originates from the Nile, Chad, Niger, Senegal, and Gambia River basins and feeds on plankton, algae, detritus, surface insects, chironomid larvae and molluscs. They have short and deep body with large eyes and usual colour is grey-black tinged with brown, with a faint network of dark black spots (Fig. 3.21). Adult fish may grow up to half meter in length and weighs up to 1.5 kg. It is oviparous and venomous.

Fig. 3.21. *Synodontis batensoda*

16. African catfish *(Heterobranchus bidorsalis)*

Also called eel-like fatty fin catfish, it is demersal and inhabits freshwater found widely in the northern half of Africa between Senegal and Ethiopia, as well as the Nile. The head is oval, snout is round with rectangular dorsum and the eyes are lateral. It is commercially fished for human consumption. The pectoral spine is smooth. The body and fins may have spots. Adult fish length goes up to 5 ft with range of weight for this species is 15-30 kg. The species has 40-46 dorsal soft rays in the back, 49-58 anal soft rays, and 62-63 vertebrae. Spawning can be induced in females by single intramuscular hormone injections of carp pituitary suspensions. An 82% survival rate of the larvae was achieved. It lives in waters of 22-28°C.

17. *Andersonia leptura*

Andersonia leptura is found in Omo, Niger, and Upper Nile Rivers. It is a species of catfish and is the only species of the genus *Andersonia*. This fish grows up to 50.0 cm (19.7 in). Previously considered to be toothless on the lower jaw but the teeth are embedded in the mucous sheath that covers the head and extends into the oral cavity, which makes the teeth difficult to see with the naked eye.

18. Giraffe catfish *(Auchenoglanis occidentalis)*

This catfish is highly adaptive, rapidly growing and will readily accept a variety of foods and is tolerant of a wide variety of water conditions. Due to high adaptivity, it is distributed throughout East to West Africa in lakes and rivers such as Nile and Lake Chad. It is inhabitant of shallow water with muddy bottom and eats plants of the floor of lakes. It lays eggs in mud nest which is guarded by male. The fish grows up to two to three feet.

19. *Danakilia franchettii*

This fish species is endemic to the saline Lake Afrera and nearby swamps in Ethiopia. It was the only member of the genus *Danakilia* until the description of *D. dinicolai* in 2010. The species is listed as endangered, due to water abstraction and mining of salt in the lake.

20. *Lates longispinis*

This is a latid fish that is endemic to Lake Turkana in Kenya and Ethiopia. It is important commercial as well as game fish. It lives in the deeper waters of the lake, eating prawns from the bottom of the lakes and feeding on characins in the mid-water column. Adult fish grows up to 10-11 inches in length. It spawns in the open water in the middle of the lake, and parental care is highly unlikely.

21. *Siluranodon auritus*

This species is known from the Nile River, previously thought that fish of this species lack teeth, it has been found that they have very reduced teeth. As the fish grows, teeth on the upper jaw are lost due to damage, while teeth on the lower jaw are overgrown by the surrounding bone. This species exhibits pedomorphosis, that is, they retain many juvenile traits into adulthood. Some of these include an absence of a dorsal fin spine and a reduced number of ribs. It reaches length up to 6-7 inches. They feed primarily on phytoplankton and zooplankton. These fish are oviparous and the eggs are unguarded.

4

Fish Biology

Feeding habits of fish are important biological factors for selecting a group of fish for culture in ponds to avoid competition for food among themselves and live in association and to utilize all the available food. Most of the time, fish will consume mostly small animals and plants that grow in water. However, it may be necessary to provide additional food if primary production of fish in the pond is not good and the fish grow slowly. Nutritionally, organic matter includes proteins, lipids (fats), and carbohydrates, as well as substances present in relatively low proportions (micronutrients), such as vitamins and minerals. Nutritional requirements vary with species. Deficiencies in vitamins can cause stunted growth, loss of appetite, cloudy eyes, weakness or tumors in fish. For this reason it is advisable to give vitamin supplements to fish from time to time.

Feeding habits

On the basis of feeding habits, there are four basic groups among fish i.e. carnivores, herbivores, omnivores and limnivores. Each group of fish needs to be fed in a particular way.

a) **Carnivores:** These are meat-eating fish. The recommended feed for the carnivores would be earthworms, red worms, tubifex worms, daphnia, larvae of mosquitoes or fruit flies, oysters, shrimps, clams and other fish. They will never damage or eat plants. Carnivores need at least 45% of protein in their food, without which they become severely malnourished. Although many of the prepared foods are spiked with extra protein to help such fish. Carnivores are happiest when they are fed live food like worms. If these worms are kept frozen, they need to be thawed and then sliced into slivers. They should be supplements in the form of flakes or granules and pellets for added nutrition.

b) **Herbivores:** These fish eat only plants. These fish need to graze very often, and whether they are fed regularly or not, they nip plant. It is good to feed these fish with fresh veggies. The fish keep nipping at these. Recommended foods for this variety are cucumber, peas and potatoes. Vegetable flakes come in a variety of flavors that may be given. Algal flakes will also be a favourite among this kind of fish. Many aquarists who like herbivores keep plastic plants in their aquarium. If real plants are used, the aquarium runs a risk of having a badly mauled garden. Care should be taken to remove the frayed plants before they start decaying and rotting in the water.

c) **Omnivores:** These fish will eat anything present such as plants as well as smaller creatures. They are also voracious eaters and aquarists can sometimes mistake their eating frenzy for hunger. It is a common tendency to overfeed these species, and they tend to pile on the fat very quickly if overfed.

d) **Limnivores:** These fish feed mainly on algae and the microorganisms. These fish are constantly eating, and can be given pellets and algae based foods. They are also known as mud-eaters. The type of food, the culture conditions and the individual fish will affect the quantity of food provided. In nature, there may be times when an adult fish starves for a day or two, or even for longer periods of time. The younger fish need more frequent feedings than the older ones. The fry have their own feeding needs. Most feeding problems arise due to overfeeding. The excess food will purify and degrade the water quality.

Sources of feed

Sources of feed in pond are naturally produced fish food inside the pond and fish food supplied from outside. Natural fish food consists of algae (phytoplankton) and tiny animals (zooplankton). Supplementary fish food is produced outside the pond and supplied to the fish regularly to increase the amount of fish food in the pond.

a) **Natural fish food:** The natural fish food in the pond consists mainly of algae. Oxygen is produced by all plants and algae in the pond with the help of sunlight. The more sunlight falls on the pond and the larger the quantity of algae, the higher will be the oxygen-production in the fishpond. The oxygen produced dissolves partly in the water and the rest escapes to the air. The oxygen level of the water varies during the day because the production and absorption of oxygen by the plants changes with the intensity and duration of light. The algae in the pond only produce oxygen when there is light. At night they need oxygen like any other plant or animal in the pond, while no oxygen can be produced due to lack of sunlight. Due to this, the quantity of dissolved oxygen in the water decreases after sunset. Normally the oxygen level is at the highest at the end of the afternoon (oxygen has been produced throughout the day) and at the lowest in the early morning (oxygen has been used up throughout the night). Shortage of oxygen is the most important death cause of fish in fisheries where the pond has been manured or fed too much. An oxygen level that is sufficiently high is important for a good fish production.

b) **Supplemented fish food:** When supplementary food is given to the fish most of it is directly eaten by the fish. The uneaten food will act as an additional fertilizer for the pond. But even in ponds receiving a high amount of supplemented food, natural fish food still plays a very important role in the growth of fish. In general, local waste products can be used as supplementary fish food. The type of food depends on the local availability and costs and the fish species raised. Typical examples of supplementary fish feeds are rice bran, broken rice, bread crumbs, cereals, cereal wastes, maize meal, guinea grass, napier grass, fruits and vegetables, peanut cake, soybean cake and brewer's waste.

Practical guidelines for feeding fish

Feed the fish at the same time and in the same part of the pond. Fish will get used to this and come near the surface of the water so it is easier to see if the fish are eating and growing well. Feeding should be done in the late morning or early afternoon when dissolved oxygen levels are high so fish have enough time to recover from the high oxygen-demanding feeding activity before nightfall. Do not overfeed the fish by observing their behaviour while feeding too much food will decay and use up too much oxygen in the pond. Stop feeding fish for at least one day before breeding, harvesting or transporting them. This enables the fish to digest the food completely. In general, fry can be starved for 24 hours, fingerlings for 48 hours and adult fish for about 72 hours.

Food Intake

The amount of food fish eats is directly related to its size, its metabolic rate, and the temperature of its environment. Smaller fishes generally have a higher metabolic rate than large fishes of the same species. Thus, small fishes generally eat proportionately more. Warm-water fishes generally require more food than similar-size cold-water fishes. A fish's body temperature and its metabolic rate is determined by the temperature of its environment. Some fishes can go long periods without eating. Some freshwater eels (*Anguilla* spp.) can survive more than a year without food. Some researchers have calculated food intake for some species. In one study, bluegill (*Lepomis macrochirus*), a species of small freshwater fish ate food between 1% and 35% of their body weight per week, depending on water temperature. Studies on anchovies (family Engraulidae) during the summer showed a food intake of about 8% to 10% of body weight per day. Levels of nutrients required by different species of fish are shown in Table 4.1.

Table 4.1. Levels of nutrients required by different species of fish.

	Nutrient percent requirement in different sizes/classes of fish				
Size/Class of fish	**< 0.5 g**	**0.5 to 10 g**	**10 to 35 g**	**> 35 g**	**Breeders**
Tilapia					
Crude proteins (%)	50	35–40	30–35	25–30	30
Crude lipids (%)	10	10	6–10	6	8
Digestible glucids (%)	25	25	25	25	25
Fibers (%)	8	8	8-10	8–10	8–10
Catfish					
Digestible proteins (%)	>27	27	29	22–24	
Common carp					
Digestible proteins (%)		27	31		

Fish Growth

Most fishes continue to grow throughout their lives. Their growth rates are determined by food supply, habitat, water quality and competition, among other factors. As long as conditions for growth are satisfactory, fish will continue to increase in length and weight throughout its lifespan. If there are insufficient resources for growth, fish stop growing, but not necessarily die. If resources become sufficient at some time in the future, fish can resume growing.

Fish growth is very much dependent on population density (abundance). Indeterminate growth allows the development of that high density, slow-growing fish populations that are often referred to as stunted populations. When .perch density is high, there is much competition for a limiting factor such as food, and growth is slow. When density is low, food is more abundant, and growth rates are substantially faster. Low density alone does not ensure fast growth for fish populations. Fish growth actually should be thought of as a reflection of food availability in relation to population size. A decrease in food base (prey) or an increase in predator fish abundance can lead to predator populations with slower growth.

Length-Weight Relationships

The relationship between total length (L) and total weight (W) for nearly all species of fish is expressed by the equation:

$$W = aL^b$$

Values of W usually have been calculated from the logarithmic (base 10) equivalent:

$$\log W = \log a + b \cdot \log L$$

A graph of log W against log L forms a straight line with a slope of b and a Y-axis (log W) intercept of log a. Invariably, b is close to 3.0 for all species. The exact relationship between length and weight differs among species of fish according to their inherited body shape, and within a species according to the condition (robustness) of individual fish.

Individual fish within the same sample vary considerably, and the average condition of each population varies seasonally and yearly. Sex and gonad development are other important variables in some species, especially percids.

Fish Age Determination

Age recognition from calcified structures: Fish scales, otoliths (earbones), spines and other bony parts are used to determine the age of individual fish. This process is similar to finding the age of a tree by counting rings in the wood. The scales, otoliths (earbones), and other bony parts of fish often contain a record of seasonal growth patterns. This is because fish grow faster in the summer than in winter, due to higher temperatures and increased food consumption. Patterns in the scales and otoliths reflect this change: summer zones are wide, and winter zones are narrow (Fig. 4.1).

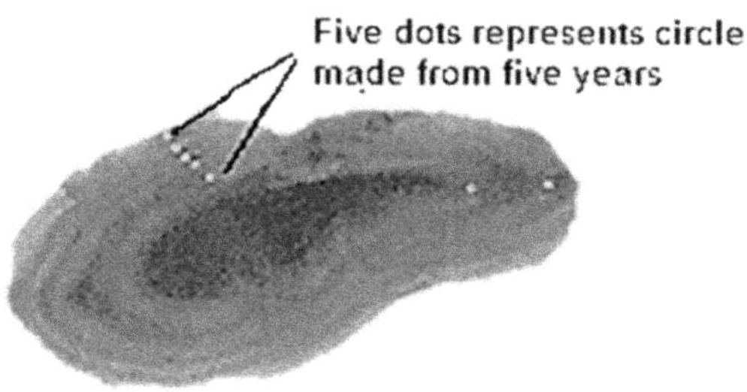

Fig. 4.1. Otolith slice. Annuli (year-marks) are indicated.

Fish age, in years, can therefore be determined by counting the number of paired summer/winter growth zones. One pair of such zones is called an annulus (plural, annuli). Thus, the process of ageing fish is similar to finding the age of a tree by counting rings in the wood.

Back calculation of length at previous ages: Growth of calcified structures in fishes is proportional to body growth. Body lengths at previous ages computed (back-calculated) from relationships of body length to length of calcified structure. Several available formulas, depending on calcified structure, are used. Growth history of the fish is needed.

Calculation of growth rates

a) Change in length or weight between samples

   i. **Absolute growth rate (A)**

$$A = \left\{\frac{l_2 - l_1}{t_2 - t_1}\right\}$$

Where, l_1 = length at time 1 (t_1), l_2 = length at time 2 (t_2)

In above formula weight can be substituted for length and it will be expressed as growth per unit time.

ii. **Relative growth rate (R)**

$$R = \frac{A}{l_1}$$

In the above formula, weight can be substituted for length and it will be expressed as growth per unit time, standardized by fish size.

5

Breeding and Reproduction of Fish

The reproductive process allows species to perpetuate themselves, and there are a diverse number of reproductive strategies in fishes throughout the world. In an aquarium or pond, successful breeding largely depends on nutrition and environmental conditions that are sometimes very specific. In the wild, these conditions might be seasonal changes, water conditions, the amount of daylight, and the availability of specific food sources. The amount of daylight is generally less important in tropical species, because hours of sunlight in tropical regions nearer the equator stay fairly constant year round. Temperate or coldwater fish, such as goldfish and koi, may be more affected by shorter and longer days of the seasons further north or south. Certain conditions often trigger a particular species to breed. For instance, during the wet season in the tropics, rains may wash extra nutrients into the swollen rivers, leading to a greater abundance of available food and plants, which can be ideal breeding conditions for fish. In aquarium and pond fish, healthy breeding stock must be of spawning age. Proper substrate, cover, temperature, pH, live foods, lighting, and number of fish are all likely considerations.

Propagation in fish

There are several methods for the breeding or propagation of cultivated fish. Suitability of methods depends on the reproduction biology of the species, on local environmental conditions and on the facilities available. There are three main methods of propagation.

1. **Natural propagation:** In this method of propagation, human intervention is least. Males and females are placed together in a breeding area such as a small pond or an enclosure where they spawn naturally. Certain species

may require some environmental manipulation for successful breeding such as the inflow of new water and a sudden rise of the pond water level for the African catfish Clarias; the presence of grassy vegetation as egg collectors nests for common carp; or the presence of artificial nests for American and European catfishes, Ictalurus and Silurus. This method is usually used, for example, to produce tilapias cheaply.

2. **Semi-natural propagation:** In this method, the female fish are first given one injection of pituitary gland extract to trigger spawning. Males and females are then placed together in a specially prepared breeding area such as a small grassy pond or an enclosure where spawning takes place. The fertilized eggs are usually collected and reared under improved conditions, either natural or artificial.
3. **Artificial propagation:** In this method males and females are given injections for ripening eggs in females and collection of sperm from males. Females are given one or more injections of chemicals to regulate the final ripening of dormant eggs in the ovaries. As soon as the eggs are ripened, they are stripped from the females. Eggs are artificially fertilized with sperm obtained from the males and reared under controlled conditions.

Modes of reproduction

The reproductive cycle of nearly all fish is regulated by environmental stimuli (day length, water temperature, water level etc.) which trigger the release of hormones by the fish brain that act on the reproductive organs of the females and the males. These organs in turn produce sperm in the case of males and eggs in the case of females. Most cultured fish species are seasonal breeders. The breeding season appears to coincide with environmental conditions most suitable for the survival of their young. Day length, temperature and rainfall are important factors involved in the regulation of the reproduction cycles. There are three basic reproductive strategies that can be used to classify fish.

1. **Oviparity:** It is the most common reproductive strategy in marine ecosystems. Oviparous fishes literally meant for, "egg-laying" fishes. Approximately 90% of bony fishes and 43% of cartilaginous fish are oviparous. In oviparous fish, females spawn eggs into the water column, which are then fertilized by males. Males and females swim close together so that the eggs are shed into a cloud of spermatozoa. For most oviparous fish, the eggs take less energy to produce so the females release large quantities of eggs. The eggs are then fertilized and develop in the environment outside the female. An egg membrane is present, and the embryonic stage is nourished entirely by the yolk. The fertilized eggs may spend long periods of time in the water column as larvae before settling out as juveniles. An advantage of oviparity is the number of eggs produced, because it is likely some of the offspring will survive. However, the offspring are at a disadvantage because they must go through a larval stage in which their location is directed by oceans currents. During

the larval stage, the larvae act as primary consumers in the food web where they must not only obtain food but also avoid predation. Another disadvantage is that the larvae might not find suitable habitat when they settle out of the water column.

Oviparous Sharks and Rays do not have the advantage of producing high numbers of eggs, however they spawn eggs that have a large amount of yolk to provide nourishment as the embryo develops. These offspring also do not go through a larval stage, but are instead laid on the seafloor.

2. **Ovoviviparity:** In ovoviviparous fish, the eggs are fertilized inside of the female. The eggs remain within the mother while they develop allowing for a greater degree of protection from predators and difficult environmental conditions than in oviparous fish. However, there is no direct nourishment provided by the mother. Another advantage of ovoviviparity is that the offspring are advanced in their development when they are born live, thus the juveniles are more likely to fend for themselves in the wild. A disadvantage of ovoviviparity is that fewer individuals are born and it takes more energy for the females to carry the eggs inside. It occurs in most Sharks and Rays, as well as species of Rockfish.
3. **Viviparity:** Similar to ovoviviparous fish, internal fertilization and development occur. However, the embryos receive direct nourishment from the mother, similar to the development of an embryo in mammals. Like ovoviviparous fish, the viviparous fish give birth to live young; however viviparous fish are fully advanced at birth allowing for a greater chance of survival. Viviparous fish are at a disadvantage if the mother dies because the offspring are likely to die and the mother is more vulnerable to predators when in labor. It occurs in some Sharks and Surfperches.

Spawning in fish

Spawn is the eggs and sperm released or deposited, usually into water, by aquatic animals. As a verb, spawn refers to the process of releasing the eggs and sperm, also called spawning. Most aquatic animals, apart from aquatic mammals, reproduce through a process of spawning. The eggs are fertilized shortly after release by males. Some fish also deposit unfertilized eggs in nests where they are fertilized and develop. Fishes with internal fertilization release free-swimming larvae, or juveniles. The ripening of eggs and spawning are controlled by hormones, nutrition of the female, and external (ecological) factors. Usually maturation and spawning are controlled by a combination of endogenous and exogenous controls and are not governed by a y-specific factor.

A majority of the world's fish species are egg layers, but there are also a lot of species that have developed into livebearers. The egg laying species will typically use some form of external fertilization of the eggs, while the livebearers perform internal fertilization. The level and type of parental care will also vary considerably between different fish species. Some are extremely devoted parents while others leave their offspring immediately, or even try to eat them. Female fish release eggs into the water (either into the water column or into a nest) and male fish fertilize eggs by releasing milt. Not all eggs are fertilized. Some fish spawn each year after reaching maturity, others spawn at intervals (every four years, for example), while others spawn only once and then die.

1. **Livebearers:** Fish reproduce by bearing live young or by laying eggs. Livebearers give birth to fully formed and functional young, called fry. A lot of the commonly kept aquarium species are livebearers. The eggs are fertilized by the male while they are still inside the body of the female fish, so called internal fertilization. These fertilized eggs are hatched within the female. Most livebearers have fewer and larger fry than egg layers, because the fry need to be more developed and large enough to fend for themselves after birth. In live bearing species, the male's anal fin has developed into a reproductive organ. This type of modified anal fin is called a gonopodium. After the fertilization, the eggs develop into fry inside the female fish. When the fry is born, they look like miniatures of adult fish, but sometimes without the striking colours of their parents. In some live bearing species the female fish can store spermatozoa (semen) from one single mating and use it to fertilize several batches in a row. This is why female livebearers sometimes give birth in aquariums where they are kept without any males.
2. **Egg scatterers:** Females scatter adhesive or non-adhesive eggs to fall to the substrate, into plants, or float to the surface. These eggs are then fertilized, and then rapidly swept away by the current. These species do not look after their brood and even eat their own eggs. The fry hatch quickly.
3. **Egg depositors:** Egg depositors usually lay fewer eggs than egg-scatterers, although the eggs are larger. There are two types of egg depositors: open water spawners and secretive spawners. Open water spawners will not hide their eggs. Open water spawners typically deposit the eggs on a flat rock, on the aquarium floor or on the leaves of broad leaved aquatic plants. Some open water spawners will dig a crater in the substrate and place their eggs inside. Secretive egg depositors want to hide their eggs, and will choose a cave, a crevice or similar as spawning site. In the aquarium they will usually appreciate turned over terracotta flowerpot. Both open water spawners and secretive spawners clean the site before they deposit their eggs, and they will usually also defend the eggs and care for them by cleaning them. Before the fry emerge, many egg depositors will move the eggs around to other pre-cleaned sites. Egg depositors are also known to guard their fry and the fry is often seen swimming around with their parents.
4. **Nest Builders:** Nest spawners construct some sort of structure, cavity, or pit in which the eggs are laid and fertilized and the embryos are defended. Pit nests can be made of a wide variety of material, but the most common are nests of gravel and rocks. Such nests are typically shallow depressions that are carefully constructed and tended by territorial males. In few species, nests are formed by the male fish by blowing saliva bubbles, and a bubble nest will often contain plant fragments. When the female has released the eggs they are carefully gathered by the male and placed inside the bubble

nest. In some species, the female will gather the eggs. In some species the eggs will float up into the nest without help from the parents.

5. **Mouth brooders:** These are also a kind of egg depositors, but the offspring is guarded inside the mouth of a parent. The eggs are often deposited in a shallow crater where they are fertilized by the male before being picked up by the male or the female fish. In some species the eggs are fertilized by the male when they have already been picked up by the female. Mouth brooders can be ovophiles or larvophiles. Ovophile or egg-loving mouth-brooders lay their eggs in a pit, which are sucked up into the mouth of the female. A small number of large eggs hatch in the mother's mouth, and the fry remain there for a period of time. Fertilization often occurs with the help of egg-spots, which are colourful spots on the anal fin of the male. When the female sees these spots, she tries to pick up the egg-spots, but instead gets a mouthful of sperm, fertilizing the eggs in her mouth. Many cichlids and some labyrinth fish are ovophile mouthbrooders. Larvophile or larvae-loving mouth-brooders lay their eggs on a substrate and guard them until the eggs hatch. After hatching, the female picks up the fry and keeps them in her mouth. When the fry can fend for themselves, they are released. Some eartheaters are larvophile mouthbrooders.
6. **Egg buriers:** Egg buriers can inhabit waters that dry up at some time of the year. The egg burying species have developed in areas subjected to seasonal draughts. The parents mature quickly and lay their eggs before dying when the water dries up. The eggs remain in a dormant stage until rains stimulate hatching. The egg burying species will not guard their offspring, since the parents are usually dead long before the rainy season begins.

Fish Life Cycle

Eggs: Most eggs do not survive to maturity even under the best conditions. Threats to eggs include changes in water temperature and oxygen levels, flooding or sedimentation, predators and disease. Once the egg is fertilized, the embryo will form inside the hardened egg. The embryo will start to develop organs, and eventually eyespots and the tail can be seen inside the egg (Fig. 5.1). The embryo will develop pigmentation spots along the body. The tail will wrap around the egg to the head. If the species lives in warmer waters, the embryo will hatch more quickly. Colder water species hatch slowly, and the eyes and pigmentation will be fully developed at hatching. The tail of the embryo will break out of the shell and the embryo becomes a free-swimming larva.

Fig. 5.1. Egg of fish

Larvae: Fertilized eggs under favourable condition hatched into larva. Newly hatched larvae have a yolk sac that is a source of nutrition for the larvae (Fig. 5.2). They absorb their yolk sac for several days until they are developed enough to feed on live prey.

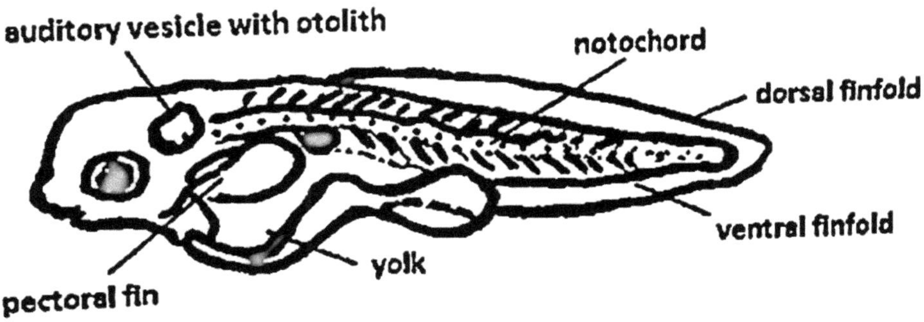

Fig. 5.2. Larva of fish

Larval development: Larval rearing takes place from hatching until the time when the larva fills up its air bladder with air; begins swimming in a fish-like manner; and starts to eat external food. The larva then becomes what is usually called early fry. During this period, fish larvae mostly develop their alimentary and respiratory organs. The yolk sac provides the material for growth and development. Its size slowly decreases until complete reabsorption, soon after the larva has started to ingest external food (Fig. 5.3). The length of this period therefore greatly depends on the initial size of the yolk sac, which varies from species to species, and on the rate of larval development, which mainly varies with water temperature. For each species, there is an optimal thermal range, similar to the one defined for egg incubation. For successful rearing, fish larvae require: (1) Suitable water temperature, with as little fluctuation as possible; (2) an oxygen-rich environment, preferably saturated, especially for passive larvae (water flow should not however be too strong); (3) a clean environment (egg shells and bad eggs should be removed); and (4) access to food of a suitable kind, well dispersed among the larvae.

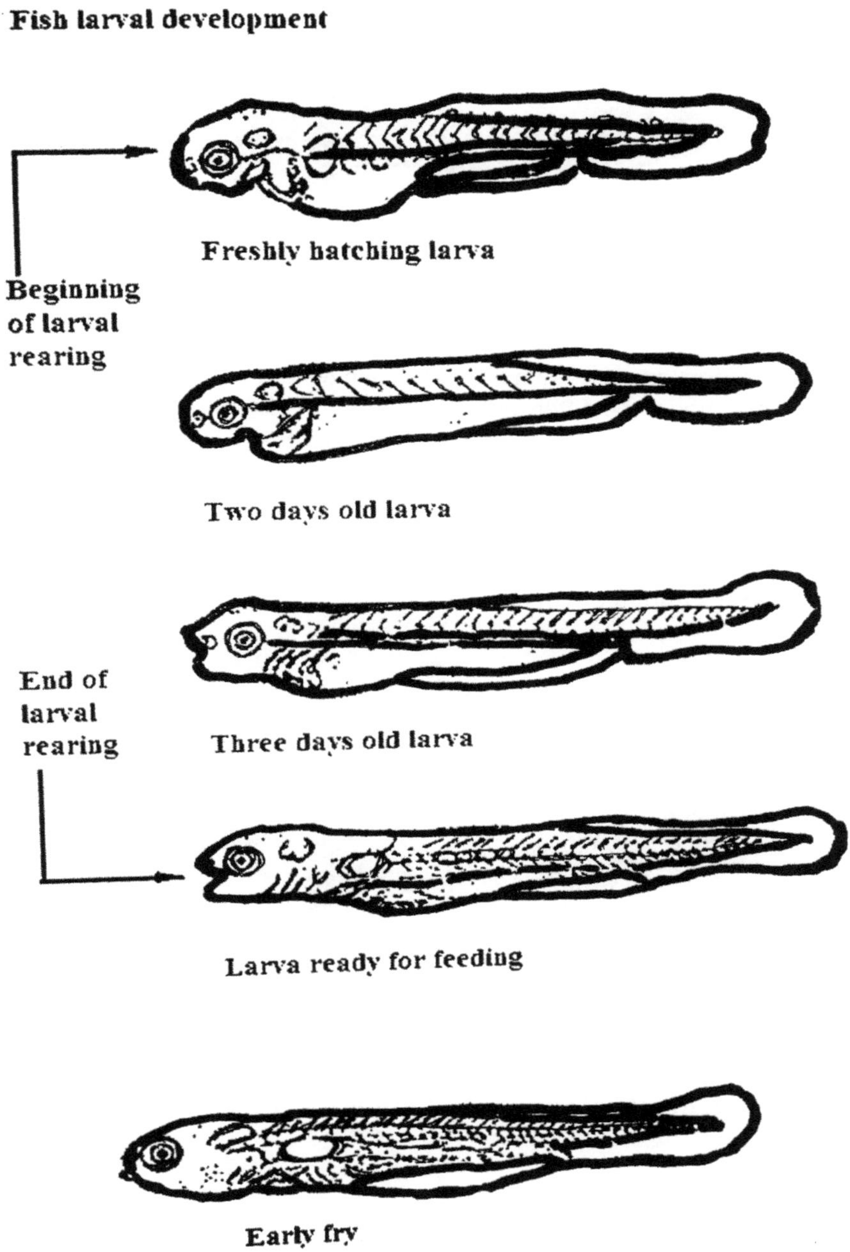

Fig. 5.3. Larval development

Fry: Fry are ready to start eating on their own. Fry undergo several more developmental stages, which vary by species, as they mature into adults (Fig. 5.4). Young fish are generally considered fry during their first few months (during their first few months to just less than one year in some species).

Fig. 5.4. Fry

Juvenile: The time fish spend developing from fry into reproductively mature adults varies among species. Most fish do not survive to become adults. Threats to survival include fluctuations in water temperature, changes in oxygen levels, competition for habitat and predators. After metamorphosis, the fish are considered juveniles and will acquire characteristics of an adult fish: body features, colouration, fins, etc. Metamorphosis also denotes full organ development; it occurs at different times for different types of fish. Juveniles are usually resistant to stress (temperature, water quality, etc.) over time. As long as the culture environment remains healthy, the fish should thrive on dry feed and show significant growth rates. Juveniles are not considered adults until they become sexually mature (Fig. 5.5).

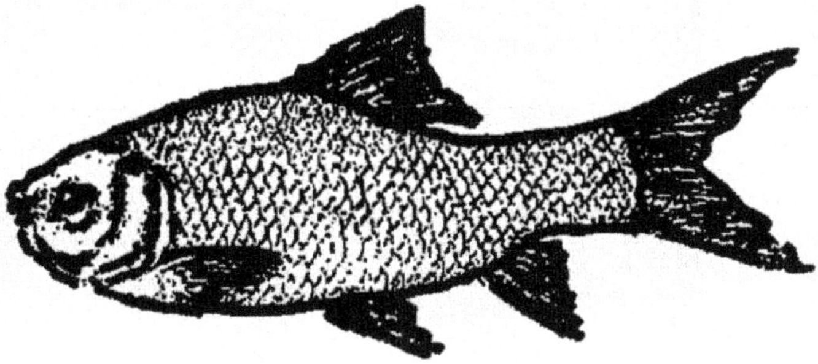

Fig. 5.5. Juvenile fish

Adult: When fish are able to reproduce, they are considered adults. The time it takes to reach maturity varies among species and individual fish.

6

Fishing Methods

Traditional fishing arts have been developed over the years to adapt to local conditions, the species of fish desired, and the size targeted. This chapter will describe some of the traditional fishing methods used around the world and consider their advantages and disadvantages. Each method shows a continuum of development with evolution resulting from modernizing factors. The introduction of any new fishing technology always demands good national management and regulation. Vessels must also be matched with new methods or gear. As gear becomes more complex, it may require upgrading of vessels in size, power, and design. The site specificity of fishing arts should always be considered.

The Ideal Fishing Gear

Some criteria for the ideal fishing gear could be: (1) Highly selective for the target species and sizes, with negligible direct or indirect impact on non-target species, sizes and habitats; (2) effective, giving high catches of target species at lowest possible cost; and (3) quality orientated, producing catches of high quality.

Classification of Fishing Gears

Based on the relative behaviour of the target species and the fishing gear, it is commonly classified in to passive and active. With passive gears, the capture of fish is generally based on the movement of the target species towards the gear (e.g. traps), while with active gears capture is generally based on an aimed chase of the target species (*e.g.* trawls, dredges). A parallel on land would be the difference between the trapping of and hunting for animals.

(A) Passive gear

This gear is stationary and it does not have to be dragged or towed to capture fish. Long lines, traps, weirs, and gill nets effectively fish by themselves. The catch is recovered by simply removing the gear from the water after a period of time.

1. Hooks and Lines Fishing

This gear generally consists of lines and hooks where natural or artificial baits are hooked to attract fish or other aquatic animals. A fish hook is a device for catching fish either by impaling them in the mouth or, more rarely, by snagging the body of the fish. Unbaited hooks or a jig may also be used. There is an enormous variety of fish hooks. Sizes, designs, shapes, and materials are all variable depending on the intended purpose of the hook. Fish hooks are normally attached to some form of line or lure device which connects the caught fish to the fisherman. The line is cast into the water where the fish supposedly are; the fish take the bait and are hauled in. Lines may be cast by ingenious methods. Hook and line fishing is inexpensive and easy. It can be used to catch fish from any boat or shoreline. A wide variety of sizes and types of hooks and lures can be used, allowing very selective fishing. The limitation of this method is that very limited number of fish can be captured per line and usually some type of bait is required (Fig. 6.1). Hook and lines come in many different forms that include hand lines, poles, long lines and trolling lines. The use of set lines can increase the number of lines deployed without requiring the constant presence of the fisherman. Such lines must be checked regularly because predators will devour any fish caught if the lines are not promptly recovered.

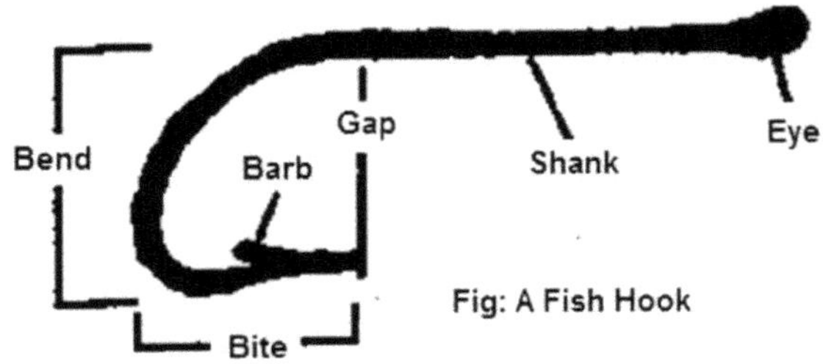

Fig: A Fish Hook

Fig. 6.1. Multiple-baited hooks on a line can increase the catch.

2. Longlines

Long-line fishing, also known as a trot line is a commercial fishing technique that uses many baited hooks hanging from a single line. It uses a long line, called the main line, with baited hooks attached at intervals by means of branch lines called snoods (or gangions). A snood is a short length of line, attached to the main line using a clip or swivel, with the hook at the other end. They can be used at the surface, suspended in the water column, or fixed on or near the bottom. Surface longlines are used to capture tuna, shark, and billfish. Subsurface and bottom-set longlines are used to catch cod, grouper, snapper, drum, bream, halibut, haddock, hake, and flatfish. An alternative to bottom-set longlines is a vertical fish stick. These hooks and lines involve low capital and energy investments and labor-intensive operations.

3. Traps

Traps, large stationary nets or barrages or pots, are gears in which the fish are retained or enter voluntarily and will be hampered from escaping. They are designed in such manner that the entrance itself became a non-return device, allowing the fish to enter the trap but making it impossible to leave the catching chamber. Pieces of fish are often used as bait. Artificial baits are also in use. Other types of traps are provided with large guiding panels made from netting to lead the fish into the catching chamber. Different materials are used for building a trap; wood, split bamboo, netting wire are some examples. The manner in which fish traps are used depends on local conditions and the behaviour of the local fish. For example, a fish trap might be placed in shallow water near rocks where pikes like to lie. If placed correctly, traps can be very effective. It is usually not necessary to check the trap daily, since the fish remain alive inside the trap, relatively unhurt. Because of this, the trap also allows for the release of undersized fish as per fishing regulations. Traps are culturally almost universal and seem to have been independently invented many times. There are essentially two types of trap, a permanent or semi-permanent structure placed in a river or tidal area and bottle or pot traps that are usually, but not always baited to attract prey, and are periodically lifted out of the water.

4. Weirs and Trap Nets

A fishing weir is an obstruction placed in tidal waters, or wholly or partially across a river, to direct the passage of fish. Weirs were traditionally built from wood or stones. The use of fishing weirs as fish traps dates back prior to the emergence of modern humans, and weirs have since been used by many societies across the world. A weir can be used to trap salmon and other fish when they attempt to swim upstream, or to trap eels as they migrate downstream. Alternatively, fish weirs can be used to redirect fish elsewhere.

Large traps can be built in shallow coastal waters to capture sizable fish such as salmon, bonito, tuna, herring, sardines, and cod. Leaders, or wings, guide fish through a slit and into a corral or catching chamber. The small opening acts as a retaining device so the fish do not escape from the corral. Weirs and trap nets have a number of advantages that favour their use in developing countries. They may be constructed of local materials and use little or no energy. Where seasonal runs occur, the catches can be enormous. The fish are live at capture, and therefore in excellent condition.

5. Gill Nets and Entangling Nets

Gillnets and entangling nets are walls of netting that are designed to catch fish by gilling, capturing the fish in the mesh by its head and gills, or entangling the entire body of the fish. These walls of nets may be set along the seafloor, anywhere in the water column, or at the surface. Entangling nets are net walls, placed transversely to the path of migrating fish. The bottom of the net is weighted with sinkers while the top is supported by floats. A single-walled net (gill net) is used to gill fish, while a triple-walled net (trammel) entangles them. A gill net is an upright wall of fiber netting. A fish, of a size for which the net is designed, swimming into the net, can only pass part way through a single mesh. As the fish struggles to free itself, the net twine slips in back of the gill. The fish is thus gilled and can go neither forward nor backward. Various mesh sizes are employed, depending on the species and size of the fish to be caught (Fig. 6.2). The mesh size determines the size of the fish caught.

The main difference between gillnets and entangling nets is that entangling nets are set to have more slack in the netting, which results in fish becoming completely entangled in the net. Conversely, with gillnets, the netting is more tight and fish only are entangled through their head.

Fig. 6.2. Gill net

6. Trammel Nets

Trammel nets are one of the most complex, yet efficient gill nets that are in popular use worldwide. Unlike single wall gill nets, which will catch a narrow range of fish sizes, a trammel net will catch a wide variety of fish sizes. A trammel is fishing net with three layers of netting suspended from a common row of floats and attached to a single bottom line that is used to entangle fish or crustacea. A slack central layer with a small mesh is sandwiched between two taut outer layers with a much larger mesh. The net is kept vertical by the floats on the head-rope and weights on the bottom-rope. A fish striking from either side passes through the large mesh outer panel, strikes the smaller mesh interior panel, and carries it through the opposite large mesh panel, forming a sack or pocket in which the fish is trapped. A trammel net is often fished by drifting. These nets may be used at the surface, in mid-water, or at the bottom. Although a single net may be deployed, usually a row of nets are set. A fisherman may choose to anchor his net or allow it to drift. In intertidal areas, the nets may be driven into the bottom and the fish collected at low tide.

(B) Active gear

Active gear has to be moved, dragged, or towed in order to capture fish. This usually requires engine-propelled boats and usually involves additional investment over passive or stationary gear.

1. Trolling

Trolling lines are simple hooked lines that are trailed from a moving vessel at a controlled depth. This may be behind a moving boat, or by slowly winding the line in when fishing from a static position, or even sweeping the line from side-to-side. Trolling is used to catch pelagic fish such as salmon, mackerel and kingfish. Bait may be artificial or natural and attracts predator fish that see what appears to be a smaller fish thrashing and turning in the water. To be effective, trolling baits and lures must have the visual ability to attract fish and intrigue them with the way they move through the water. Most trolling lures are designed to look and behave like dying, injured, or fast moving fish. The use of outriggers can increase the number of lines that can be trolled and helps keep them from becoming tangled. Trolling offers numerous advantages to small-scale fisheries. Multiple trolling can be performed from a reasonably small craft. Changing sinker weights allows fishing at graduated depths. The use of artificial bait avoids the capture or purchase of live bait.

2. Seining

A seine is a fishing net that hangs vertically in the water with its bottom edge held down by weights and its top edge buoyed by floats. Seine nets can be deployed from the shore as a beach seine, or from a boat. Seines are long nets with meshes small enough to prevent the desired fish from gilling (filtering nets). They are generally set in a semicircle and dragged over a smooth bottom by means of long ropes (sweeps). In this way, the fish are herded into the net and hauled onto the beach or on board.

3. Beach seines

Beach seine is a traditional fishing method where fish are encircled from the shore with a long net dragged by a rowing boat, and hauled up onto the beach. One end remains on shore, while the rest of the net is set in a curved path and brought back to the beach. Once the second drag line is delivered to shore, the hauling begins. The bottom and the water surface act as natural barriers for the fish encircled in the net. The wings may often be hundreds of meters long. Large beach seines, however, are costly, and their use is restricted to large stretches of smooth, shallow bottoms with fairly mild surf. The net is species-indiscriminate and may catch juveniles of large-sized fish. Small two-man beach seines are often used for catching live bait or small fish. The method has a much more localised impact compared to industrialised fishing methods; but nets of any kind by nature are non-selective and fishing tends to occur in or near estuaries which are important breeding and nursery zones for many fish species.

4. Boat seines

These seines are hauled from a boat. A vessel anchors one end of the seine and sails in a circle, releasing the net, and returns to the anchor. The net is then hauled into the boat. With small seines, this fishing technique can be used by smaller vessels without mechanization almost anywhere there is a smooth bottom.

5. Purse seines and ring nets

Purse seines are common type of seine named such because along the bottom are a number of rings. A line (referred to as a purse-line) passes through all the rings, and when pulled, draws the rings close to one another, preventing the fish from "sounding", or swimming down to escape the net. This operation is similar to a traditional style purse, which has a drawstring. The purse seine can be set with one or two boats and must be fished quickly. Those that are operated with two boats are called ring nets. Light may also be used to attract the target species. The purse seine is a preferred technique for capturing fish species aggregate close to the surface such as sardines, mackerel, anchovies, herring, certain species of tuna and salmon soon before they swim up rivers and streams to spawn (aggregation). Hauling can be done manually, and the catch is live. Nevertheless, purse seines are costly and require highly skilled operators.

6. Cast nets

Cast, or throw nets are small round nets with weights on the edges which is thrown by the fisher. It is a good tool for capturing large fish without damaging them. A cast net is made of a flat circular piece of small-mesh netting, heavily weighted along its periphery with sinkers. Sizes vary up to about four meters in diameter. Usually a series of strings runs from the outer edge through a central ring to join into a single pulling rope. A cast net is not very easy to make, but can be bought from a specialized store. Handling of a cast net requires skill (Fig. 6.3). The net is thrown by hand in such a manner that it spreads out on the water and sinks. Fish are caught as the net is hauled back in. A cast net can be used either from the banks, in the water, or from a boat.

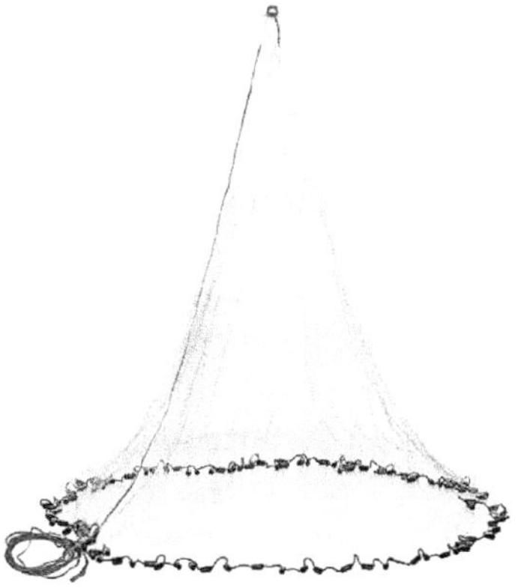

Fig. 6.3. Cast net

7. Spears and harpoons

This is one of the most ancient ways of active fish capture. Capture with spears and harpoons depends on visual observation of the target species, which is then impaled by the spear or harpoon from a relatively short distance. Basically, the spear or harpoon is designed for easy penetration of the target organism, but the spear head is equipped with barbs or flukes that hold the prey when it is hit. Common target species with this fishing method are flat fish, sword fish, tunas and whales.

Fishing boats

Traditional fishing vessels have evolved to complement the sea conditions and fishing methods unique to each particular region. Like fishing gear, boats have passed the test of time. Nevertheless, traditional craft are not without their problems. They often have a very limited range of operation and are not able to go beyond heavily fished near shore areas. Many will sink if swamped, providing no reserve of safety. Customary building materials are often unavailable. Deforestation in many coastal areas has created a scarcity of quality wood for dugout canoes and larger craft.

Traditional boats can be improved, often without radically altering the basic design; a respect for tradition will increase their acceptance. New vessels should have improved fishing capabilities. Increased seaworthiness and better fuel performance would permit fishing further offshore for previously unexploited species. Working and storage space could be increased, creating better working conditions and facilitating an increased catch. In areas without harbors, beachable craft are a priority. Improved designs should also help ensure the safety of the crew by including a second means of propulsion and sufficient buoyancy so that the vessel remains afloat when flooded. Cost effectiveness is a fundamental requirement. The value of the daily catch must exceed the operational costs and help amortize the construction costs within a reasonable time. In essence, the boat should require low investment, use minimum fuel, catch as much fish as possible, and have a long service life. A fishing boat may be described as a floating platform used to transport the crew, gear, and cargo to and from the fishing grounds and to support the crew and equipment during the fishing operation. Some of the major factors that affect the design of this platform include:

- Available funds
- Available materials
- Skills for building and maintenance
- Size limitations dictated by water depth or requirement for beaching
- Distance to fishing grounds
- Fuel costs
- Type and quantity of gear used
- Vessel speed requirements

- Number of crew, standard of accommodation, cooking facilities
- Methods of bait and catch preservation
- Safety features

Overfishing

Overfishing is a form of overexploitation in which fish stocks are depleted to unacceptable levels, regardless of water body size. Resource depletion, low biological growth rates, and critically low biomass levels result from overfishing. For example, overfishing of sharks has led to the upset of entire marine ecosystems.

Billions of people rely on fish for protein, and fishing is the principal livelihood for millions of people around the world. For centuries, our seas and oceans have been considered a limitless bounty of food. More than 85 percent of the world's fisheries have been pushed to or beyond their biological limits and are in need of strict management plans to restore them. Several important commercial fish populations (such as Atlantic bluefin tuna) have declined to the point where their survival as a species is threatened. Target fishing of top predators, such as tuna and groupers, is changing marine communities, which lead to an abundance of smaller marine species, such as sardines and anchovies.

Causes of overfishing

Lack of protected areas: Just 1.6% of the world's oceans have been declared as marine protected areas (MPAs), and 90% of existing MPAs are open to fishing. MPAs are important because they protect habitats such as coral reefs from destructive fishing practices. No-take zones allow depleted fish populations to recover and provide refuge for endangered species such as marine turtles. Protected areas allow stressed reefs the ability to recover from climate change impacts, such as bleaching. These benefits translate to improved food security for people who rely on the ocean for their daily sustenance and livelihoods.

Open access fisheries: A main problem of overfishing is the "open access" nature of fisheries. Because there are no or few property rights there is a lack of incentive for fishermen to leave fish in the water.

Poor fisheries management: A lack of management oversight, government regulations, and traceability of fishing activities has long been a problem in the fishing industry. Current rules and regulations are not strong enough to limit fishing capacity to a sustainable level. This is particularly the case for the high seas, where there are few international fishing regulations, and those that exist are not always implemented or enforced. Many fisheries management bodies are not able to adequately incorporate scientific advice on fish quotas, and customs agencies and retailers cannot always ensure that the fish entering their country is caught legally and in a sustainable way.

Illegal fishing: One key dimension of the overfishing crisis is illegal, unregulated, and unreported fishing. It occurs across all types of fisheries, within national and international waters, and small scale to large industrialized operations. Illegal fishing accounts for an estimated 20% of the world's catch and as much as 50% in some fisheries. The costs of illegal fishing are significant, with the value of pirate fish products estimated at between $10-23.5 billion annually.

Subsidies: Many governments still continue to subsidize their fleets, allowing unprofitable operations to subsist, and overfishing to occur. Today's worldwide fishing fleet is estimated to be up to two and a half times the capacity needed to catch what we actually need.

Impacts of overfishing

Economic loss: Fishing is integral to economies around the world. Overfishing threatens coastal nations down to the local level, devastating communities whose chief source of labor and revenue hinges on healthy, plentiful stocks of fish.

Marine life imbalance: Targeted fishing of top predators (such as billfish, sharks and tuna) eventually disrupts marine communities, causing increased abundance of smaller marine animals at the bottom of the food chain. This in turn has impacts on the rest of the marine ecosystem, such as the increased growth of algae and threats to coral reef health. Overfishing is also closely tied to by catch, another serious marine threat that causes the needless loss of billions of fish, along with marine turtles and cetaceans.

Decreased food security: Coastal communities around the world depend on fish as their primary source of protein. Overfishing threatens their long-term food security, particularly in developing countries.

Pollution: Oil and liquid spills, chemical and solid elements discharged into the water by fishing boats, vessels and trawlers often hurt marine life. It is very easy to think that the oceans are so big and these are not real threats, but a bit of pollution by thousands of trawlers everyday contribute to something very big and disturbing. Water pollution has very devastating consequences.

7

Construction of a Fish Pond

A fish pond is a controlled pond, artificial lake, or reservoir that is stocked with fish and is used in aquaculture for fish farming, or is used for recreational fishing or for ornamental purposes. Fishes can be grown in any pond but a pond specially dug for fish culture has some important features. Such ponds have a regular shape, a flat bottom with a slight slope along its length. Fish ponds are different depending upon the purpose of fish culture.

Types of ponds

Nursery pond: These are smallest and shallowest ponds built in an area of 0.02-0.05 hectare with water one meter deep.

Rearing pond: It is 0.08-0.2 hectare in size with water about 1.5 – 2 meters deep. Nursery and rearing ponds can be seasonal.

Stocking pond: It is a large pond, often 0.2 to 2 hectares. It should have a water depth of 2.0 to 3.5 meters. Such ponds can be perennial or seasonal.

Marketing pond: It is small but quite deep pond used to keep fish from stocking pond for sale as and when demand comes. Size of this pond can be 0.05–0.01 ha with water level of 3-4 m in summer.

Brood stock pond: Brood stock ponds (0.2-0.4 ha) are perennial and have a water depth of 2 m in summer.

Quarantine pond: It is a pond meant to first place fish brought in from outside for verification of disease free status. It is small (0.02 ha) but perennial (1.5 m deep).

Site selection

The first step or the most important preconstruction activity is to select a correct site as careful site selection is a pre-requisite in pond construction. Improper site selection may lead to difficulties in holding water in the pond; high seepage; dike erosion; low productivity of the pond, resulting low yields and economic loss; inability to drain water completely, and difficulties in harvesting.

Factors for a suitable site selection

The most important factors while selecting a suitable site are space availability and topography of the site, water supply and quality, and soil quality. Other site characteristics which are also important include vegetation cover, accessibility, proximity to home, multiple uses of the ponds, proximity and size of the market and availability of inputs.

1. **Space availability and topography:** The site should at least have a space of 200 m^2 to construct a pond. It is better to select flat land or lands with a slight gradient. Sites with slight gradients (0.5 to 3 percent is better. Avoid sites with gradients more than 5 percent) have the advantage of obtaining water into the pond and drain water out from the pond by gravity. A site having large undulations and rocks and with large trees should be avoided. This type of areas will increase the construction cost and also prevent good sunlight into the pond.
2. **Water supply and water quality:** The site should be adjacent to or in close proximity to a suitable water source in order to fill the pond easily. The source of water should have adequate amount of water with required quality to supply water into the pond throughout the year or at least throughout grater part of the year. The water should not be acidic and should be free from pollutants such as waste and pesticides. Streams, large rivers, small rivers, lakes and reservoirs can be used as water sources. Stream and river water is generally rich in dissolved oxygen than lakes and reservoirs. With respect to state of pollution all these water sources can have same pollution problems, but reservoirs and lakes are relatively slow than streams and rivers in recovering from the pollution state.

   The most important water quality parameters in freshwater ponds are temperature, pH value, dissolved oxygen. Temperature influences almost all the physiological activities of fish/shrimp such as respiration, growth, feeding, molting, disease resistance. In general the suitable range for tropical fish is 25 to 30°C. The dissolved oxygen in water is one of the most important water quality parameter to maintain a healthy pond environment. The dissolved oxygen level of 5.0 to 6.0 mg/liter is better for many fish. The pH value tells whether water is acidic or otherwise (basic). The pH of pond water is a good indication of health of fish and pond environment. For most of fish a pH value between 6 and 8.5 is better.
3. **Soil quality:** Soil quality should be considered in two ways *i.e.* as physical quality and chemical quality.

Physical quality: Soil has particles of various sizes, namely, sand, silt and clay. Among these three types sand is the largest and clay is the finest. The relative amount (percentages) of these three sizes is known as soil texture. Pond soil should have enough clay to hold water and prevent erosion of pond dike. However, 100% clay is not suitable for pond construction, since the pond dikes crack when expose to sunlight.

Chemical quality: Pond soil should not be acidic because acidic-soils reduce the pond productivity. Growth of algae, a natural food for many fish and essential for a good pond environment, may be greatly reduced. Acidic-soils make the pond water acidic which in turn retards growth of fish and causes stress situation favouring infections and diseases.

Avoid sites with rock outcrops, gravel beds, sandstone and limestone and beware of sandy soils and termite mounds. Preference should be given to soils such as sandy clay, silty clay loam and clayey loam.

4. ***Local topography:*** The site should be such where water drainage will be possible by gravity, the earthwork is minimum and where it will be easy to balance the volume of earth to be excavated and that to be filled in. Such sites are available on gently sloping ground, where the slope is 0.5 to 3 percent. Avoid slopes greater than 5 percent. If you have to use horizontal land, it will be more costly to build drainable ponds. Also, the size of the selected site should be large enough for immediate purpose and, if necessary, for future expansion. A regular shape will make it easier to plan.
5. ***Vegetation cover:*** Open woodland, grassland, old paddy fields or land covered with low shrubs permit easier and cheaper construction. Avoid the areas having big trees or a dense population of smaller trees.
6. ***Accessibility and proximity to home:*** There should be a good accessibility to the site by a road. This will help in good management of the pond and marketing. To make an easy pond management and to protect them against poaching it is always best to live near the ponds.
7. ***Multiple uses of the ponds:*** It is sometimes advantageous to be able to use your ponds for purposes other than fish farming such as livestock watering, gardening or domestic use.
8. ***Proximity and size of market:*** Once harvested, your fish should preferably be sold fresh, as soon as possible and with the least costs. You should know in advance how many fish you will be able to sell in one day and plan your pond sizes and harvests accordingly.
9. ***Availability of inputs:*** Regular inputs such as feed ingredients and juvenile fish should be available locally. Availability of spare parts and supplies is also important.

Pond layout

After selecting the site of fish farm, the physical planning is made, in which decision on layouts, detailed design and earthwork is taken. Pond layout can be done either in a series or parallel. The advantage of arranging the ponds in a series is cost effective when compared to arranging in parallel. However, it has the disadvantage of difficulties in maintaining a healthy pond environment as it has a greater risk of spreading disease and contaminations from one pond to the other.

Align the pond direction. Wind plays a role in fishpond design. Strong wind generates waves and the waves break on the dikes, it may erode the sides of the dikes. To minimize this, position the longer pond dimensions (longer pond axis) parallel to the direction of the main prevailing wind direction so that the wave action would be on shorter length of dikes and erosion would be less.

Ensure protection of pond from flood. If the fish pond site is prone to flooding, construct a diversion canal along the perimeter dike to divert runoff water during heavy rains. Construct a larger and higher perimeter dike to prevent inflow of water.

Design of the pond

Pond bottom, pond dike and pond outlets are important features of a fish pond that should be properly designed.

1. **Pond bottom**: The bottom of the pond should be flat and sloping towards the outlet or drainage gate with a gentle gradient. For small ponds a gentle slope of the pond bottom of about 0.5% to 1.0% from the water inlet to water outlet to ensure easy and complete drainage of the pond is good.
2. **Pond dikes**: Dikes are the most important part of a fish pond, as they keep the necessary volume of water impounded and form the actual pond; their design and construction is particularly important. Any pond dike should have three basic qualities: (1) It should be able to resist the water pressure resulting from the pond water depth; (2) should be impervious, the water seepage through the dike kept to a minimum; and (3) it should be high enough to keep the pond water from ever running over its top, which would otherwise rapidly destroy the dike. These points can be ensured as noted below.
   a) **Resistance to water pressure:** Newly built dikes should be protected against erosion by planting or seeding a grass cover on the crest of the dikes, on their dry side and on their wet side down to the normal water level of the pond.
   b) **Ensuring impermeability**: Impermeability of the dike can be ensured by using good soil that contains enough clay, building a central clay core when using pervious soil material, and a cut-off trench when the foundation is permeable. Application of good construction practices with appropriate thickness of dikes is very important.
   c) **Choosing the right height**: The height of the dike depends on the depth of water to be kept in pond. The upper part of the dike should never be under water. Part of the calculated dike height is lost during settlement, taking into account the compression of the subsoil by the dike weight and the settling of fresh soil material. Therefore, a settlement allowance which usually varies from 5 to 20 percent of the construction height of the dike should be given while deciding the height of the dike of a fish pond.

Dike outlet structures: Outlet structures are built for two main reasons: (1) To keep the water surface in the pond at its optimum level, which usually coincides with the maximum water level designed for the pond; and (2) to allow for the complete draining of the pond and harvesting of the fish whenever necessary.

3. **Pond outlets:** Outlet structures are built for two main reasons: (1) To keep the water surface in the pond at its optimum level, which usually coincides with the maximum water level designed for the pond; and (2) to allow for the complete draining of the pond and harvesting of the fish whenever necessary. In addition to these major features, a good outlet should also ensure as far as possible that:
   - the amount of time necessary to drain the pond completely is reasonable;
   - the flow of the draining water is as uniform as possible to avoid disturbing the fish excessively;
   - there is no loss of fish, especially during the draining period;
   - water can be drained from the top, bottom or intermediate levels of the pond;
   - any reasonable excess of water is carried away;
   - the outlet can be easily cleaned and serviced; and
   - the construction cost and maintenance are relatively low.

Functions of pond outlet: The functions of the pond outlet are to drain the pond completely in reasonable time, the flow of the draining water is as uniform as possible to avoid disturbing the fish excessively; there is no loss of fish, especially during the draining period; water can be drained from the top, bottom or intermediate levels of the pond; any reasonable excess of water is carried away; the outlet can easily be cleaned and serviced; and the construction cost and maintenance are relatively low.

Construction of pond outlet: An outlet comprises a collecting area on the inside of the pond, from which the water drains and into which the stock is collected for harvest. The means of water control include any drain plugs, valves, control boards, screens and gates. Pond outlets can be built in various ways, using different materials such as bamboo, wood, bricks, cement blocks or concrete. There are four main types, viz. simple cuts through the dike, simple pipelines and siphons, sluices, monks.

1. **Simple cut through the dike:** Very small rural ponds can be harvested by cutting the dike open at one of the deepest points of the pond.
2. **Simple pipe outlet:** For small-size and shallow ponds, a straight pipeline with a small diameter can be used as a water outlet. The pipe should be laid down at the lowest point of the pond before the dike is built. According to availability and cost, the pipe can be a bamboo pipe, galvanized iron pipe or plastic pipe.
3. **The sluice gate:** A sluice gate consists of a protected opening in the pond dike that can be easily closed with wooden boards to regulate water

level and can be screened to avoid fish losses. Whenever required, it can discharge excess water continuously.

4. **The monk outlet:** It consists of a vertical tower closed with wooden boards to regulate the water level. The water is discharged through a pipeline buried under the dike. A screen keeps the farmed fish from leaving the pond

Transportation of water on a fish farm

Several different kinds of structures may be used to transport water on a fish farm. The most common one is the open canal. The other common structures include: (i) simple aqueducts to transport water above ground level; (ii) short pipelines to transport water above or under another structure such as a water canal or an access road; and (iii) simple siphons to transport water over an obstacle such as a pond dike. Different types of open water canals are used on fish farms to transport water, usually by gravity for four main purposes listed below.

1. **Feeder canals**: These are used to supply water from the main water intake to the fish ponds. Water feeder canals, or supply canals, connect the main water intake to the various fish rearing facilities of the fish farm. While planning and designing feeder canals, it should be kept in mind that the main feeder canal should bring the water to the farm site by gravity at the highest possible level. The level of the canal bottom should ideally be at least 10 cm higher than the normal water level in the pond it supplies.
2. **Drainage canals**: Drainage canals are built to carry the water draining from the fish ponds away from the farm site, usually into a lower natural channel.
3. **Diversion canals**: These divert excess water away from barrage ponds. A diversion canal should be built to divert excess stream water around a barrage pond if the pond is built where there is a likelihood of floods. Such a canal should therefore be deep and wide enough to evacuate the largest flood waters. The canal should be at least 5 m away from the pond banks
4. **Protection canals**: These are required to divert water runoff away from the fish ponds.

Construction of a dug-out pond

A pond is usually dug in the ground and can be made of earth or building material like concrete. Dug-out ponds, entirely obtained through soil excavation, are the simplest to build. There are two main types of dug-out pond depending on the water supply. These include: (1) Dug-out ponds fed by rain and surface runoff, commonly found in relatively flat, well-drained terrain such as the low point of a natural depression; and (2) dug-out ponds fed by springs or seepage. The latter is commonly found in areas where the groundwater table is close to the surface, either permanently or seasonally.

1. Selecting soil for dug-out ponds

To build a rain-fed dug-out pond, it is essential to have enough impervious soil at the site to avoid excess seepage losses. The best sites are those where fine-textured clays and silty clays extend well below the proposed pond depth. Sandy clays extending to adequate depths are satisfactory. Porous soils, either at the surface or at the depths should be avoided for rain fed dug-out pond. A seepage dug-out pond should have the soil having a thick water-bearing layer as well as permeable enough to provide the required water. It is best to observe the site during a complete annual cycle to check on the possible variations of the water table elevation with the season.

2. Preparation of site

i. Mark the area to be cleared using stakes. This should include the total area of the pond to the outside limits of the pond dikes and, in addition, an area of two to three metres to serve as a work space and for walkways beyond the dikes.

ii. Clear all vegetation from the marked area. Also remove all shrubs and trees within 10 metres of the cleared area.

iii. Next, at the very centre of the cleared area, mark the pond area to the outside limits of the pond dikes using heavy string or cord. Remove the surface soil from this area and store it for later use.

iv. Now mark the inside limits of the pond bottom using heavy string or cord. When staking out the pond bottom, indicate on each stake the depth of excavation from ground surface to pond bottom.

v. Dig to the designed depth within the limits of the pond, cutting the sides vertically. Transport the waste soil to the planned areas. There are two easy ways to dispose of waste soil material. If there is enough space around the pond, the waste soil can be spread there. Limit the thickness of spread soil to 1 m at most and slope it gently away from the pond; make a pile of waste soil near the pond, but be sure to leave at least 4 m between the toe of the pile and the pond. The sides of piled soil should have a gentle slope of 3:1 or more. Clearly mark the limits of the areas where the excavated material will be spread or piled.

vi. Shape the sides of the pond to the desired slope and finish the pond bottom and the horizontal dike tops. Remove any excess soil.

vii. Bring back the surface soil to cover the waste material and the dike tops.

viii. Then plant or sow grass all around the pond to prevent erosion.

ix. Water control structures such as a feeding canal, inlet pipe, outlet sluice, spillway or drainage canal may be provided for dug-out ponds.

When the construction site has been prepared, the fish pond construction can be initiated. To construct it, the fish pond dike and construction of water control structures needs special attention.

3. Construction of the dikes

Construction of the dikes is the most important component of a fish pond construction, as they keep the necessary volume of water impounded and form the actual pond; their design and construction is particularly important.

Foundations of the dike: After clearing the site, removing the surface soil and marking out the position of the dike, the foundations of the dike should be prepared. The surface of the dike's foundations needs to be well compacted, so that the dike can be solidly attached without any risk of it sliding away. The foundation soil should contain an adequate layer of impervious material at the surface,

Preparing for the construction of the dikes: When the inner and outer limits of the pond have been staked, clear any remaining vegetation from the area. Remove the surface soil only from the area of the dike bases, as staked out above, and store it close by. Treat the surface of the foundations of the dikes as described above. Build the water control structures, as necessary. Place the outlet entrance at an elevation low enough to ensure complete drainage of the pond along the sloping bottom.

Finishing the dikes: The dikes are constructed with sides that look like staircases. To reform these dikes with smooth side slopes and to finish their construction, one should proceed in the following way. On the top of each dike, set out the planned dike crest width, measuring half of its value on either side of the Centre line and marking the limits with wooden pegs and lines. Starting from the top of the dike, obliquely cut the end of each soil layer on the wet side of the dikes following a slope that joins the limit of the dike crest to the bottom limit of the layers, until reaching the staked-out limit of the dike base. Repeat this cutting on the dry side of the dikes. Transport the soil removed, as necessary. Remove all stakes and lines. Bring back some of the surface soil on the top of the dikes and on the dry sides.

4. Construction of pond outlet structures

In most cases, outlets have three main elements: (1) A collecting area on the inside of the pond, from which the water drains and into which the stock is collected for harvest; (2) the water control itself, including any drain plugs, valves, control boards, screens and gates; and (3) a device for getting the water to the outside of the pond such as a pipe or a cut through the wall, and/or an overflow structure. When designing and constructing an outlet structure, one should pay particular attention to the following points:

a) Design a water discharge capacity large enough so that the pond can be drained within a reasonable amount of time, from a few hours for a small pond to one to two days for a large pond.

b) Design the elevation of the bottom of the outlet structure low enough to ensure complete drainage of the pond, so that on the pond side, it is at least 10 cm lower than the lowest point in the pond; it slopes away from the pond, preferably with a slope equal to or greater than 1 percent; and at its end, it is at least 20 cm higher than the bottom of the drainage canal.

c) Design its total length so that the water will be discharged well away from the outside toe of the dike to avoid damaging it by erosion.

d) Plan for the outlet to be built before or right after the beginning of the dike construction, depending on the type of pond.

e) If there is an outlet pipe through the dike, it is always best to build at least one anti-seepage concrete collar around it. Place it so that it will be integrated with the dike; build it perpendicular to the pipe; extend it at least 15 cm from all sides of the pipe; and make it at least 10 cm thick.

f) When building the dike above the pipes, be sure to compact the earth well around them.

g) Remember that small pipes can become easily blocked, particularly inside the pond. Therefore avoid using pipes with a very small diameter; protect the entrance of all pipes with a screen, and keep this screen clean through regular checks.

Select the right size and quality of pipes to be used. For very small diameters, one can use bamboo, galvanized or plastic pipes; for small diameters, plastic pipes are prepared; for medium diameters, asbestos cement pipes are preferred and for large diameters, reinforced concrete pipes are preferred.

Placing and fixing outlet pipes

In general, in stable soil with well-constructed dikes and smaller pipes, no special precautions are required, apart from ensuring that pipe trenches are level and that the pipe will not be damaged. For longer and larger pipes such as those used in monks, some fixing or foundation may be required. For very small rural ponds, simple outlets can be built by using a cut in the dike at one of the deepest points of the pond. It is rebuilt when the pond has to be filled again.

5. Final check of the pond structures

After the construction of pond is completed, it is essential to check that the structures so constructed will function properly. This includes the water intake, the canals, the pond inlet and outlet; strength of the dikes as well its stabilization and enough impervious nature. For maximum security and efficiency, one should proceed in the following way. Fill the pond with water very slowly and up to a maximum depth of 0.40 m at the outlet.

i. Close the water supply and keep water in the pond for a few days. During this period, check the dikes carefully. Repair crevices and collapsed sections, compacting well.

ii. Drain the water completely and leave the pond dry for a few days. Keep checking the dikes and repair them as necessary.

iii. Fill the pond again very slowly and up to a maximum level about 0.40 m higher than the previous time.

iv. Close the water supply. Check the dikes and repair them as necessary. After a few days, drain the pond completely.

v. Repeat this process of filling/drying until the water level in the pond reaches the designed maximum level.

vi. Check and repair the dikes as necessary.

vii. If there is a limited water supply it will not be possible to follow the above procedure. In such a case, fill the pond very slowly and gradually, closing the water supply at regular intervals and checking on the dikes carefully

8

Management of Fish Farm Ponds

Ponds are complex ecological systems and require personal commitment and insight for productive management. No two ponds are exactly alike. The purpose of good fish pond management includes enhancing food availability for fish, controlled harvesting to maintain the balance of predator and prey populations, controlling weeds, and preventing situations that may cause fish kills.

Factors critical to fish pond management

Plankton and water quality along with the fish populations are major critical factors influencing fish farm management.

1. Plankton

Plankton is classified as phytoplankton (plants) and zooplankton (animals). Both phytoplankton and zooplankton are important in fish pond management. Plankton in the water of a pond are important because they creat oxygen in a pond. Fish need oxygen to survive, and oxygen should be made available to fish in dissolved form. The source of dissolved oxygen is either the air or through the process of photosynthesis. Aquatic plants, primarily phytoplankton and other algae, release oxygen directly into the water as a by-product of photosynthesis, the most important source of oxygen in water. Also the phytoplankton at the bottom of the aquatic food chain is eaten by zooplankton and insects. Small fish eat the zooplankton and insects. Small fish are food for larger fish. An adequate phytoplankton population is essential for producing a large and healthy fish community.

The colour or clarity of pond water can be related to plankton populations or to suspended sediments and organic matter. Productive water i.e. the water that will support healthy fish populations has a green tint that is produced by chlorophyll pigments contained in the billions of phytoplankton suspended in the water. The dark or black coloured water is indicative of decayed phytoplankton and the fish in such water are stressed or die.

Sediments (silt, sand, or dirt) washed into ponds after heavy rains can also change pond colour. Normal colour should return within a few days as the particles settle. Ponds that receive too much sediment can become unproductive.

2. Water Quality

Pond dynamics are also affected by water quality. Factors such as pH, alkalinity, and dissolved oxygen affect fish health and pond productivity. Some aspects of water quality fluctuate daily, weekly, or monthly. Dissolved oxygen and pH cycle can change each day the alkalinity over a period over a period of time, ranging from several weeks to months, depending on the pH of the watershed or soils on the bottom of the pond.

a) **Dissolved oxygen:** Photosynthesis is critical to the production of oxygen in a pond. That is why dissolved oxygen levels rise throughout the day while there is no oxygen production at night. In a well-managed pond, nighttime dissolved oxygen levels should not fall below 3 or 4 parts per million (ppm or mg/l). Oxygen levels below 3 ppm stress fish, and many species may suffocate and die when oxygen levels fall below 2 ppm.

b) **pH:** It varies over the course of a day as a result of respiration and photosynthesis. The carbon dioxide released from respiration reacts with water, producing carbonic acid. During nighttime the pond becomes more acidic and pH is lowered. During daylight, phytoplankton use carbon dioxide in photosynthesis. This reduces acidity and increases pH. The pond pH normally fluctuates between 6.5 and 9. If the pH drops below 5 or rises above 10, fish may become stressed and die.

c) **Alkalinity:** It is related to pH. Alkalinity can increase the availability of carbon dioxide and other nutrients to phytoplankton. Waters of low alkalinity generally originate from acid soils. Alkaline water originates from soils with good quantities of limestone. Alkaline water (50 to 300 ppm as $CaCO_3$) is the most desirable for fish production. Acid pond soils can be neutralized with applications of agricultural limestone.

Basic principles of fish pond management

Following principles should be kept in mind for good pond management.

i. Proper pond construction and watershed management
ii. Removal of unwanted and overpopulated species of fish
iii. Liming and/or fertilization
iv. Fish species selection and stocking
v. Harvest and record keeping
vi. Evaluation of pond balance

vii. Weed control

viii. Other beneficial management practices

1. Pond construction

One of the first principles of good pond management is the proper construction of the pond. In poorly constructed ponds, water levels may change dramatically if there is seepage. Soils for pond construction must contain a minimum of 20% clay, and the dam should be constructed with a compacted clay core. Trees or other woody vegetation should not be permitted to grow on pond dams. Ponds should have a drain to regulate water levels easily.

Shallow ponds, less than 2½ feet deep, stimulate aquatic weed growth by allowing sunlight to reach the pond bottom. To remedy this problem, pond banks should be built with slopes of 2:1 or 3:1 ratios (horizontal distance to height). In addition, erosion and contamination from the watershed may make pond management difficult or impossible.

Livestock can cause severe erosion damage on pond banks and levees. The eroded sediments slowly fill the pond and create shallow areas enhancing weed growth. In addition, animal wastes may wash into the pond during periods of heavy rainfall. This can cause water pollution or nutrient overload problems. To prevent this from happening, locate livestock watering areas below the pond, do not allow livestock to graze or roam on watershed land, and fence the pond to keep cattle away.

Ponds should also be separated from agricultural row-crops or fields by a grass barrier. Pesticides, herbicides, and contaminated soils or vegetation can wash into a pond and kill fish. By placing grass strips 50 to 100 feet wide around the pond, soil erosion can be reduced and chemical runoff from neighboring pastures and fields be prevented.

2. Fish removal

In poorly managed fish pond, fish populations often become imbalanced or contaminated with unwanted species. Typically, unmanaged ponds become crowded with small, stunted or bullhead sized fish. The best remedy is to eliminate unwanted fish. Rotenone is a registered aquatic chemical which can be used to kill fish. Rotenone dissipates from the water within 3-20 days depending on water temperature and weather conditions. Generally, it is safe to stock fish 2 weeks after applying rotenone during spring, summer, and autumn.

3. Pond fertilization

3.1 Purpose of fertilization

The fresh and clean water contains fewer nutrients. In absence of nutrients, no organism develops. Therefore, some nutrient in the form of manure or fertilizer is introduced in fresh water of a fish pond, so that with the help of sunlight some reaction take place and plant or animal origin organisms (phytoplankton, zooplankton) develop which are the natural food of cultivable fish. Therefore, to produce these organisms abundantly, a certain quantity of manure is used regularly year round. Fertilizing the fishponds increase fish production by a factor of two or three. Once fertilization program is initiated, it should be continued, or fish growth may become stunted due to reduced food supply.

3.2 Liming before fertilization

Ponds should be limed before fertilizer is applied. Liming is important because it increases pH and alkalinity. Fertilization will not stimulate a good phytoplankton bloom if alkalinity is below 20 ppm. Check the alkalinity in the pond before applying fertilizer. If alkalinity and pH are low, the addition of powdered, agricultural limestone should raise pH and alkalinity. Quick or slaked lime should be applied to increase alkalinity because these compounds can cause rapid pH changes which may kill the fish. The amount of lime needed depends on chemical characteristics of bottom sediments or mud. A way to estimate the amount of lime required in ponds is to apply 1¼ to 1½ times the amount of agricultural lime used for crops in nearby areas.

3. 3 When to Fertilize

One simple method used to determine when to fertilize is to measure the clarity of pond water. The depth of light penetration in water is a good indicator of the phytoplankton density or bloom. If light penetration is six inches or less, it needs fertilization.

3.4 How to fertilize

Granular fertilizers should not be broadcast directly into the pond because the granules sink to the bottom. If granular fertilizers are used, they should be placed on a platform (e.g. a sheet of plywood) situated 12 inches underwater. Granules placed on the platform will slowly dissolve and promote a bloom. If a liquid fertilizer is to be used, it should be diluted and sprayed or splashed into the pond. Apply the fertilizer evenly over as much of the pond surface as possible.

To fertilize the pond, water temperatures should have a minimum of 60°F. Fertilization should stimulate a phytoplankton bloom within two weeks. If a bloom does not appear, fertilize the pond again and continue fertilizing at two-week intervals. Do not fertilize more than 3 times. After a bloom has developed, fertilize the pond as necessary to maintain it. Do not fertilize ponds with an aquatic weed problem because the fertilizer stimulates weed growth only. The nutrients are absorbed by unwanted vegetation, not by phytoplankton. In such case, weed should first be controlled before fertilization.

3.5 Kinds of fertiliser

There are two major kinds of fertilizer: organic and inorganic.

Organic: Any manure produced by organism or animal is called organic manure *e.g.* cow dung or poultry litter. Such manure contains many elements of which nitrogen and phosphorous are most important to produce organisms in the pond water. The organisms or living animal manure contains little or meager amount of nitrogen and phosphorous, therefore, such manure are used in considerable quantity to make it effective.

Inorganic: A by-product of chemicals in the form of crystal or liquid is called inorganic fertiliser. Such fertiliser contains nitrogen and phosphorous in concentrated form. The concentration of nitrogen and phosphorous differs from one commercial brand to other. As the inorganic fertiliser contains nitrogen and phosphorous in concentrated form, so they are used in less quantity than the organic manure.

3.6 Dose of fertilizer

As the time approaches to use or reuse the fish pond, an initial dose of manure is applied at the rate of 100-200 kg of cattle dung or 50 kg of chicken litters per kanal. In case, the organic manure is not available, then only it is recommended to use inorganic fertiliser at the rate of 8-12 kg of nitrogen and 8-12 kg of phosphorous per kanal. The organic or inorganic fertiliser is broadcasted throughout the pond. With the broadcasting of manure, the pond is filled with fresh and clean water after screening with fine wire gauze.

The newly filled water is left for few days. By then the effect of fertiliser is distinctly seen with the change of water colour to light or deep green. The greenish colour of the water is the effect of the manuring. The colour is the indication about the growth of unicellular and multicellular microscopic plant cells – phytoplankton and zooplankton.

With the stocking of fingerlings/yearlings, the developed natural food of fish is consumed. Accordingly the colouration of the pond water starts changing to normal water colour or muddy colour if additional manure or fertiliser is not applied. Therefore, to provide nutrients continuously in the water, application of manure is repeated. It is always better to observe the water colour and as its colour starts changing to light or lighter colour, second or third or fourth application of manure need to be undertaken at the rate of initial dose. As such there is no hard and fast rule on the amount of manure because the effect of manure varies from one place to other place depending on various factors e.g. quality of soil, quantity and quality of water and also depends on the intensity of the sun light.

The use of less quantity of manure fails to produce phytoplankton and zooplankton adequately in the pond water. Under such condition the stocked fingerlings/yearlings do not get adequate food and the fish do not show good growth. Therefore, to start fish culture, the pond water area need to be measured and accordingly the quantity of manure is calculated and applied regularly. The excessive use of the manure is again not at all useful as it deteriorate the water quality and harms the stocked fish. Sometime, it pollutes the water to that level that the stocked fish start dying due to oxygen deficiency. Therefore, the use or reuse of manure should be done judiciously depending on soil, the quantity and quality of water and atmospheric temperature.

4.1 Species selection and stocking

The choice of fish to be stocked depends on the pond owner's goals. However, it is important to understand that all the different kinds of fishes are not cultivable as they have different feeding habits. Some of the fish feeds on only plant origin food, so they are called herbivorous while other fish feeds on insects and its larvae are called insectivorous. Some other fish feed on only fish, they are called carnivorous and while some other fish feed on anything available in the pond ecosystem and are called omnivorous. The different kinds of fish besides carnivorous can be cultured with other kinds of fish as they coexist together without competing with other fish for food. But the carnivorous fish feeds on the other fish and thus it lowers down the fish production. Therefore carnivorous fish is never included together with other fish in culture practice. The carnivorous fish is cultured in mono species system with supplementary feed. Due to supplementary feed, the production of carnivorous fish turns out expensive and again it remains beyond the capacity of the mass of the people. But the herbivorous and omnivorous fishes are easily cultured together and these fishes are mostly of Carp family and are called Cyprinids

Some of the examples of selection of species and stocking are given below.

i. The largemouth bass and bluegill sunfish combination is the most common strategy for stocking ponds for recreational fishing. Channel catfish can be added to a bass-bluegill pond. However, catfish will compete with bass and bluegill for natural foods and lower the number of bass and bluegill caught. Blue catfish may be stocked instead of channel catfish. Blue catfish are better predators than channel catfish and will compete with bass for bluegill.

ii. The places where the cattle or poultry manure (cattle dung and chicken litter) are abundantly available at low cost to fertilise the fish pond for the maximum production of phytoplankton. For such case the Silver Carp (35%) has been considered as major fish while Grass Carp (15%), Common Carp (10%), Rohu (15%), Mori (10%) and Thaila (15%) can be the other stocking fish.

iii. The place where the grasses are cultivated as green fodder and are abundantly available to feed, Grass Carp (35) is considered as major fish species, while Silver Carp (20), Common Carp (10), Rohu (10), Mori (10) and Thaila (15) are the other fishes suitable for stocking.

iv. The places where the availability of manure or poultry litter and grasses are meager or not available then the process need to be based on the supplementary food for which the Common Carp is considered as major fish. The production of supplementary food is made with many different ingredients derived from agricultural crops and their byproducts.

5. Harvest and record keeping

Ponds should not be fished for one year following stocking. After the first season, bass are often easy to catch. The most common problem in small ponds is removing too many bass. To maintain good fishing, one must carefully control how many pounds of fish are removed each year.

When bass are over harvested, the pond becomes overpopulated with stunted bluegill. If this happens, it is difficult to restore the balance of predator (bass) and prey (bluegill) in the pond. It may be necessary to poison the fish and start again. As a general rule, fertile ponds can sustain an annual harvest of 25-35 pounds of bass per acre. If the pond is infertile, do not remove more than 10-15 pounds of bass per acre. Do not begin bass fishing in a new pond before bass spawn in the spring, when the water is above 60°F. By practising catch and release with the bass, successful angling is more often. Bluegill should be harvested also. A good general rule is to remove 10-15 bluegill for each bass taken or four pounds of bluegill for each pound of bass.

Catfish may be removed when they reach a size that satisfies the pond owner. Catfish must be stocked periodically to replace individuals that have been removed. Catfish spawns do not usually survive when bass and bluegills are present in a pond. Large catfish fingerlings (8 inches or longer) should be stocked into ponds with established bass bluegill populations to minimize bass eating small catfish.

6. Evaluation of pond balance

Ponds should be checked every 1 to 2 years to ensure that fish populations are in balance. Pond balance can be evaluated from catch records about the number, species, and size of each fish caught. Balance can also be checked with a 10 or 15 foot minnow seine (a seine is a fishing net) that hangs vertically in the water with its bottom edge held down by weights and its top edge buoyed by floats). Try to seine several shallow areas of the pond. Record the size, number, and species of fish caught in the seine. If fish catch includes both young bass and recently hatched bluegill fry in the seine, the pond is most likely balanced. The pond is out of balance when no young bass or bluegill fry but many intermediate-size bluegill (4 to 5 inches long) are caught in the seine. If large numbers of undesirable fish species are caught, it is time to poison the pond and start over.

7. Weed control

If left unchecked, weeds can take over the entire pond and remove the nutrients required for phytoplankton production. Aquatic weeds can be controlled using physical, chemical, or biological means. Physical control of plants by hand removal is one method. Another option is to use herbicides (chemical control). However, many herbicides are not approved for aquatic use because there is oxygen depletion. Therefore selection of chemical should be done wisely considering the type of weeds, dose of chemical and method of application.

One of the simplest and most economical long term methods of controlling rooted aquatic vegetation in new or recently treated ponds is to stock grass carp (biological control). These fish are primarily plant eaters once they reach a length of 10 inches. During warm weather, grass carp can eat 30-40% of their body weight in weeds daily.

8. Other beneficial management practices

Ponds turn over: This is one cause of fish killing. Pond turnover is related to pond stratification or layering. In a fish pond there is stratification of fish. Stratification occurs when surface water warms faster than deep water. The warm layer is lighter and does not mix with the cool, deep water. The cool water near the bottom becomes stagnant and does not circulate. In the deep, cool water oxygen becomes depleted and toxic compounds may be produced by bacteria and decaying organic matter. A turnover occurs when the upper layer cools quickly and mixes with the stagnant layer. The resultant mixture may not contain enough oxygen to support fish. Turnovers usually take place after a cold, heavy rain or the sudden passage of a cold front. Immediate or preventive aeration may save the fish. Fish kills can also be caused by oxygen depletions resulting from phytoplankton bloom die offs or decomposing vegetation killed by herbicide applications.

Fish shelters: A good way to increase fish reproduction is to place nesting structures in the pond. Fish spawns can be encouraged by furnishing breeding areas throughout the pond. If the pond has a silty bottom, spawning beds are necessary for successful fish reproduction. Spawning beds are made by building a frame or box around 4 to 6 inches of sand and gravel. Place beds at several locations around the shoreline in 2 to 5 feet of water.

Supplemental feeding: Providing supplemental, commercial fish feed is a way to increase the growth. Supplemented feed should be offered in the same area and at the same time each day. A good general rule is to supply what the fish will eat in 10 to 15 minutes. Do not feed the fish more than 15 pounds of feed per acre each day.

9

Fish Preservation Methods

Preservation is the processing of foods so that they can be stored longer and fish preservation is a very important aspect of the fisheries. Normally the fish farms or other fish capturing sites are located far off from the market place and there is chance of fish decomposition and the uncertainties of their sale in market. When the fishes are caught in numbers, greater than the amount of consumption, their preservation becomes a necessity for their future use. Fresh fish will spoil very quickly. Once the fish has been caught, spoilage progresses rapidly. In the high ambient temperatures of the tropics, fish will spoil within 12 hours. Preservation is done in such a manner that the fishes remain fresh for a long time, with a minimum loss of flavour, taste, odour, nutritive value and the digestibility of their flesh.

Freshness of Fish

Freshness is usually judged in the trade entirely by appearance, odour and texture of the raw fish. Since assessment depends upon the senses, these factors are known as sensory or organoleptic. The most important things to look for the freshness of fish are:

- The general appearance of the fish including that of the eyes, gills, surface slime and scales and the firmness or softness of the flesh;
- Odour of the gills and belly cavity;
- Appearance, particularly the presence and absence of discolouration along the underside of the backbone.
- Presence or absence of rigor mortis or death stiffening; and
- The appearance of the belly walls.

Causes of Spoilage of Fish

In the cooler regions of the world the fish preservation is not required for a few days after their capture. This is because, the temperature is low enough to discourage the bacterial growth and so the spoilage of fishes is minimized. In tropical regions, the hot climate favours rapid growth of bacteria and so the spoilage of fish flesh becomes inevitable. Landed fishes may ordinarily remain fresh for not more than 8 hours and begin to decompose rapidly after that. The decomposition or spoilage of fish flesh occurs mainly due to various chemical, microbial and the enzymatic action.

a) **Microbial action:** Some bacteria are naturally present in the living fish but their multiplication and growth is limited by the general metabolic reactions of the fish (low pH of gut, anaerobic environment on the gut and its enzymes, acid in the viscera which often digest the bacteria and cause the gut condition to be favourable for their growth). When a fish dies, these metabolic actions are slowed down and microorganisms begin to multiply. The bacteria lining the gills penetrate the flesh and the vascular system. Those lining the gut penetrate the nearby tissues through the peritorieuna. Bacteria in the slime penetrate the skin into the surrounding tissues. The powerful gut thus giving way for bacteria to enter into the tissues. These bacteria secrete digestive juices and enzymes which breakdown the tissues and cause spoilage of the fish. The end result of microbial invasion of the tissues is the loss of fresh flavour and odour of the fish replacing it with a sour and stale odour which changes to ammoniac, putrid and faecal odour at the later stage of spoilage.

b) **Enzymatic action:** Enzyme spoilage is known as autolysis i.e. self digestion. It is a process whereby enzymes against which the fish is normally protected alive, under optimal conditions for enzymatic activity, post mortem, digest the fish tissues such enzymes are present in the gut, on the skin and in the tissue. Autolysis causes off odours, off flavour and softening of flesh and tissues. It causes general disruption and permission of movements of enzymes and oxygen in the muscle. Such enzymes include cathepsins and proteolytic enzymes. They make the fish unpalatable, unattractive and unfit for consumption. Gutting should be carefully and thoroughly done and belly cavity thoroughly washed (Athepsin in fish is more active in fish than in meat hence autolysis is faster in fish). The breakdown of amino acids (lysine, histidine and) into toxic compounds such as cadaverine and $CO_{2,}$ histamine and CO_2, and putrescine and CO_2, respectively, is undesirable to consumer. Shellfish spoil faster than true fish due to higher content of non- protein N- compounds such as Arginine phosphate.

c) **Chemical action:** The chemical action involves oxidation of fat, contained within the fatty tissues of the fish. It is more pronounced in fat fishes (*e.g.* oil sardine, mackerels, catla, trout, grass carp etc.) which as a result become decolourised. The oil starts getting oxidized as soon as it comes in contact with the atmospheric air, which is known as rancidity. The colour of the fat and its viscosity changes and the fish becomes strong tasted. Methods employed to prevent rancidity include application of antioxidants like polyphenols or other viscous fluid and minimizing exposure of fish to atmospheric air.

Methods of Preservation

Preservation is the processing of foods so that they can be stored longer. It can be done, both for short and long duration. When the preservation is required for a long period of time, the fishes are passed through the cleaning, gutting and conservation and storage.

Cleaning: To clean fish, first of all one needs good and clean tools. Personal hygiene is also important. During cleaning, the caught first are fish washed thoroughly in cold, clean water to remove bacteria, slime, blood, faeces, and mud, etc. from the body surface of the fish. It is being done under proper sanitary conditions.

Gutting: After cleaning, the fishes are cut along their mid ventral side, and their visceral organs are removed. By removing viscera, the bacteria in the gastro intestinal tract and enzymes of visceral organs are removed along with it to prevent bacterial decomposition and enzymic autolysis respectively.

Conservation and storage: Conservation is necessary to keep the dead fish in fresh condition for quite a long time. This is achieved by employing any one of the methods like freezing, drying, salting, smoking and canning.

Cooling and Freezing

Of the many processing methods used to preserve fish, only freezing can maintain the flavour and quality of fresh fish. Freezing greatly reduces or halts the biochemical reactions in fish flesh. The storage life of fish or fish product depends on the acidity and water content of the product. External influences such as oxygen (from the air), micro-organisms, storage temperature, light and water secretion are all also important determining factors. Fresh fish spoil very quickly in the high ambient temperatures of the tropics. If we want to keep fish more than one day, we will have to preserve it. Another preservation method is to cool or freeze the products.

There are two possibilities for storing fresh fish at low temperatures:

i. **Cooling:** Rapid cooling and holding of fish at temperatures between 2 and –2°C takes place immediately after the fish have been harvested, which inhibits the growth of microorganisms

ii. **Freezing:** The key to freezing is rapid reduction of the temperature to between –2 and –7°C. This temperature range represents the zone of maximum ice crystal formation in the cells of the flesh. If water in the cells freezes quickly, then the ice crystals will remain small and cause minimal damage to the cells. However, slow freezing results in the formation of large ice crystals and the rupturing of the cell membranes. When slow-frozen flesh is thawed, the ruptured cells release water (called drip) and many compounds that provide certain flavour characteristics of fish, resulting in a dry, tasteless product. Fish that passes through the zone of maximum ice crystal formation in less than one hour will generally have minimum drip loss upon thawing.

Once fish is frozen, it must be stored at a constant temperature of –23°C or below in order to maintain a long shelf life and ensure quality. A large portion of fresh fish is water (e.g. oysters are more than 80 percent water). Because the water in fish contains many dissolved substances, it does not uniformly freeze at the freezing point of pure water. Instead, the free water in fish freezes over a wide range, beginning at approximately –2°C. The amount of remaining free water decreases until the product reaches a temperature of approximately –40°C. Fish held below that temperature and packaged so as not to allow water loss through sublimation can be stored for an indefinite period. Unfortunately, there are relatively few commercial freezers capable of storing fish at -40° because of the tremendous variation in energy costs. Fish are therefore normally stored at –18 to –29°C, resulting in a variable shelf life ranging from a few weeks to almost one year.

Drying

Drying is the removal of water from fish. Since water is essential for the activity of all living organisms its removal will slow down, or stop, microbiological or autolytic activity and can thus be used as a method of preservation. When moisture contents reduce upto 10%, the fishes are not spoiled provided they are stored in dry conditions. Fish drying is achieved either naturally or by artificial means.

i. **Natural drying:** Where drying has evolved as a traditional method of preserving fish, the action of the sun and wind is used to effect evaporative drying. Sun drying is a popular way of processing small fish. For drying, fishes are put on the drying rack in sun light, and turn the fish once or twice a day to dry evenly. It takes 3-4 days to finish the process, and the fish should be taken away from the rack at night or in the rain. The process, however, has a number of disadvantages. It is slow and results in much loss, through putrefaction. It can be carried out only in dry, well aerated climate receiving sunshine which is not too hot. It thus depends upon the environmental factors and availability of space. Lastly only the thin fishes can be preserved by this method, because the fat fishes have much flesh allowing bacterial decomposition to continue in deeper parts of their body. An additional disadvantage is that dried fishes require a long soaking period to restore water and that the sun dried fishes are not usually relished.

ii. **Artificial drying:** In recent times, the controlled artificial dehydration of fish has been developed in some industrialized countries so that fish drying can be carried out regardless of weather conditions. In this method, the killed fishes are cleaned, gutted and have their heads removed. They are then cut lengthwise to remove large parts of their spinal column, followed by washing and drying them mechanically.

Salting

Salting is the preservation of food with dry edible salt. This is an inexpensive method when salt is cheap, as no electricity is necessary and storage can be at room temperature. Fish quality and nutritional value are reasonable after salting.

Storage life is long. Salting has been used for thousands of years to preserve marine products. It has no adverse effect on the value of fish protein. It is related to pickling (preparing food with brine, i.e. salty water), and is one of the oldest methods of preserving food. Salt inhibits the growth of microorganisms by drawing water out of microbial cells through osmosis. Concentrations of salt up to 20% are required to kill most species of unwanted bacteria. Dry salting, wet salting and mixed salting are the three methods employed in salting of fish.

i. **Dry salting:** Dry salting is the simplest method and is used primarily for fish with high water content. In this process the fish is first rubbed in salt and packed in layers in the tubs and cemented tanks. The salt is applied in between the layers of fishes in the proportion of 1:3 to 1:8 salt to fish. The proportion of salt to fish varies with the fish since the oily fish require more salt. At the end of 10-24 hours the fishes are removed from the tubs and washed in salt brine and dried in the sun for 2 or 3 days. Large fish lose about one third and small fish about one half of their dressed weights.

ii. **Wet salting:** The wet-salting methods (brine and pickle) are recommended for tropical applications, especially with fatty fish. The cleaned fish are put in the previously prepared salt solution. It is stirred daily till it is properly picked. In some fishes like seer, black pomfret, Indian salmon etc., the gut is removed and filled with salt in 1: 3 proportions. First the salt is filled in the gut region of the fish and stacked; on the following day further addition of salt is done since the salt settles down at the bottom. Finally the process is repeated to ensure the proper filling up of salt and left undisturbed for 7-10 days allowing the liquor to flow off. In another method, the gut is removed and the salt is applied in one lot and they are arranged in bamboo baskets. The fishes preserve in wet salting process are to be consumed before the rain sets in and the fishes are marketed without drying.

iii. **Mixed salting:** In this process, simultaneous use of salt and brine is followed. The salting process is continued till the concentration of salt in the surrounding medium equalizes with the concentration of salt in the fish tissue. The salting process may affect the shape, structure and the mechanical features of muscle tissue.

Some of the factors involved in salting of fish which play an important role are purity of salt, quantify of salt used, method of salting and weather conditions like temperature, etc. At a salt concentration of 6-10 percent in the fish, the activity of most bacteria that cause spoilage will be inhibited. Since fish contain 70-80 percent water, the amount of brine used must be adjusted accordingly. During the process the small fishes are directly salted without being cleaned. In the medium and large sized fish the head and viscera are removed and longitudinal cuts are made with the help of knives in the fleshy area of the body.

Smoking

Smoked fish is fish that has been cured by smoking. Foods have been smoked by humans throughout history. It is another traditional preservation technique that is used toprepare fish products with long storage lives. Smoke contains substances that kill bacteria, thus helping to preserve the product. The heat also dries the fish. Often fish are salted before they are smoked. In tropical countries, fish are generally heavily smoked at relatively high temperatures so that they are also cooked.

The burning of wood or sawdust to produce smoke is extremely complex since the smoke is the result of incomplete combustion and this will vary with the source of the fuel and the ventilation of the fire. A slow burning fire will produce much more smoke than a small intense fire. Wood smoke is a mixture of gases, vapours and droplets. Droplets form the visible part of the smoke although the invisible vapours contribute to the characteristic smell. It has been shown that it is mainly the vapours that are taken up by fish during smoking. The substances in the vapours dissolve in the liquid on the surface of the fish and the rate of uptake depends on the moisture on the surface of the fish and the rate of flow of the smoke.

In cold smoking, first a temperature of 38°C is raised from a smokeless fire. After this heating, cold smoke at a temperature below 28°C is allowed to circulate past the fish. In hot smoking, temperatures may remain between 60-110°C for 4-12 hours. This is usually long enough to eliminate the non-sporulating spoilage bacteria. However, the spores of *Bacillus subtilis* and *B. mesentericus* survive even with longer periods of smoking. The bactericidal action of the smoke is considerably increased by the presence of salt in the fish. The smoke has to be wet and dense. Good controls are necessary over density, temperature, humidity, speed of circulation, pattern of circulation and time of contact with fish of the smoke. The phenol content of the smoke acts as an antiseptic and it also imparts a characteristic colour and flavour. Some condensation of tars and resins also adds to the taste. Strict hygienic conditions are maintained throughout this operation.

Canning

The canning process is a sterilization technique that kills microorganisms already present on the fish, prevents further microbial contamination, and inactivates degradative enzymes. In canning micro-organisms are killed through heat. It is generally well known that food carries micro-organisms which cause spoilage if left unchecked. These microorganisms are to be eliminated and the entry of other is restricted. The canning process involves pre-treatment of fish, preparation of can, filling and closure of the can, technique of heating the filled cans to kill micro-organisms without damage to fish, finally cooling, cleaning and storage of the product.

Because the severe thermal conditions of canning cause the disintegration and discolouration of the flesh of many species of fish, only a few types of fish are available as canned products. The most common types are tuna, salmon, herring, sardines, and shrimp. The thermal processing does not have a detrimental effect on the high-quality protein of the fish. In addition, these species are often canned with their bones left intact. The bones become soft and edible, significantly increasing the level of calcium present in the fish product. Tuna is an exception; because of special handling considerations, the bones of tuna are removed prior to canning. Tuna is normally caught far offshore and must be frozen and held for some period of time prior to canning. During this freezing and holding period unsaturated fatty acids are oxidized, causing the tuna to become rancid. The rancidity is removed by precooking, and the bones are removed at this time in order to facilitate the cutting and preparation of the meat for canning.

Demerits of Fish Preservation

Although the preservation and processing constitute a very important aspect of the fish industry, it has certain drawbacks as well, particularly with respect to retaining quality of fish flesh These are discussed briefly.

i. If proper hygienic measures are not taken during the processes like washing, guttation and evisceration, etc. more harm would be done to the preserved material, owing to increase in the bacteria population.

ii. Freezing brings about denaturation of flesh. This is because of ice crystals formed during chilling and causing mechanical damage to the muscles. Cell walls burst, structure gets deformed and the flesh loses much of flavour and taste. The flesh also becomes dehydrated and losses texture.

iii. Incomplete or poor preservation leads to decarboxylation of histidine of fish flesh into histamine. This and some other related substances, collectively called saurine, are common causes of food poisoning.

iv. Drying reduces weight, nutritive value and the digestibility of the flesh.

v. Excess salting allows growth of salt tolerant bacteria, causing pink eye spoilage of fish flesh.

vi. Salting combined with smoking results in loss of protein, about 1 to 5% due to salting and 8 to 30 % due to smoking.

vii. Smoking also accelerates rancidity of fat and so reduces digestibility of fat products.

viii. Canning leads to much loss of vitamin B_1, panthothenic acid, vitamin-C and pteroxylglutamic acid.

Transporting Live Fish

Transporting live fish is a common practice on many fish farms. It is done after harvesting fish in the wild; to take fish to short-term live storage. The duration of transport varies, depending on the distance to be covered. From the river, transport time is usually longer, varying from a few hours to one or two days. On the farm, transport time is usually very short (from a few minutes up to a half-hour).

Live fish are generally transported in water. Water quality changes during transport, as the concentration of chemicals changes. Dissolved oxygen is essential for fish to breathe. Bacterial activity and oxidation processes also require oxygen that is present in organic matter. Oxygen consumption increases with temperature. Dissolved oxygen consumption by small fish up to 1 kg is higher than for larger fish. Oxygen consumption for resting fish is lower than for stressed or active fish. Ammonia is excreted by fish and produced by bacteria in different forms. The most toxic form, free or non-ionized ammonia, increases as water temperature and pH increase.

Carbon dioxide is produced by fish as a by-product of respiration. Bacteria also produce carbon dioxide. Carbon dioxide exists in different forms; the most toxic form, free carbon dioxide, increases as water pH decreases. Other changes in water quality that may take place during transport include:

- Increasing water temperature in warm climates increases oxygen consumption and the content of toxic free ammonia.
- Increased carbon dioxide content and thus decreased pH, reduce the amount of toxic free ammonia but increase the amount of toxic free carbon dioxide.
- Suspended solids from fish waste increase.

Water should be kept cool, so that fish and bacteria will be less active, consume less dissolved oxygen, and produce less ammonia and carbon dioxide. Ice may be used if necessary. Fish should not be exposed to a sudden change in temperature. Water should be clear and free from silt or suspended solids, in order to reduce stress on fish's gills, reduce bacteria in organic solids, and reduce the risk of low oxygen levels that result from the decomposition of organic material. As far as possible, touching fish should be avoided with hands, since this will destroy the mucus on the fish's body, and also avoid keeping them out of the water for too long. For short and medium transport, use clay pots or barrels, buckets or basins, or inflated plastic bags. For a long transport, use plastic bags inflated with oxygen or with air if there is no oxygen.

As much as possible, keep each breeder in his own bag and limit the density of juveniles. Although this will increase the volume of material to be transported, it will substantially reduce mortality risk. Do not put too much water in the bag. Bags should be filled to a level just above the fish. In general, bags should include 1/3 water for 2/3 air or oxygen.

Before medium and long-term transport, fish should be kept without food when they are taken from the ponds, and kept there long enough so that their digestive tracts are completely empty. This way, the water in which they are transported remains cleaner. The minimum duration of the fasting period depends on the water temperature and the species. As much as possible, the transport water should not be allowed to get dirty. The fish should be carefully cleaned with clean water before they are loaded into the transport container. Place the containers in the dark and keep them safe from sudden noises in order to keep the fish quiet during transport. Fish should be kept cool during transport, so it is best to transport them at night or early in the morning. Similarly, avoid putting containers in direct sunlight and place them in the shade. Containers can be covered with bags or wet tissues to increase the cooling effect of evaporation. Do not feed fish during transport. During long stops, if the fish seem disturbed or start to come to the surface of the water to breathe instead of remaining calmly at the bottom, or when transport lasts more than 24 hours without oxygen being added, replace the water with fresh, well oxygenated water. If necessary, the amount of oxygen can be increased in the water by agitating it with hand.

Fish should not be too crowded so that they will not run out of oxygen. Three or four 2 cm long fish can be put into a half liter bag, but that same bag can only hold one 8 cm fish. Moreover, fighting between individuals can cause wounds which may kill the fish. If a fish dies in a bag or a container, it should be removed quickly. After transport and before the fish are released into the water, the container should be placed in the new water to equilibrate the temperature between the water in the bag and the water in the pond. Then, water from the pond should be added to the container a little at a time to complete the fish's acclimatization before they are released.

Fish Products and Byproducts

Fish oil is recommended for a healthy diet because it contains omega-3 fatty acids, eicosapentaenoic acid (EPA), and docosahexaenoic acid (DHA), precursors to eicosanoids that reduce inflammation throughout the body.

Fish sauce is a condiment that is derived from fish that have been allowed to ferment. It is an essential ingredient in many curries and sauces. Tatami iwashi is a Japanese processed food product made from baby sardines laid out and dried while entwined in a single layer to form a large mat-like sheet.

Fish meal is made from both whole fish and the bones and offal from processed fish. It is a brown powder or cake obtained by rendering pressing the whole fish or fish trimmings to remove the fish oil. It is used as a high-protein supplement in aquaculture feed. Fish emulsion is a fertilizer emulsion that is produced from the fluid remains of fish processed for fish oil and fish meal industrially. Fish glue is made by boiling the skin, bones and swim bladders of fish. Fish glue has long been valued for its use in all manner of products from illuminated manuscripts to the Mongolian war bow.

Isinglass is a substance obtained from the swim bladders of fish (especially sturgeon). It is used for the clarification of wine and beer. Surimi refers to a Japanese food product intended to mimic the meat of lobster, crab, and other shellfish. It is typically made from white-fleshed fish (such as Pollock or Hake) that has been pulverized to a paste and attains a rubbery texture when cooked.

Fish hydrolysate is ground up fish carcasses. After the usable portions are removed for human consumption, the remaining fish body – guts, bones, cartilage, scales, meat etc. are put into water and ground up.

A shimmery substance found on fish scales, most usually obtained from herring and one of many byproducts of commercial fish processing, can also be used for pearlescent effects, primarily in nail polish, but is now rarely used due to its high cost, bismuth oxychloride flakes being used as a substitute instead.

10

Fish Population Dynamics

Fish population is the group of fish of the same species that are alive in a defined area at a given time. Fish stock is a part of a fish population usually with a particular migration pattern, specific spawning grounds, and subject to a distinct fishery. A fish stock may be treated as a total or a spawning stock. Total stock refers to both juveniles and adults, either in numbers or by weight, while spawning stock refers to the numbers or weight of individuals that are old enough to reproduce. In theory, a unit stock is composed of all the individual fish in an area that are part of the same reproductive process. It is self-contained, with no emigration or immigration of individuals from or to the stock. On practical grounds, however, a fraction of the unit stock is considered a "stock" for management purposes (or a management unit), as long as the results of the assessments and management remain close enough to what they would be on the unit stock. A stock can be defined as a group or population that maintains and sustains itself over time in a definable area. It is a population of organisms which share a common gene pool, and is sufficiently discrete to warrant consideration as a self-perpetuating system that can be managed.

Fish population dynamics

Fish population dynamics is the study of fish populations and how fishing mortality, growth, recruitment, and natural mortality affect them. In other words, fish population dynamics may be defined as the changes/ fluctuation in number of fish in a population and the factors responsible for these changes including the rate of loss and replacement of individual in the population and any other regulatory forces tending to keep the number in population steady at least to prevent excessive changes. It deals with the rate of reproduction, rate of growth, rate of mortality, rate of recruitment etc.

Fish population dynamics play a vital role in management and development of fisheries resources. The ultimate goal of study of this subject is to attain maximum sustainable yield. However the set of objectives and the mode of function of study of fish population dynamics are as follows:

- To determine the level of abundances of major fish species.
- To determine the parameters of growth, recruitment and mortality of the major fish stock.
- To know about the proper management and conservation system of fish stock.
- To determine the current level of catch and fishing effort.
- To develop fish life and thereby increasing the productivity.
- To obtain the highest potential economic benefits in the long run.
- To identify all the factors that affect the fish and its ecology, growth, food, reproduction, mortality etc.
- To determine the maximum sustainable yield of the major fish stock.
- To identify the breeding ground, breeding season and nursery ground of major fish stock.

Components of fish population dynamics

Following are the areas of study under fish population dynamics:

1. **Population structure:** Population may be defined as the group of fish of the same species that are alive in a defined area at a given time. It is interbreeding group of individuals of single species that occupy in a specific area at a specific time. Population model is a component of a stock assessment model, made up of formulations that describe how the population changes from one time period to the next. The types of population models vary depending on the species life history and on data availability. Population structure can roughly be classified as age/size structured or biomass based, deterministic or stochastic, density-dependent or density-independent, spatially structured or spatially aggregated, equilibrium or non-equilibrium.
2. **Age:** The number of years of life completed, here indicated by an Roman or Arabic numeral, followed by a plus sign if there is any possibility of ambiguity (age 1, age 1+). Fish may be divided into age class which is a group of individuals of the same age range in a population. The age 0 group includes the fish in their first year of life. A fish born in April of a given year remains in the age 0 group until April of the following year. The term usually refers to a year class in long lived annually breeding species, but shorter units of time are also used, particularly in the tropics. A breakdown of the different age groups of a kind of fish in a population or sample is called as age structure or frequency.

3. **Abundance of fish:** It is the total number of a kind of fish in a population; this is rarely known, and usually estimated from the relative abundance. Abundance Index is a relative measure of the weight or number of fish in a stock, a segment of the stock (*e.g.* the spawners), or an area. Often available in time series, the information is collected through scientific surveys or inferred from fishery data.

4. **Growth of fish:** Usually an individual fish's increase in length or weight with time. Also may refer to the increase in numbers of fish in a population with time. It may be represented by growth model which is a mathematical description or representation of the size of a living organism at its various ages. The Von Bertalanffy growth model is commonly used in fish stock assessments.

5. **Recruitments of fish:** The amount of fish added to the exploitable stock each year due to growth and/or migration into the fishing area. For example, the number of fish that grow to become vulnerable to the fishing gear in one year would be the recruitment to the fishable population that year. This term is also used in referring to the number of fish from a year class reaching a certain age. For example, all fish reaching their second year would be age 2 recruits. Recruitment overfishing is a situation in which the rate of fishing is (or has been) such that annual recruitment to the exploitable stock has become significantly reduced. The situation is characterized by a greatly reduced spawning stock, a decreasing proportion of older fish in the catch, and generally very low recruitment year after year. If prolonged, recruitment overfishing can lead to stock collapse, particularly under unfavourable environmental conditions.

6. **Fish mortality:** It measures the rate of death of fish. Mortality occurs at all life stages of the population and tends to decrease with age. Death can be due to several factors such as pollution, starvation, and disease but the main source of death is predation (in unexploited stocks) and fishing (in exploited ones). Mortality rate is the rate at which the numbers in a population decrease with time due to various causes. Mortality rates are critical parameters in determining the effects of harvesting strategies on stocks, yields, revenues etc. The proportion of the total stock (in numbers) dying each year is called the "annual mortality rate."

7. **Fish marking and tagging:** Marking an individual or group of individuals (e.g. by clipping a fin, injecting a dye, inserting a tag) in order to identify it when recaptured. Tagging allows the study of growth, mortality, and migration as well as the estimation of the stock size.

8. **Fishery models:** Model in fisheries science is a description of something that cannot be observed. Often a set of equations and data used to make estimates. Modeling is the construction of physical, conceptual, or mathematical simulations of the real world. Models help to show relationships between processes (physical, economic, or social) and may be used to predict the effects of changes in the components of a system.

9. **Overfishing and under fishing:** According to the National Standard Guidelines of USA, overfishing occurs whenever a stock or stock complex is subjected to a rate or level of fishing mortality that jeopardizes the capacity of a stock or stock complex to produce maximum sustainable yield (MSY) on a continuing basis. Overfishing is occurring if the maximum fishing mortality threshold (MFMT) is exceeded for 1 year or more. In general, the action of exerting fishing pressure (fishing intensity) beyond the agreed optimum level. A reduction of fishing pressure would, in the medium term, lead to an increase in the total catch. Under fishing is the level of fishing pressure which is operated along with the forces of natural mortality causing insufficient total mortality to prevent excessive survival of young and to moderate severe food competition among adults.
10. **Fishery management and regulations:** Fishery management is the integrated process of information gathering, analysis, planning, decision making, allocation of resources, and formulation and enforcement of fishery regulations by which the fisheries management authority controls the present and future behaviours of the interested parties in the fishery in order to ensure the continued productivity of the living resources. Fisheries management authority are the body which makes the decisions on how the fishery is carried out, and is responsible for all ancillary services, such as statistics gathering, assessment, monitoring, control and surveillance, consultation with fishers and other users of the sea, and resource allocation or determining the conditions of access to the fishery. Fisheries management organization institution responsible for fisheries management, including the formulation of the rules that govern fishing activities.

Importance of studying fish population dynamics

Fish population dynamics is the only subject that has a direct relation with fish production, growth, mortality etc. Hence, undoubtedly, it casts the main role in proper management and gaining of maximum sustainable yield. Its importance in the field of fishery in short may be noted as follows.

- Fish population dynamics is the only subject that describes fish population and its stock which helps a lot in fishery management.
- It provides the population structure which gives us the vivid description about the number and amount of different sizes, age and length.
- It deals with the age structure of fish and helps in the determination age of fish.
- It helps us to get the techniques of separating fish stock.
- It helps in the estimation of abundance of fish which helps in culture management.
- It provides us the regulation of the proper management of fish production.
- It helps controlling over fishing and also avoid under fishing.

- It deals with over-all provisions, rules and regulation for fishery management which helps in betterment and sound management of total fisheries resources of a country.
- It provides us different fishery model which helps in attaining Maximum Sustainable Yield.
- It helps in the estimation of total fish production.
- It helps in growth measurement both relative and absolute.
- It helps in recruit measurement and the measurement of variation in recruitment.
- It helps in mortality measurement, total mortality, natural mortality and fishing mortality etc.

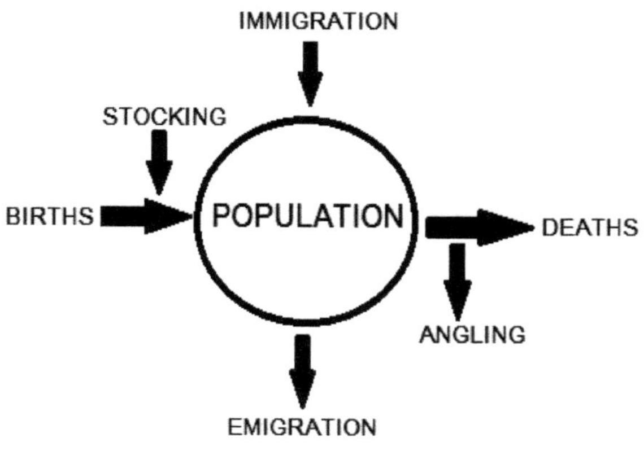

Fig. 10.1. Fish population dynamics

Fish population dynamics is not a static subject (Fig. 10.1). It is always changing from time to time with respect to different factors that affect the growth, mortality, production etc. The points noted below show that this subject is really not a static one but is always on dynamic motion and changes.

- Fish population dynamics mainly deals with growth, mortality and production etc. which are always changing.
- Physico-chemical and biological factors are always acting differently on growth, mortality, production of fish by which the population structure is always changed.
- Subsets of a species or a population (stock) are not always in static condition.
- The application of different fisheries management and conservation techniques keeps the population on dynamic motion.
- Fisheries rules and regulation are always being changed to meet different needs which always keep the population changing.

Techniques to study fish population dynamics

The main criteria or techniques that are used to separate stocks are briefly described below.

1. **Demographic parameters:** These include growth and mortality rate, age at maturity, fecundity, frequency of spawning etc. may differ between populations.
   i. **Growth rate:** It may be annual or seasonal. The increase in weight of a fish per year (or season), divided by the initial weight.
   ii. **Mortality Rate:** The rate at which the numbers in a population decrease with time due to various causes. Mortality rates are critical parameters in determining the effects of harvesting strategies on stocks, yields, revenues, etc. The proportion of the total stock (in numbers) dying each year is called the "annual mortality rate."
   iii. **Age at maturity:** It refers to the ability, on average, of the fish of a given age or size to reproduce. Maturity information, in the form of percent mature by age or size, is often used to compute spawning potential.
   iv. **Fecundity:** The potential reproductive capacity of an organism or population expressed in the number of eggs (or offspring) produced during each reproductive cycle. Fecundity usually increases with age and size. The information is used to compute spawning potential.
   v. **Spawning frequency:** It is the number of times of release of ova, fertilized or to be fertilized in given period.
1. **Difference in behaviour:** Behavioural differences such as reproductive behaviour may provide various mechanisms between stocks.
2. **Location of spawning ground areas:** Particular stocks are used particular spawning ground/area such as Hilsa and Salmon.
3. **Physiological parameters:** Different types of physiological parameters are taken into account.
4. **Marking and tagging:** It involves in capturing applying a mark of some sort, release and eventually recapturing. It indicates the movement and range of the stocks. Tags may be of different kinds. Some are noted below.
   - Micro-wire tags: 4 mm in length inserted into nasal and body cavity of fish. The tags are banded and numbered in binary code. Tags invisible from outside present indicted by metal detector and code read from X-rays.
   - Latex tags: It is used under the skin.
   - External tags: It is most commonly used in fish. Example dorsal surface near fin, jaw tags etc.
   - Fin clipping: It is primarily used in fresh water or just clips a few fin rays.

11

The Meaning of Disease in Fish

Disease is a departure from typical normal state of health of a living organism. It is any phenomenon which causes a population to be abnormal or disadvantaged. A disease may be caused by genetic disorders, physical injury, nutritional imbalance or other factors such as pollution, pathogens or combination of these possibilities. The reasons for the occurrence of disease outbreaks are varied, representing complex interactions between the host and the disease causing situation. In the cases of host-pathogen interactions, the onset of the disease represents a decrease in the resistance of the host and an increase in numbers and/or virulence of the pathogens.

The successful transmission of a disease requires the presence of sufficient number of susceptible fish per unit volume of water and the presence of the organisms in sufficient numbers. Frequently adverse environmental factors are required to initiate infection. Commonly, outbreaks of bacterial diseases follow shipping, handling or environmental changes such as periods of suboptimal oxygen concentrations. Overcrowding leading to disease is quite likely in commercial ponds of fishes. Overcrowding with low oxygen and high secreted ammonia is the major cause of disease, and ciliated protozoa can be leading pathogens as aeromonads and other bacteria might be. Viruses are much less often causes of disease. Nonetheless, viruses like Salmon Anaemia Virus cause millions of dollars of quick losses without considerations of environmental deterioration. The waters of some streams and lakes are also being acidified by industrial pollutants like sulfides. Excess nitrogen is being transported by rivers into estuaries and coastal waters that lead to long term declines in coastal fisheries. Over extraction of freshwater by pumping in many places can lead to salination and invasion of salt tolerant fishes as in the Rio Grande.

Within the fish farms, outbreaks of disease may begin suddenly, progress rapidly, usually with high mortalities and disappear with equal speed (acute disease). They may develop quite slowly with less severity but persists for greater periods (chronic disease). Four major groups of diseases may be described. These are: (1) Sporadic diseases which occur sporadically in comparatively few members of a population; (2) Epizootics which involve large scale outbreaks of communicable animal diseases occurring temporarily within limited geographical areas; (3) Panzootics which occur over large areas; and (4) Enzootics that persist or reoccur as low level outbreaks in certain areas. All these factors must be considered in any investigation of the fish diseases.

A disease may be infectious or non-infectious. The formers are caused by microorganisms such as bacteria, viruses, fungi etc. while the latter are not caused by microorganisms but by other causes such as nutritional deficiencies, intoxications, and low or high oxygen levels.

Some major diseases of fish are listed below. These are described in detail in other sections.

Infectious diseases

Table 11.1. Important infectious diseases of fish

Bacterial diseases	Viral diseases	Fungal diseases	Protozoan diseases
1. Furunculosis	Channel catfish virus disease (CCV)	*Saprolegnia* infection	White spot disease
2. Epizootic ulcerative syndrome	Spring viraemia of carp virus (SVCV)	*Icthiophonus* infection	Costiasis
3. Columanris disease	Swim bladder inflammation	*Branchiomyces sangtimis* infection (gill rot)	Trichodinosis
4. Fish tuberculosis	Lymphocystis virus	*Penicillium piscium* infection	Myxosporidiosis
5. Bacterial kidney disease	Infectious pancreatic necrosis viral disease	*Nephromyces piscium* infection	
6. Bacterial gill disease		*Pullularia* infection	
7. Pseudo kidney disease		*Aphanomyces* infection	
8. Enteric red mouth disease			
9. Red pest			
10. Red spot disease			
11. Edwardsiellosis			
12. Tail rot			
13. Fin rot			

Non-infectious diseases

1. Gas bubble disease
2. Disease due to low oxygen level in water
3. Disease due to CO_2
4. Disease due to abnormal pH of water
5. Disease due to ammonia in water
6. Intoxications

12

Non-infectious Fish Diseases

Non-infectious diseases in fish can be broadly categorized as environmental, nutritional, or genetic.

1. **Environmental diseases:** These are the most important in commercial aquaculture. Environmental diseases include low dissolved oxygen, high ammonia, high nitrite or natural or man-made toxins in the aquatic environment. Proper techniques of managing water quality will enable producers to prevent most environmental diseases.
2. **Nutritional diseases:** Nutritional management of fish is very important. Fish require balanced and high quality diets. Most fish do not synthesize some of the diet components like ascorbic acid and therefore adequate supplementation is necessary. Proper storage of feeds in a cool, dry place is another factor necessary to minimize nutritional degradation. Availability of high quality diets especially in developing countries is another constraint which may cause a disease in fish.
3. **Genetic abnormalities:** It include conformational abnormalities such as lack of a tail or presence of an extra tail. Most of these are of minimal significance; however, it is important to bring in unrelated fish for use as brood stock every few years to minimize inbreeding.

A. Diseases due to poor water quality

For successful fish production, abundant water of good quality is important. Major interrelated water quality factors that influence the fish health and the associated disease conditions are briefly discussed below.

1. Dissolved oxygen depletion

Dissolved oxygen (DO) is one of the most important parameters in aquaculture. Maintaining good levels of DO in the water is essential for successful production since oxygen (O_2) has a direct influence on feed intake, disease resistance and metabolism. A sub-optimal level is very stressful for fish and shrimp. It is therefore important to keep DO at optimum levels of above 4.0 ppm. The DO concentration in water goes up as the temperature goes down, and decreases when salinity increases. One of the sources of oxygen in pond water is photosynthesis while the other is diffusion or transfer from air to water. Wave action or mechanical aeration is forcing this oxygen diffusion.

Five-day biochemical oxygen demand (BOD_5) is an important water quality variable that reflects the oxygen demand of pond aquaculture and it is defined as the amount of dissolved oxygen (DO) needed by aerobic biological organisms in the water to break down organic material present at a constant temperature during a 5-day period. The BOD_5 of pond aquaculture effluents usually ranges from 5 to 20 mg/l. The greater the BOD, the more rapidly oxygen is depleted.

Oxygen depletion is the most common cause of fish kills. It occurs when the demand of oxygen is more than it is produced in environment. It is a problem during warm period and not during winter as algal growth in winter is restricted and cold water has more oxygen. It is important to anticipate oxygen deficiency before fish begin to die otherwise it is difficult to stop a fish kill.

Aquatic animals, plants, and decaying organic matter consume oxygen. Aquatic plants are primary producers of oxygen. Sunlight affects the photosynthesis and therefore the amount of oxygen in pond water fluctuates daily. Oxygen levels are usually highest at midday and lowest just before sunrise. Mismanagement of ponds by overstocking, overfeeding, overfertilization, pollution from barns and feedlots, or chemical treatment of aquatic weeds can result in oxygen depletion and fish kills especially during warm period. The top water layer in fish pond has oxygen producing algae and wind action also contributes oxygen to this layer. Most of the fish are in top layer. The middle layer has low level of oxygen while bottom is stagnant with little oxygen. Mixing of these layers of water can cause oxygen depletion. Such mixing is triggered by heavy rains, strong winds blowing for long periods in one direction, and rapid cooling in the fall. In a pond with an excessive bloom of algae, several days of reduced light and calm weather can result in not enough oxygen being produced to meet the demands of respiration and decay. Chemical treatment of aquatic weeds may also result in oxygen depletion.

Oxygen depletion is manifested by fish swimming to the top and gulping of air at night or early in the morning. If oxygen depletion has not reached to lethal level, fish are seen on the surface in early morning but returns to deeper water as oxygen level increases during the day. Fish being fed suddenly stop eating is another indication of oxygen depletion.

Testing the oxygen level in a pond by oxygen test kits and meters is an excellent way to detect a developing problem. Tests of oxygen levels in ponds should be made at dawn or shortly thereafter. If oxygen is less than three parts per million (ppm) in the top three feet of water, immediate action should be taken.

The needs of fish for oxygen vary according to species, age and culture conditions. Most warm water fish need oxygen dissolved in water at a rate of at least one ppm for survival and more than three ppm for comfort. Oxygen at five or more ppm provides the best growing conditions.

Under the oxygen depletion conditions immediate corrective measures should be taken. Water replacement is very effective but may not be practically feasible. Mechanical aeration of the water is the effective method and can be done by using commercially available aerators like paddle wheel aerator, large volume pumps, bush hog mower and outboard motors. While doing mechanical aeration, it is important not to disturb the bottom mud. Bottom mud contains a large amount of organic material and decomposing bacteria that will contribute to oxygen depletion problems if mixed with water. Chemical treatments like adding six to eight pounds of potassium permanganate per acre-foot or 50 to 100 pounds of triple superphosphate per surface acre or 50 pounds of builders or hydrated lime per surface acre are also effective to enhance oxygen level.

Proper pond management always helps to preventing oxygen depletion. After the emergency has passed, cause of oxygen depletion should be found. Oxygen depletion makes the surviving fish more susceptible to diseases and parasites and therefore surviving fish should be watched closely during the few weeks following oxygen depletion to determine if treatment is necessary. If a high percentage of the fish have died as a result of oxygen depletion, the pond should be restocked.

2. Super-saturation of water with gases leading to gas bubble disease

Gas bubble disease refers to the development of gases in fish's bloodstream. This can occur when its aquarium or pond water is supersaturated with gases. Gases involved are carbon dioxide, nitrogen and oxygen. A gas saturation level of above 110% is usually considered to be a problem.

Fishes are cold-blooded creatures, meaning their body temperature depends on the temperature of their environment. The water they live in and their bloodstreams can become supersaturated with gases when there is a sudden rise in water temperature or a sudden rise in pressure. On sudden increase in temperature, the gases in water are released and are trapped within the water. Supersaturating gas condition also arises from faulty water pumps with leaking gaskets causing sucking of air into the pump, compression and its distribution to aquaria. Similarly, pond or tank water can become supersaturated with gases when they are filled with well water through a submerged hose.

The disease is manifested by bubbles just under the surface of the skin, in the gills, fins and eyes of animal. Fins may be mottled due to gas bubbles. There may be haemorrhages on fins due to occlusion of small blood vessels by gas bubbles and gas emboli can reach brain or heart and fish can die suddenly with no other signs. Gas bubble disease damages the fish's tissue, which if extensive, can even lead to the fish's death.

Gas bubble disease can be prevented by slowly heating up water when it is added to the aquarium. Also, do not submerge the hose when filling up a pond.

Instead, spray water from above, as this will allow all the gases to harmlessly release into the air.

3. Carbon dioxide toxicity

The primary sources of carbon dioxide in fish ponds are derived from respiration by fish and fish pond biota (microscopic plants and animals). Decomposition of organic matter is another major source. During day time, carbon-dioxide is lowest while during the night it is produced by pond organisms and accumulates to a maximum (usually around 10-15 mg/litre) at dawn. Water sources can contain 4 ppm CO_2. Levels of 20 ppm represent a critical concentration above which carbon dioxide is a problem. At 140 ppm with an oxygen level of 10 ppm, fish may die.

The problem with potential toxicity of carbon dioxide can be related to the daily fluctuating pattern of dissolved oxygen and carbon dioxide concentrations. Toxicity of carbon dioxide is enhanced by low dissolved oxygen concentrations. Fish are able to get rid themselves of carbon dioxide through the gills in response to difference in carbon dioxide concentration between fish blood and surrounding water. If environmental carbon dioxide is high, the fish is unable to reduce internal carbon dioxide concentrations resulting in accumulation in fish blood. This accumulation reduces the oxygen carrying capacity of haemoglobin and may cause the fish to feel stress similar to suffocation.

The density of algae bloom has an important effect on the magnitude of daily fluctuation of oxygen and carbon dioxide. Carbon dioxide problem are more likely as the thickness of algae bloom increases. Application of an algaecide is another cause as well as high density of fish. Summer is the time of year when carbon dioxide is most likely to be a problem in fish ponds.

Carbon dioxide can be removed temporarily by chemical treatment of pond water with liming agents such as quick lime (calcium oxide), hydrated lime (calcium hydroxide) or sodium carbonate. These agents chemically react with carbon dioxide and increase alkalinity and pH. Amount of a liming agent to apply to a pond can be calculated by formula given below:

Pounds of liming agent to add = Carbon dioxide concentration (mg/liter) x pond area (acres) x average depth of water (feet) x factor for a liming agent

The liming agent factors for quick lime, hydrated lime and sodium carbonate are 3.45, 4.57 and 6.48, respectively.

4. Ammonia toxicity

In aquatic systems, ammonia accumulates as a result of normal metabolism of proteins by the fish where it is excreted through gill tissues and in faeces . Ammonia also enters the pond from bacterial decomposition of organic material such as uneaten feed or dead phyto or zooplanktons. High levels of ammonia are also a result of insufficient water flow for the amount of fish stocked.

Total ammonia nitrogen (TAN) is composed of toxic (unionized) ammonia and non-toxic (ionized) ammonia. Only a fraction of TAN exists as toxic ammonia and a balance exists between ionized and non-ionized ammonia. Increase in temperature and pH of water increases the proportion of toxic form of ammonia. Assimilation of ammonia by plankton algae is important in reducing the amount of ammonia coming in contact with fish. That is why ammonia increases in the fall and winter because of reduced algae populations.

Dangerous short-term levels of toxic un-ionized ammonia which are capable of killing fish for over a few days start at about 0.6 mg/liter (ppm). Chronic exposure to toxic ammonia levels as low as 0.06 mg/liter (ppm) can cause gill and kidney damage, reduction in growth, possible brain malfunctioning and reduction in oxygen carrying capacity in fish.

Treatment of high TAN concentrations is difficult in large pond culture systems. Pumping fresh water into the pond is one approach but not practical and economical. Maintaining high dissolved oxygen levels by aeration will slightly reduce the toxic effect. Increased aerobic bacterial activity and temporary reduction of feeding rates are recommended.

Prevention of high TAN is a better approach to problem due to ammonia. The use of lower feeding rates and good feeding practices play a big role in keeping TAN levels low. Fish should not be overfed and it should be ensured that the fish are consuming feed that has offered.

Ammonia is toxic to fish. Toxicity varies with particular species. Lower safe value is 0.02 ppm. Higher levels, over 0.3 ppm probably interfere with respiration resulting in physiological oxygen depletion. Ammonia in water is a predisposing factor to bacterial gill disease. Aquarium fish when transported in sealed bags face ammonia problem. Addition of clay granules reduce ammonia levels because they are ion exchangers and buffer the water.

5. Hydrogen sulphide poisoning

Hydrogen sulphide is a colourless, toxic gas, is a by-product of the deterioration of organic matter, usually under anaerobic conditions. Anaerobic soils with moderate to high organic concentrations can be a significant source of H_2S, which is toxic to shrimp and fish even at low concentrations since it hinders their respiration. Without oxygen, some bacteria can respire by using sulfur, and this is another source of hydrogen sulfide. The smell is one of rotting eggs. If the bottom soil becomes black and a rotten egg odour is recognized when sediment is disturbed, it indicates anaerobic conditions and the presence of H_2S. Hydrogen sulfide is highly toxic in the unionized form and this toxicity is comparable to that due to ammonia.

H_2S is very toxic to fish. Lethal levels of hydrogen sulphide can be reached during the harvest of fish from ponds with a thick layer of degenerating organic matter. The signs are respiratory and neurological like spinning, flipping and fearlessness may be seen just before death occurs. Losses may be great and they will continue after the H_2S is long gone.

Whenever hydrogen sulphide poisoning is suspected, fish should be removed before disturbing any gravel or sand. Also, to neutralize some of the hydrogen sulfide, a weak dose of Potassium permanganate may be effective. Still, housekeeping, and finding the source of the anaerobic bacteria is the priority. However, the unionized form is predominant at low pH (< 8) and high temperature. At pH 7.5 approximately 14% of the sulfide is in the toxic H_2S form and at pH 6.5 about 61%. Therefore, sulfide concentrations should be below 0.002 ppm.

Many marine species live in close proximity to sediments that often contain H_2S. Some even live in them. The range of susceptibility to H_2S poisoning varies among such species.

6. Nitrite toxicity

Nitrite (NO_2^-) is another form of nitrogenous compound that results from feeding and can be toxic to shrimp and fish. Nitrite is an intermediate product of the transformation of ammonia into nitrate by bacterial activity. The absorbed nitrites from the gut bind to haemoglobin and reduce its ability to carry oxygen.

An increase in CO_2 may decrease the pH to a value below 6.5, which can lead to toxicity of nitrite through the formation of nitrous acid (HNO_2). At 2 ppm and above, nitrites are toxic (injurious or lethal) to many fish and shrimp.

7. Fluctuation in hydrogen ion concentration

The term pH is a mathematical transformation of the hydrogen ion (H^+) concentration; it is conveniently expressed as the acidity or basicity of water. Each change of one pH unit represents a ten-fold change in hydrogen ion concentration. Pure water exposed to air has an acidic pH of about 5.6 because carbon hydroxide hydrates in water to form carbonic acid which dissociates to hydrogen ion and bicarbonates. The pH of freshwater ecosystem can fluctuate considerably within daily and seasonal and time frames. Freshwater animals including fish have evolved to tolerate a relatively wide environmental pH range. Fish can tolerate wide ranges of pH *i.e.* from 5–9. Desirable pH range for fresh water fish is 6.5–7.5 and for marine fish 8.3. Animals can, however, become stressed or die when exposed to pH extremes or when pH changes rapidly even if the change occurs within a pH range that is normally tolerated. Sudden change in pH is common when the fish from transport tank/vessel is shifted to pond water. Sudden increase in pH can stress or kill aquatic animals like channel cat fish fry are very sensitive to such a sudden change. Problems with high pH are common in aquaculture especially in fry nursery ponds and in ponds to grow freshwater prawn.

Under pond culture conditions, there are pH fluctuations due to the respiration process of algae. During dark, algae utilize oxygen and gives off CO_2 as their normal respiration. This CO_2 acidifies water. That is why in early morning, pond water is having acidic pH, as low as 6.5. This pH shifts to as high as to 8–9 by afternoon.

In most aquatic environments, daily photosynthesis is about equal to respiration and pH will usually remain within a range tolerated by fish. However, when plants or algae are growing rapidly, more carbon dioxide is removed each day by photosynthesis than is added each night by respiration. As a result, pH may rise to abnormally high levels during the afternoons and may even remain high through the night. High pH is most common in recently filled and fertilized ponds. High pH in aquaculture ponds appears to occur more frequently and with great severity in waters with low hardness and moderate to high total alkalinity.

In general, preventing or managing around pH problems will be more effective than trying to correct the problems after they occur. High pH can be corrected simply by adding an acid to increase that concentration. However, this approach reduces the pH temporarily. The long term solution to high pH problems in ponds is to alter pond biology so that the net daily carbon dioxide uptake is zero. This can be done by reducing photosynthesis or increasing respiration. Another way to minimize problems caused by high pH in freshly prepared ponds is to prepare ponds as early as possible, preferably several weeks before stocking. Balancing the hardness and alkalinity can be made by adding gypsum (calcium sulphate). Hardness deficiency should be corrected before stocking, preferably as soon as the pond is filled.

An emergency treatment that quickly reduces the high pH is the application of alum (aluminium sulphate). This safe, relatively inexpensive chemical reacts in water to form an acid. A safer, longer lasting way to reduce high pH is to add carbon dioxide, which acts as acid in water. Carbon dioxide level can be increased by adding organic matter such as cracked corn, soybean meal or cottonseed meal to ponds. Generally, applying about 15 pounds per acre daily for about a week prevent pH from rising to undesirable level.

The remedy of sudden change in pH is to measure the pH of water in transport tank and that of pond and fish are transferred only when the pH of receiving water is very near, or below, that of transport tank water. Pond pH is usually lowest a few hours after dawn, so this is usually the best time to transfer fry.

8. Salinity

Salinity represents the total concentration of dissolved inorganic ions, or salts, in water. It plays a significant role for the growth of culture organisms through osmoregulation of body minerals from that of the surrounding water. For better survival and growth an optimum range of salinity should be maintained in the pond water. If salinity is too high, fish and shrimp will start to lose water to the environment. Younger shrimp appear to tolerate a wider fluctuation of salinity than the adults. Drastic changes of salinity may also alter the phytoplankton fauna and their population densities and lead to instability of the ecosystem.

9. Hardness

It refers to the concentration of calcium and magnesium in water. Water can be classified by the degrees of hardness as soft (0-75 mg/l), moderately hard (75-150 mg/l), hard (150-300 mg/l) and very hard (over 300 mg/l). Hard waters have the ability to buffer the effects of heavy metals such as zinc or copper which are toxic for fish and shrimp. Thus, hardness is a crucial parameter in maintaining good pond "balance".

10. Temperature variations

Temperature is another important water quality parameter. It can affect fish and shrimp metabolism, feeding rates and the degree of ammonia toxicity. Temperature also has a direct impact on biota respiration (O_2 consumption) rates and influences the solubility of O_2 (warmer water holds less O_2 than cooler water) Every 10°C increment in temperature doubles the rate of metabolism, chemical reaction and O_2 consumption.

Temperature range for fish life varies from just above freezing to 35-49°C (96°-104°F). Fish body temperature is 0.5°C above the temperature of the environment. However each species has an optimal growth temperature range. Trout, catfish, gold fish can tolerate low environmental temperature otherwise most tropical species will die when temperature drops below 10°C (50°F). Fish can tolerate upward changes in temperature better than downward changes. Fish respond to an increase in environmental temperature by increasing the respiration rate as well cardiac output. Fish eventually die from abnormally high temperature because of lack of oxygen and malfunction of enzyme systems. Signs of temperature shock include rapid respiration followed by collapse.

Temperature cannot obviously be controlled in a pond. Aquatic animals modify their body temperature to the environment and are sensitive to rapid temperature variations. For each species, there is a range of temperature conditions. It is therefore important to adapt fish and shrimp progressively when transferring them from tank to pond.

11. Intoxications

Heavy metals such as zinc, copper, mercury, nickel, lead, cadmium etc. enter fish culture system by industrial pollution. In hard water (300ppm $CaCO_3$) and pH 8.0 heavy metals precipitates as carbonates or sulphates. In soft water and low pH water(less than 100ppm as $CaCO_3$), the metals are in their ionic form and are more toxic to fish. Pollutants like chlorinated diphenols, insecticides, herbicides or sewage pollutants either directly damage the gills or skin leading to metabolic asphyxia or they may be concentrated within the body and cause liver and kidney damage.

12. Algal toxins

Algal toxins produce severe losses in pond culture. Algal toxins follow a period of elevated temperature. Small fish die first after erratic swimming movements and convulsions followed by death. High temperature means toxin produced during the bright day light and thus pH of pond will also be high as CO_2 is used by algae.

B. Nutritional diseases

Nutritional diseases may occur due to inadequate nutrition, poor quality of feed, or faulty feeding practices. The causes and remedies of such diseases are discussed below.

1. Vitamin deficiency diseases

Classic ascorbic acid deficiency (broken back or sway back disease) is caused by vitamin C deficiency. Due to deficiency of this vitamin, bone development is improper resulting in deformation of the spinal column and the backbone of the affected fishes get bent.

Folic acid deficiency (no blood disease) has been referred to as nutritional anaemia of catfish, and is caused by bacterial contamination of feed. Affected fish become anaemic with poor growth and may die. If nutritional anaemia is suspected the feed should be changed to a new bag from a different source immediately. The condition seems to disappear when the deficient feed is discarded and a new feed is provided.

Pantothenic acid deficiency has been associated with clubbed gills, also referred to as nutritional gill disease. Acute thiamine deficiency has been associated with neurologic signs, including convulsions and death; chronic deficiency has resulted in loss of equilibrium, oedema, and poor growth.

Riboflavin deficiency has been associated with vascularization of the cornea, hyperpigmentation, clouding, and haemorrhage in the eyes. Vitamin B complex (thiamin, biotin, niacin, and pyridoxine) deficiency can cause brain, spinal cord and nerve disorders in fishes. These deficiencies have been associated with neurologic abnormalities, including spasms and convulsions.

Vitamin A deficiency has been associated with poor growth and retinal atrophy. Vitamin E deficiency has been related to myopathy, including muscular deformities. Choline and inositol deficiency have been linked to poor growth.

2. Deficiency/excess of proteins, fats, carbohydrates and minerals

Insufficient dietary proteins lead to reduced growth rate, poor reproduction and increased susceptibility to infectious diseases. Reduced or abnormal amino acid intake in fish/shrimp results in reduced biosynthesis of vital substances like enzymes, hormones and certain pigments. Protein deficiency is manifested by anaemia and reduction of growth. Tryptophan or sulphur amino acid deficiency causes cataract.

Deficiency of fats and /or fatty acids leads to growth retardation, reproductive problems and colouration abnormalities in skin. If unsaturated fatty acids go rancid, peroxides and other toxic compounds are produced and may produce a syndrome of muscular dystrophy as seen in Vitamin E deficiency. High fat intake leads to fatty liver/obesity; deficiency of linolenic acid leads to malpigmentation and fin erosion

Excessive soluble carbohydrates may cause hyperglycemia and enlargement of liver; fish become lethargic, darkening of colour and poor appetite. This might cause increased susceptibility to diseases from bacteria, fungi and parasites. Deficiencies in carbohydrate levels and minerals are rare.

Eye cataracts due to zinc deficiency, anaemia due to low iron, skeletal deformities due to phosphorus deficiency. However, iodine deficiency can cause goiter in fish that is characterized by swelling behind the lower jaw of the fish. Skeletal muscle abnormalities have been associated with selenium deficiency and rancid feeds.

3. Incorrectly stored feed

Improperly stored feed is another reason fishes acquire nutritional disorders. Dry feed should be stored in a cool, dry place and replaced after two months. Improperly stored feeds may be subject to contamination by mycotoxins. Aflatoxin produced by fungal contamination with *Aspergillus* spp, causes hepatomegaly and hepatocellular carcinoma in rainbow trout. Fish feeds should be replaced frequently: for dry foods, every 6 months; for wet or semi-moist foods, every 1–2 months.

4. Improper feeding

The methods and rates of feeding vary with species, age, system, and water temperature. A maintenance diet is generally considered to be 1–2% of body wt/day, whereas a diet for growth may be 3–5% of body wt/day. Some ornamental species may require more than this. Feeding behaviour can be an important indicator of health. Vigorous feeding is desirable, and a sudden decrease in appetite should be cause for alarm. To minimize size variation within a population, feed should be distributed over as broad an area as possible. Smaller, more frequent feedings are preferable to one large feeding, especially for young fish. Professional aquarists should be encouraged to periodically weigh valuable fish, keep an estimated weight for total fish biomass in individual tanks or exhibits, and weigh feed for these animals.

5. Feed toxicity

Nutritional disorders caused by toxins found in food occur frequently in aquarium fishes. The most common of these is the aflatoxin produced by the growth of the mold *Aspergillus flavus* in the stored food. Aflatoxin causes tumours and is fatal in fishes. Store the fish food hygienically and replace it every two months, or when mold appears in it.

Prevention of nutritional disorders

To avoid nutritional disorders, store feed properly in cool and dry place, use feed by expiration date, feed correct amount of feed to fish, do not keep them underfed, use feed from reliable sources, get the feed sample analyzed from time to time, and the suspected bad feed should not be used; it should be discarded.

13

Bacterial Diseases of Fish

Bacteria are unicellular prokaryotic cells ranging in size from 1–2x1–4 micrometer or less. They may be motile or non motile and can grow on artificial media. They are visible only under microscope. The major characteristics of bacterial cells are their size, shape, structure and arrangement. They may be spherical (cocci) or rod like (bacilli). These may be arranged in groups, pairs, chains or singly. Examination of shape and arrangement under the microscope helps in identifying different types of bacteria. The bacterial cells are colourless, however, they can be stained with certain dyes like crystal violet and carbol fuchsin by a method called as Gram's staining. Accordingly, they may be Gram positive (take violet colour of crystal violet) or Gram negative (take pink colour of carbol fuchsin).

Bacteria may be classified as: (1) Aerobic due to their ability to grow in the presence of oxygen but not in its absence; (2) anaerobic, which grow in the absence of oxygen but will die in the presence of oxygen; (3) facultative anaerobes that are able to grow either aerobically or anaerobically; or (4) microaerophilic bacteria which grow best in the presence of trace of free oxygen and often prefer an increased concentration of CO_2.

Depending on the temperature required for their growth, bacteria are grouped as: (1) psychrophilic which grow best at temperature below 20°C, usually quite well at refrigeration temperatures; (2) mesophillic that grow best at temperature between 25–40°C; or (3) thermophilic which grow best at high temperature between 55–65°C.

Bacteria which are capable of producing disease in fish are almost always present either in the surroundings, on the surface of the fish, or within the fish where they are present in the intestine or other internal organs. In a case, where bacterial pathogens are associated with a fish but not found in water, they are called as obligate bacteria *e.g. Aeromonas salmonicida.*

The approach to the diagnosis of a bacterial infection should be to first exclude water quality or environmental problems, which could be the cause of mortality. Secondly, exclude the presence of external or internal parasites. If water quality is good with the absence of heavy parasitism, then a bacterial problem should be suspected. Bacterial infections do not arise spontaneously but are the result of some stress to fish which makes them more susceptible to bacterial infection. Bacterial problems are more during warmer months.

1. Fish tuberculosis

Tuberculosis in fish is not as old disease as in mammals. Both fresh water and marine fishes suffer with this infection.

Etiology: Several species of *Mycobacterium* causing fish tuberculosis are known and some of them are given below.

M. piscium: Common in most cases of fish tuberculosis.

M. fortuitum: Pathogenic to a range of cold blooded animals as well as cattle and humans.

M. salmoniphilum: Pathogenic to salmonaedae. They produce yellow to violet pigments.

M. marinum: Infects marine fishes only. Pathogenic to humans where it causes ulcerous and tuberculous skin lesions.

M. platypoecilis: Highly pathogenic for Platys.

M. anabantid: Paradise fishes most commonly affected.

All members of genus *Mycobacterium* are acid fast, Gram positive, non-motile pleomorphic bacilli. Optimum temperature for growth is 25°C except *M. marinum* at 30–33°C.

Transmission: The reservoir of TB organisms is the aquatic environment and possible transmission is by ingestion of contaminated food and debris.

Symptoms: Lack of appetite, progressive thinness, and sluggish movements are main symptoms. Skin defects including blood spots, wounds that may ulcerate and produce cavities, falling of fin rays, loosening and falling of scales are the other symptoms which are noticed in the progressive stage of the disease. Diseased fishes show faded colours and keep their fins folded.

Post-mortem changes: In the internal organs, small, dirty-grey knots (nodules) containing necrotic tissue of blackish colour are formed. These nodules grow and push aside the normal tissue. Infection may spread to skeletal system causing deformities like crooked spine. Tubercles may occur in all internal organs, like intestine, kidney, liver heart, spleen, and are more dangerous than those on skin and muscles. Death is due to reduction of body resistance and emaciation.

Diagnosis: Clinical symptoms and pathological lesions help in suspecting the disease. Demonstration of acid fast bacteria in diseased fish can be done by examining internal organs especially intestine, liver and kidneys.

Control: There are two approaches. Clinically diseased fishes should be removed from pond and destroyed by incineration or burying in quick lime because of expensive treatment that includes prolonged use of chemotherapeutic drugs. Chemotherapy can be attempted with chloramine B or T, cycloserine, ethambutol, streptomycin, isoniazid, kanamycin, ampicillin, tetracycline etc. Chloramine B or T-10 mg/liter of water is given for an exposure period of 24 h after which water should be changed. Streptomycin is administered at the rate of 10–20 µg/g of fish per day given orally in food or 10 mg/litre of water. The dose of isoniazid is 3–5 µg/g of fish per day, given orally in food or 3–5 mg/liter of water.

2. Bacterial kidney disease

Bacterial kidney disease (BKD) is a chronic bacterial disease first reported in wild Atlantic salmon populations in the rivers Spey and Dee in Scotland in 1933. Outbreaks can occur throughout the year, but generally accompany rising water temperatures in the spring.

Etiology: *Renibacterium salmoninarum* which is Gram positive, asporogenous, non motile, non acid fast bacilli frequently occur in pairs. Grow rapidly at 15°C, slow growth at 5 and 22°C but no growth at 37°C. The organisms produce creamy, shiny, smooth, round and raised colonies of about 2 mm in diameter on KDM2 at 15°C for 20 days.

Transmission: The exact source of infection is unclear, but may include clinically or asymptomatically diseased fishes which excrete organisms in faeces. Vertical transmission of the bacteria is also reported.

Symptoms: *R. salmoninarum* appears to be a most unaggressive organism, devoid of much production of toxin, yet it is severe problem in salmonids. Infection can result in significant mortalities in both wild and farmed salmonids; Losses are generally chronic, occurring over an extended period. Nearly all age groups of fish can be affected, although the disease is rare in very young fish. External signs include exopthalmia, swollen abdomen. Blood filled blisters on the flank and presence of ulcers/or abscesses.

Pathology: Internally lesions develop in the kidney, liver, spleen, and heart. Kidney becomes swollen, a false membrane covering may be found on internal organs. This membrane consists of layers of fibroblasts, histiocytes, degenerating leucocytes with macrophages and fibrin. Haemorrhages occur on the muscles especially those lining the peritoneum.

Diagnosis: Clinical cases can be diagnosed by FAT or culture of organisms while asymptomatic cases need full bacteriological examination. Isolation and identification of bacteria from kidney can be made on Kidney Disease medium (KDM2) by incubation at 15°C for 8 weeks. Histological examination of kidney tissue reveals the presence of large number of bacilli. Immunodiffusion test can detect soluble antigen in infected tissue.

Control: This disease has been regarded as one of the most difficult fish disease to treat.However, some success with erythromycin, sulphonamides, chloremphenicol, lincomycin, rifampcin has been reported. Sulphdiazine at a rate of 250 mg/kg body weight of fish/day for 15 days, or erythromycin 100 mg/kg body weight/day for 21 days through feed are effective. Prevention measure includes disinfection of egg surfaces by iodophores @25–100 mg/liter for 5 min. Heat killed or formalized suspension of bacterial cells may be used as vaccine with adjuvant.

3. Enteric red mouth disease

It is a septicaemic disease affecting a wide variety of fish of all ages. Initially this disease was diagnosed in rainbow trout but other trouts and salmonids are also affected. This disease has been responsible for causing greater financial losses of trout farming industry.

Etiology: *Yersinia ruckeri* which is Gram negative, slightly curved rods which are motile. There are several serotypes of the bacterium, but the serotype responsible for enteric red mouth disease is the Hagerman strain, serotype O1a, which is considered to be the most virulent. Salmonid blood spot disease is another disease caused by this agent.

Transmission: The disease causes septicaemia as bacteria spread through the body via the blood. Outbreaks usually begin with low mortalities that slowly escalate.

Symptoms: One of the most common symptoms is reddening in the mouth and throat, which is caused by subcutaneous haemorrhages. Other symptoms include inflammation and erosion of the jaws and palate, darkening of the skin, haemorrhages around the base of the fins, bilateral exopthalmia, and a tendency for sluggishness.

Post-mortem changes: Internally, there may be haemorrhages in the muscles, body fat and in the intestine which also contains a yellow fluid. There is slight enlargement of kidney and spleen.

Diagnosis: By isolation of the pathogen from kidney on tryptophan soya agar or BHI agar following incubation at 20–25°C for 48 h whereupon round raised off white but shiny colonies of 2–3 mm diameter develop.

Control: Chemotherapy involves use of sulphamerazine @ 200 mg/kg body weight of fish /day for 3 days followed by oxytetracycline 50 mg/kg body weight of fish for 3 days. Oxytetracycline and tiamulin are other drugs which can be used. For salmonid blood spot, methylene blue 1g/kg body weight for 5 days is given followed by oxytetracycline, 66 mg/kg body weight of fish/day for 10 days and then a repeat dose of methylene blue. Dietary supplements such as vitamins and vaccine (phenol inactivated vaccine) administered orally via food may be useful.

4. Furunculosis

Etiology: *Aeromonas salmonicida* which is Gram-negative, psychrophilic, non-motile facultative anaerobic rods occurring singly, in pairs or short chains. Optimum growth temperature is 22–25°C but can grow at 5°C. They can be grown on artificial media like nutrient agar or tryptone soya agar. Most of the strains produce brown-water soluble pigment in media containing 0.1% tyrosine or phenylalanine. Both salmonids and non-salmonids fishes can affected. However, in non-salmonids, the disease may manifest in a different way.

Transmission: Water, mud, fish farm implements, carrier or infected fishes are the sources of infection. The organisms can survive in river water for 24 h to 19 days and in sea water for 24 h to 8 days. Survival in mud of fish farm is upto 29 days while on farm implements upto 6 days. Routes of transmission are lateral, *i.e.* contact with contaminated water or infected fishes, or vertical by contaminated water. Gills, anus or injured surface are ways through which organisms are taken by fish host.

Symptoms: This disease occurs in the form of acute, sub-acute and chronic forms. The name furunculosis is named because of sub-acute or chronic form of the disease in which lesions in musculature resemble to boils, i.e. furuncle (which is a pathological term in which affected part is filled with pus and raised areas will be seen). However, this is misnomer because lesions are actually not furuncle but resemble to them.

Per-acute furunculosis: This form is confined to fingerling fishes. The infected fish becomes dark in colour and may quickly die without external symptoms except as mild exopthalmia. Losses due to this form are extremely heavy

Acute form: This is the most common form in growing fish and adults which is manifested by general septicaemia accompanied by darkening of colour, lack of apetite, lethary and small haemorrhages at the base of the fins. Being of short duration, fishes usually die within 2–3 days and causes heavy mortality.

Sub-acute and chronic form: This is more common in older fishes characterized by lethargy, slight exophthalmia, blood shot fins, bloody discharge from the nares and vent, multiple haemorrhages in the muscles and other tissues.

Pathology: In acute form, haemorrhages occur over the abdominal walls, viscera and heart. The spleen is enlarged. Bacteria occur in the blood, disseminated throughout the tissues and in lesions. In sub-acute form, haemorrhages are seen in liver, swelling of the spleen, necrosis of kidneys. Mortality is low and fish may survive, although survivors have scar on tissues in the vicinity of the lesions.

Diagnosis: Diagnosis is based on gross clinical signs and lesions. Confirmation is done by isolation and identification of pathogen which produce characteristic brown diffusible pigment in tryptone soya agar. Serological diagnosis is done by slide agglutination test or passive agglutination test.

Control: Therapeutic measures include use of sulphonamides (like sulphamerazine) orally with food at a dose of 22 g/kg of feed/day for 2 weeks, or chloramphenicol and oxytetracycline 5–7 g/100kg of fish/day for 5–10 days, or furazolidine 25–75 mg/kg of fish /day for up to 20 days. Prophylactic steps include maintenance of good quality water, disinfection of fish farm equipments and utensils especially when disease outbreak occurs, and stocking of disease resistant fishes at the farm.

5. Carp erythrodermatitis (CE) and Cutaneous ulcerative disease

These are two other disease conditions that occur in gold fish due to *Aeromonas salmonicida*. Infection starts at the site of injury of the epidermis. A haemorrhagic inflammatory process develops between epidermis and dermis. This red inflammatory zone gradually extends as the infection spreads. The breakdown of tissue leads to the formation of central ulcer, which may occur in any location on the body surface but most frequently located in the flanks.

6. Columnaris disease

It is one of the oldest known diseases of warm water fish and is a leading cause of mortality in pond raised catfish.

Etiology: The causative bacterium is known by different names like *Bacillus columnaris*, *Cytophaga columnaris*, *Flavobacterium columinare* and *Flexibacter columnaris*. *Flavobacterium columinare* are Gram-negative pigmented motile rods and the striking characteristic is the formation of columnar or dome shaped masses of bacteria with a bit of material transferred to slide. Most species of fresh water fishes are liable to attack by columnaris disease. Fishes like channel cat fish, *Ictibus bubalus* (buffalo fishes) and crapples are more susceptible. The disease is world- wide in distribution, attacks fishes at comparatively higher temperature. Optimum temperature for growth is 77–90°F. It is rarely injurious at temperature below 60°F.

Transmission: Infection occurs through injured skin, the injury may be very slight.

Symptoms: This disease is easily recognized, being distinguished by well-defined symptoms. Ordinarily, the first indication of the disease is the appearance of a grey white spot on some parts of the head, gills, fins or body, which is usually surrounded by a zone with a distinguished reddish tinge. Brown to yellowish-brown lesions (sores) are found on the gills, skin and fins. The bacteria attach to the gill surface and spread to cover individual gill filament. This results in cell death. On the fins, the outer edges becoming lighter in colour which gradually extends towards the base. The fins may become weak and rough and ragged in appearance. The skin loses its natural shiny appearance.

A characteristic lesion due to these bacteria is a pale white band encircling the body and is called as a saddleback condition. As the infection progresses, a yellowish brown ulcer is formed in the center of the band. Another interesting form of columnaris disease is called as Cotton Mouth, which is observed in ornamental tropical aquarium fishes. These fishes are often shipped in small cans for longer distances. During transportation due to rubbing of nose against walls of cans, the fish is injured. The lesions thus formed become infected with *F. columinare* which extend into the mouth and forms a felted mass of bacteria over the surface which is light yellowish in colour. This form of disease is fatal. The lesions of the disease usually appear within 24 h and death comes within 48–72 h afterwards.

Diagnosis: Symptoms like yellowish-brown growth of bacteria on mouth, gills and skin are diagnostic for the infection by *F. columinare*. Scraping of the affected part on examination under microscope reveals long thin rods, their flexing and gliding movement and the formation of haystacks (columns on the surface of tissue). Isolation and identification on the medium (Selective Cytophaga agar, Hsu Shotts medium) having neomycin (5 mg/litre) and polymyxin (200 units per ml). Being gliding bacteria, they spread over the surface of culture plate in a rhizoid pattern.

Control: The control measures include dipping the fish at the time of handling in 1:2000 copper sulphate solution for 1–2 minutes. Two to three dippings at 12–24 h intervals are necessary. Dipping the fish in 1:5000 solution of malachite green for 10–30 seconds is also useful. Sulphadiazine and sulphamerazine when mixed with the daily ration at the rate of 12 g/100 lb of fish for first 7 days and half of this rate for the succeeding 7 days effectively control the disease. Terramycin medicated feed is effective for the external and internal infection when administered at the rate of 25 to 37.5 mg of active ingredient per pound of fish for ten days.

7. Bacterial gill disease

Bacterial gill disease is characterized by the presence of large numbers of filamentous bacteria on the gills accompanied by fusing and clubbing of the gill filaments. All species of Salmonadae are susceptible to this infection. Other fishes like black basses and crappies may also become infected.

Etiology: The disease is caused by *Myxobacterium*, which are Gram negative, pigmented rods and occur in the form of long, thread like filaments which usually lie side by side in a more or less continuous layer on the surface of the gills.

Transmission: Carrier fish in the rearing units or a contaminated water source probably introduce the disease. However, epizootics are almost always associated with a deterioration of environmental conditions like abundance of fish, increased feeding rates and crowding of fish.

Symptoms: Disease is not characterized by any well defined symptoms other than the appearance of the gills, general sluggishness and loss of appetite in fish. In early stage of the disease, the gills are swollen and congested and appear as deep red than usual colour. Later, the gills' filaments become more or less fused and the tips become enlarged and distinctly lighter in colour. Most constant symptom that can easily be recognized is the increased secretion of mucus by the gills, debris becomes entangled in the mucus, gills are clogged and respiration is interfered. In advance stage, the fish usually succumbs in a short time after the appearance of fungus on the gills.

Diagnosis: Diagnosis is done from the clinical signs and detection of large numbers of filamentous bacteria on the gills. The affected gills should be homogenized on a slide, spread, and staining by methylene blue to demonstrate filamentous organisms by examination under oil immersion. The condition is differentiated from columnaris disease where there is extensive necrosis and erosion of gill filaments but such lesion is seldom present in this disease.

Control: Maintenance of a high quality environment is of utmost importance in the prevention of bacterial gill disease. Population level should be kept at lowest feasible levels to reduce the effects of crowding. The application of good sanitation practices is important. Immediately on the first appearance of the disease, the fish should be dipped in a 1:2000 solution of copper sulphate for 1 min and then transferred to running water. In established disease condition, dipping on two successive days may be necessary to destroy all bacteria. Dipping in pyridyl mercuric acetate (PMA) as 1:500,000 solution for 1 h and 1:250,000 solution for 20–30 min for more sick fishes should be used. Potassium permanganate ($KMnO_4$) with certain precautions at l-2 ppm can be used. Quaternary ammonium compound as one-hour flush treatment has been found effective in situations where hardness has limited the use of other compounds.

8. Enteric septicaemia of catfish

Enteric septicaemia of catfish is a highly infectious bacterial disease. Several non-catfish species can also be affected including sea bass, salmon and trout. The disease is also known as Hole in the Head Disease.

Etiology: The disease is caused by *Edwardsiella ictaluri*, which belongs to the family Enterobacteriaceae. The bacterium can survive three to four months in pond water, mud and vegetation.

Transmission: Horizontal transmission via the faecal - oral route, cannibalism, and contact with contaminated water and materials used in handling infected fish are known to spread the disease.

Symptoms: Disease occurs primarily in spring and autumn seasons when the water has temperatures between 18°C and 28°C. The disease occurs as acute septicaemic form and chronic encephalitis form. Lethargic swimming, abnormal behaviour as alternating listless and active swimming, disorientation and swimming in spirals, loss of appetite and the protrusion of head out of the water are the signs which can be observed in affected fish. Exophthalmos (pop eye); swollen abdomen ('pot-belly') and ascites (fluid in the abdominal cavity) in acute septicaemic form and swelling on the top of head with occasional exposure of the brain (a hole in the head) are other important signs. Surviving catfish carry the bacterium, which also seems to be able to survive in the intestinal tracts of other fish species.

Pathology: Acute septicaemic form reveals pale gills, dark skin, multiple white spots on the skin, ulcers in head and flanks, haemorrhages at the base of the fins, around the mouth, and on the throat, operculum and abdomen. Gross pathological signs in the chronic encephalitic form include granulomatous inflammation of the brain.

Diagnosis: A presumptive diagnosis can be made based on the clinical signs alone but PCR, indirect immunofluorescence, bacterial culture and ELISA can be used to definitively diagnose the disease.

Control: Various management practices like reducing stress, using proper nutrition and feeding practices, and administering drugs and chemicals correctly can help. Enteric septicaemia infections can sometimes be controlled or managed by offering feed containing some antibiotics like oxytetracyclin, for 10–14 days and then followed by a 21-day withdrawal period before slaughter; Romet (sulfadimethoxine-ormetoprim) for five days followed by a three-day withdrawal period before slaughter; or Aquaflor (florfenicol) as antibiotic feeds for 10 consecutive days. A withdrawal period of 12 days is recommended.

9. Edwardsiellosis

Edwardsiellosis is a disease that frequently occurs at high water temperature and it is also associated with organic pollution. Fishes like salmon, channel cat fish, mullet, carp, flounder, eel and tilapia are affected.

Etiology: *Edwardsiella tarda*, a Gram negative, rod shaped motile organism, is the etiological agent.

Transmission: The bacterium has the ability to live outside the host in pond water and mud. The presence of these organisms increases with a rise in temperature and increased organic matter. Mammals, birds, reptiles and amphibians are the carriers.

Symptoms: The disease occurs as a mild to severe condition, but clinical signs of infection differ slightly between species of fish. There is severe hyperaemia with bloody congestion of fins in Eels with acute infection of *E. tarda.* In flounders, external gross lesions of edwardsiellosis include darkening, abdominal distention, prolapsed rectum, exophthalmia, lens opacities and abscesses around eyes. In channel cat fish, the only external signs of disease are the presence of small cutaneous lesions of approximately 3–5 mm in diameter, located in the posterio-lateral regions of body. With progression of the disease, abscesses develop in the muscle of the body and tail. These abscesses may become large and develop into gas filled hollow areas. From the surface, these are seen as poorly pigmented, convex swollen areas which, if punctured, emit foul odour. This condition has given rise to the name emphysematous putrefactive disease of cat fish. The disease causes severe economic losses in fish processing plant as the diseased fishes stop production because of noxious odour. Loss of pigmentation, swollen abdomen filled with ascetic fluid, protruded haemorrhagic anus, opaqueness to the eyes, small white nodules may be observed in the gills, kidney, liver and spleen and occasionally in the intestine. These nodules are packed with bacteria.

Pathology: Liver, kidney, spleen and musculature show lesions which include pale colouration, abscess formation and ascites. Macrophages are prominent in all lesions and neutrophils are seen in large numbers in abscesses. Bacteria are present in large numbers in all lesions except long-standing granulomas.

Diagnosis: Characteristic symptoms and lesions especially in cat fish are characteristic. Isolation and characterization of causative bacteria and tests like direct FAT and slide agglutination test can be used.

Control: Oxytetracycline 55 mg/kg fish/day for 10 days is used. Mortality is reduced within 48–72 h of initial treatment. Prophylaxis by vaccination (formalin killed cells) is helpful if there is initial stage of development. The vaccine can be administered by bath immersion.

10. Red spot disease

This disease was originally observed in eels and was referred as Sekiten byo which means red spot. Now the disease has also been described in other species like Baltic herring (*Clupea harengus membras*), gill head sea bream, black spot bream (*Pagellus bogaraveo*), orange-spotted Grouper (*Epinenephalus coioides*) and cod.

Etiology: *Pseudomonas anguilleseptica* is the causative agent. They are Gram-negative non sporing, motile, pigment producing rods.

Transmission: The pathogen enters the host either through the oral route or through broken or abraded skin. Damaged gills also provide a route of infection. Carrier fishes may play role in spreading the disease.

Symptoms: Typically the disease manifests itself by the presence of petechial haemorrhages in the skin of the mouth region, opercula and ventral side of the body. Haemorrhages in eyes can be seen in some species. Abdominal distension is another sign. Sekiten byo is recognized to be prevalent in brackish water, when the water temperature is between 20° and 27°C. There is heavy mortality in this disease.

Pathology: Small petechial haemorrhages may develop in the peritoneum; liver may be pale and haemorrhaged. The kidney may be soft and liquefying and intestine is full of yellowish exudate.

Diagnosis: It is done by isolation of *P. anguilliseptica* which is readily achieved from blood, kidney, liver and spleen on nutrient agar supplemented with 10% horse blood or nutrient agar containing 0.5% NaCl and adjusted to a pH 7.4. Incubation should be at 20–25°C for at least 7 days when small (<1 mm in diameter) round raised entire shiny pale-grey colonies develop.

Control: By raising the water temperature in fish holding areas to 26–27°C and keeping the water at this temperature for 2 weeks, followed by reducing it to approximately 21°C, further outbreaks are checked at least for few months. Chemotherapy can be tried by using nalidixic acid, oxolinic acid, or piromidic acid which are considered as effective drugs.

11. Infection due to *Pseudomonas fluorescens*

It is a dominant component of the freshwater ecosystem. It has been considered as a fish spoilage organism but it has been reported to cause disease in a wide range of fish species including silver carp, bighead, gold fish, grass carp, black carp.

Etiology: *Pseudomonas florescens*, which are Gram-negative, non sporing, motile, pigment producing rods cause the infection.

Transmission: The disease is likely to be spread through water, which will serve as the primary reservoir of infection. The disease is especially troublesome at low temperature *i.e.* approximately 10°C where sometimes there is 100% mortality. The stress factors increase the susceptibility.

Symptoms: The organism is associated with fin or tail rot, in which the infected area is eroded away. Haemorrhagic lesions occur on the skin and at the base of the fins. Ascetic fluid accumulates in peritoneal cavity and petechiae on gills, liver and in the lumen and sub-mucosa of the gut.

Diagnosis: Isolation of causative agent can be done on the standard bacteriological media by incubation at 22–28°C for 24–48 h.

Control: Being a stress mediated condition, removal of the stress, such as caused by adverse water quality, may help in the avoidance of this infection. Bath treatment with malachite green 1–5 mg/litre of water/hour or benzalkonium chloride 1–2 mg/liter of water/h is effective.

12. Red pest

Vibrio anguillarum is of major importance to salmonid fish culture industry and the disease due to it is known as Red pest of eels.

Etiology: *Vibrio anguillarum* is a Gram negative, motile rod, usually curved, comma shaped organism. It has a single polar flagellum.

Transmission: The pathogen is spread by contact with scavenging as well as cultured fish.

Symptoms: There is skin discolouration, presence of red necrotic lesions in the abdominal muscle and erythema (bloody blotches) at the base of fins, around the vent and within the mouth. The gut and rectum may be distended, and filled with clear viscous fluid. Changes to the eyes include distension and cloudiness and periorbital swelling. Exophthalmia may be evident. The disease can in severe cases cause the fins and the tail to rot away. Red pest disease can infect a healthy fish but is much more common in fish with other health issues.

Post-mortem changes: Haemorrhage in intestines, body cavity, spleen and muscle; distended mucoid and necrotic intestine and petechiation are important lesions. Splenomegaly with white/grey lesions is found.

Diagnosis: Presumptive diagnosis can be made from clinical signs especially characteristic red spots, swollen and dark lesions on the skin that bleed and ophthalmic changes; although some acute and severe cases die without clinical signs. *V. anguillarum* may be readily recovered from infected tissue by use of tryptone soya agar, nutrient agar and brain heart infusion agar supplemented with sodium chloride at 0.5%-3.5% with incubation at 15–25°C for a period upto 7 days.

Control: Chloremphenicol, nitrofurazone, oxalinic acid, sulphamerazine and oxytetracycline are effective. Formalin inactivated vaccines are available and can be given in food, by bathing/immersion, spraying and by anal and oral intubation. Good basic hygiene and farm husbandry practices may be helpful.

14

Viral Diseases of Fish

Viruses constitute a large and heterogeneous group of infectious agents, which are alike in that they are obligate intracellular parasites for the cells. They are very small in size as comparison to bacteria; the largest virus is less than one fourth of the size of typhoid bacteria. They require host cell for replication, i.e. they cannot be maintained on artificial medium. Viruses may contain RNA or DNA but not both where as bacteria have both. Each virus has a protein coat, which surrounds the nucleic acid which may or may not be further surrounded by an envelope. Viruses are not sensitive to the antibiotics. Antibiotics and other drugs may, however, be used to control secondary bacterial infections. Management techniques that minimize stress and crowding, biosecurity measures, and temperature manipulation hold the greatest promise for control of piscine viral diseases.

1. Channel catfish virus disease

Channel catfish virus disease (CCVD) is a highly contagious herpes virus infection of channel catfish that occurs during the warm part of the year. The disease is almost exclusively restricted to fish under 4 months age and in severe epizootics losses upto 100% may occur. Survivors of disease outbreaks should be regarded as carriers of virus.

Etiology: CCVD is caused by a herpes virus. It is known to affect Blue and Channel catfish. The disease mainly occurs in fish that are less than one year old (fry and fingerlings) or smaller than 15 cm in length.

Transmission: CCVD is thought to mainly spread vertically, from brood stock to young fish via the egg. Horizontal transmission of the disease also occurs directly from the virus shed in water, and from the virus carried by animal vectors. The disease is also strongly influenced by environmental stressors. Mortality rates are highest where water temperature exceeds 27°C and declines with a reduction in temperature.

Symptoms: Decreased interest in food is often the first sign and it can be followed by high mortality in fry and juveniles. Erratic swimming due to loss of equilibrium, spiral movements and hanging vertically in the water. Fish may also stay motionless with the head pointing up and their tail down. Brief episodes of hyperactivity followed by extended periods of lethargy and large congregations of fish at the sides of the pond are also symptoms that can be seen. Mortality rates in exposed fish can increase to greater than 95 per cent.

Pathology: Abdominal distension, exophthalmos (pop eye), haemorrhages of fins, skin, musculature and internal organs like liver and kidneys are seen. Lesions appear to begin in the posterior kidney but subsequently necrotic lesions develop in the liver, the spleen, the digestive tract and pancreatic tissue. Kidneys become enlarged and pale. Virus also causes degenerative changes in nervous tissues and erythrocytes. Brain neurons are vacuolated and shrunken and surrounding nerve fibers are oedematous.

Diagnosis: Infected catfish are found to produce neutralizing antibodies. If the fish is immunized with live virus, the neutralizing activity develops reaching a peak at 60 days post infection and then dropping to a low level at 120 days. Fish suffering from CCVD often show a decreased interest in food. This is often the first sign and it can be followed by high mortality in fry and juveniles.

Control: Use of virus free brood stocks of channel cat fish is the only option as there is no effective and preventive measure.

2. Infectious pancreatic necrosis

It is an acute, highly contagious viral disease, primarily of young salmonid fish hold under intensive rearing conditions. Primarily a disease of salmonids and the disease is mostly reported in atlantic salmon and brown trout. Non salmonid species like carp, roach, bream, pearch etc. can be affected.

Etiology: Infectious pancreatic necrosis virus (IPNV) is an RNA virus of Birnaviridae family, having icosahaderal symmetry and a diameter of 59 nm. The virus has several serotypes but cross react with each other and there is a quite wide variation within each strain.

Transmission: A large number of virus particles are excreted by non clinical carriers in faeces and in seminal or ovarian fluids. These are also detectable in kidney and therefore in urine. Vertical transmission from mother to offspring and horizontal transmission through cannibalism is possible.

Symptoms: Onset is sudden, affecting the larger and more robust fry and fingerlings in a population and causing sharp rise in mortality. In early stage, thin, stringy faecal pseudocasts are formed which commonly shed 1-2 days before the appearance of acute clinical disease and death. Infected fish rotate about their long axis, alternatively with a prostration. During the terminal stages, affected young ones are darker than normal, exopthalmic and show distended abdomen. Gills are pale and haemorrhages may be present at the base of the fins. This disease has been observed during hatchery cultivation of fishes. In hatchery populations, a sudden and usually progressive increase in the daily mortalities, particularly in the faster growing individuals, is often the first sign of an outbreak. Mortality may reach to 90% or more. Fishes surviving an acute IPN infection have significantly reduced growth rate.

Pathology: Viscera of affected fish have haemorrhages, liver and spleen pale, stomach whitish and devoid of food. It is unusual to find food anywhere in the digestive tract. A clear to slightly cloudy white gelatinous material and sloughed epithelial cells in stomach and intestine is pathognomonic. The hind gut and rectum may contain a watery yellowish fluid. Pancreas is the major target organ where sever necrosis can be observed in acinar cells. Intestine shows acute enteritis in the form necrosis and sloughing of the epithelium.

Diagnosis: Clinical disease may be characterised by a swollen abdomen or eyes, darkening of the skin, spiral swimming and faecal casts trailing from the vent. Internally there may be pancreatic necrosis, a catarrhal exudate in the intestine and haemorrhages in the visceral organs. IPNV is an Aquabirnavirus the presence of which can be confirmed by isolation in tissue culture and identification by enzyme linked immunosorbant assay (ELISA), antibody neutralisation or polymerase chain reaction (PCR).

Control: An antiviral drug, 1-D ribofluranosyl-1,2,4-triazole-3 carboxamide (Virazole) 10 µg/ml causes a substantial reduction in the yield of IPN virus in infected tissue culture. Application of Povidone-iodine(complex of polyvinylpyrrolidone and elemental iodine) is beneficial. Most effective method is protection from exposure to virus.

3. Spring viraemia of carp

Spring viraemia of carp (SVC) is an infectious viral disease of carp (*Cyprinus carpio*) and other cyprinid fish species. The common carp is the principal host. The disease is commonly prevalent in those areas which experience low water temperatures.

Etiology: It is caused by a rhabdovirus.

Transmission: The virus is known to be shed through faeces and mucus casts of infected fish and blood-sucking parasites. It is transmitted by water and by movement of live infected fish.

Symptoms: Clinical signs of the disease with pathological lesions become evident after an incubation period at 20 days post infection. The main clinical signs of SVC are gathering of fish at water outflows, darkening, petechial haemorrhages, loss of balance, exopthamos and abdominal dropsy. Internally fibrinous peritonitis, petechial haemorrhages over viscera and necrotic enteritis. High mortality can occur in all age groups of fish at water temperatures between 10 and 17°C, especially in spring. However, fry can be affected at temperatures as high as 23°C.

Pathology: After the entry of virus through gills, where it starts to multiply, the virus spreads via blood stream to produce viraemia. Target organs are kidney, liver, spleen, heart and alimentary tract.

Diagnosis: SVC virus multiplies in endothelial cells in blood capillaries, haematopoietic tissue and cells of the nephron. Clinical characteristics of affected fish are impairment to the salt water balance, which occurs in association with oedema and haemorrhage.

Control: Control is based on prevention of movement of fish and equipment from infected farms to uninfected locations, and by appropriate hygiene measures. There is strong protective immunity in fish which have survived outbreaks of this infection.

4. Viral haemorrhagic septicaemia

Viral haemorrhagic septicaemia (VHS) is a disease of fresh and marine water environment and has been recorded most commonly in farmed rainbow trout (*Oncorhynchus mykiss*), salmonids, grayling (*Thymallus thymallus*), whitefish (*Coregonus* spp.), pike (*Esox lucius*) and turbot (*Scopthalmus maximus*). It causes high mortalities and fish production is highly affected.

Etiology: The causative agent is a novirhabdovirus.

Transmission: The virus can be transmitted by diseased fish, by non-symptomatic carriers, and can be found in gonadal fluids of broodstock. Birds, blood-sucking parasites and equipment may also be a source of infection.

Symptoms: Acute to chronic disease in all ages of fish can be seen with high susceptibility in young fish. The disease signs include pale gills, dark body colour, ascites (fluid in the body cavity), exophthalmos (bulging eye), and in some cases an intermittent period of erratic spiraling behaviour and rapid respiration.

Pathology: Haemorrhage is often evident in the eyes and skin, and also in the viscera including the intestinal submucosa and skeletal muscle. In many fish a less dramatic pathology is noted.

Diagnosis: A presumptive diagnosis of VHS can be made if mortality among susceptible groups is high, particularly fingerling or yearling rainbow trout, and most of the typical major signs and behavioural changes are present. Confirmed diagnosis can be achieved by virus isolation followed by enzyme linked immunosorbant assay (ELISA) or indirect fluorescent antibody test (IFAT).

Control: As with many viral diseases of fish, there is no specific treatment or cure for VHS.

5. Infectious hematopoietic necrosis

It is an infectious viral disease of salmon and trout having great economic significance for fresh water fish farms.

Etiology: A rhabdovirus of the genus Novirhabdovirus, known as infectious hematopoietic necrosis virus (IHNV) is the cause of this disease.

Transmission: Fish survived of this infection act as reservoir. Infected fish shed virus particles in the faeces, urine and external mucus. The virus has spread across the countries through shipment of fry and eggs. It can be transmitted through water, by movement of fish, contact with contaminated untreated waste material and by equipment.

Symptoms: Fish become lethargic, having exophthalmic eyes, dark external surface, pale gills, haemorrhages at the base of the fins and distended abdomen. Fry and small fingerlings of salmonid species becoming infected very readily, and there may be mortality as high as 100% in fry.

Pathology: Internally, the fish becomes anaemic, ascetic and a mucus-like fluid replaces food in the digestive tract.

Diagnosis: Isolation of IHNV virus from spawning fish, pyloric caeca, intestine and ovarian/seminal fluid, should be attempted and its identification by enzyme linked immunesorbant assay (ELISA), indirect fluorescent antibody tests (IFAT), polymerase chain reaction (PCR) or antibody neutralization assays is possible.

Control: Good hygiene, the use of virus-free water supplies, disinfection of eggs from farms with IHNV and identification of carrier state of brood stock followed by disinfection of eggs of such stock are good control measures.

6. Lymphocystis

Lymphocystis is a chronic viral infectious disease of many wild and cultured marine and fresh water fish species like striped bass (*Roccus saxatilis*) from Chespeake bay, Tilapia species from East Africa, exotic aquarium fishes such as black tailed humbug, the black crapple. The virus does not affect catfish , cyprinids or salmonids. The disease is worldwide in distribution occurring in freshwater and marine species from both cold and warm water environment.

Etiology: The causative agent of this infection is a DNA virus known as Lymphocystivirus or Lymphocystis disease virus (LCDV) belonging to the family Iridoviridae. The virus particles range in size from 200-259 nm in diameter. This virus is considered to be less pathogenic than their iridoviral relatives. There is insignificant mortality but it affects the fish growth and reduces their marketability.

Transmission: Simple contact like fish-to-fish contact or contact with infected tissues, external trauma, dermal abrasion and wounding facilitates establishment of infection. In addition, crowding, shipping, and other stressors help in causing disease outbreaks. There is no vertical transmission.

Symptoms: The behaviour of affected fish is essentially normal and impact on the host is slight. In this disease there is hypertrophy of connective tissue cells resulting in macroscopic nodules often located on the fins, skin or gills. These may be cream to gray-coloured and appear during the course of the disease and may last for weeks. Pop eye (exophthalmia) due to lymphocystis masses in or behind the eye can be observed.

Pathology: Internally, pathology with lymphocystis virus is not common. Connective tissue cells of nodules have pathogenic cytoplasmic inclusions. This disease is rarely fatal.

Diagnosis: The disease can be suspected by observing the wart like growths on the fins, skin, or gills. Microscopic examination of wart like growth is a strong tentative diagnosis which reveals round to oval, grape, or balloon like structures, often in clumps. Histopathology, electron microscopy, or molecular methods are the other options of diagnosis. Due to the presence of lymphocystis nodules, the disease can be confused with fresh water white spot disease caused by *Ichthyophthirius multifiliis*, digenean trematodes ("grubs"), heavy infection with Epistylis (a stalked, ciliated, protistan parasite) or epitheliocystis (an intracellular bacterial disease). Some skin neoplasias (cancers) may also be confused with lymphocystis.

Control: It is usually a self-limiting disease, and fish is clear of nodules after a few weeks in warm water fish species. Currently, there is no good treatment that will speed up recovery from this disease. Good water quality/chemistry, good nutrition, correct population densities, optimal social groups and removing other stressors are helpful. Quarantining of new fish for at least 1–2 weeks and daily observation of these fish during this time alerts for any potential outbreak of lymphocystis. Application of potassium permanganate (100 mg/L or higher), formalin (2,000 mg/L or higher), or sodium hypochlorite at 200 mg/L for 15 minutes at 25°C inactivate the iridoviruses.

7. Koi herpes virus disease

Koi herpes virus disease (KHVD) is a herpesvirus infection capable of inducing a contagious and acute viraemia in common carp (*Cyprinus carpio*) and its ornamental subspecies, the koi carp and is responsible for explosive losses. Other cyprinid species of fish have been shown to be susceptible.

Etiology: The virus is an enveloped virion containing a double stranded DNA genome of approximately 295 kbp. It has a morphology typical of herpesviruses and formally classified as the species Cyprinid herpes virus

Transmission: KHVD can be transmitted by direct contact with infected fish, with fluids from infected fish or water and material from infected system.

Symptoms: Symptoms of the koi herpes virus usually only manifest during warm weather when the water temperature is between the mid of 60 to 80°F. Typical symptoms include bloody or discoloured gills; sunken eyes, pale or bloody patches on the skin and damage to the internal organs. Affected fish remain near the surface, swim lethargically and may exhibit respiratory distress. The virus causes heavy morbidity and mortality. Morbidity of affected populations can be 100%, and mortality 70–80%, but the latter can be as high as 90 or 100%

Pathology: Gill, kidney, and spleen are the organs in which the virus is most abundant during the course of overt infection.

Diagnosis: Confirmation of a KHV infection is only possible using biomedical techniques, such as testing the fish's blood serum for antibodies that the fish produces in response to the KHV infection.

Control: Because KHV is highly contagious, quarantining new fish and isolating any suspect fish is extremely important. Chemotherapy is not applicable.

8. Fish pox

Fish pox (also known as carp pox) is a fish herpes virus that normally only affects cyprinid fishes, including koi and goldfish. It is not particularly infectious and is not life-threatening. It is one of the oldest diseases seen in fish. As the disease weakens the fish with infection and lesions, it leaves the fish susceptible to secondary infections by other microorganisms. The fish also become disfigured by the disease.

Etiology: The Carp pox is caused by the virus herpesvirus-1 or HPV-1, which affects the fish's skin.

Transmission: Mode of transmission is unknown; however, it is probably direct.

Symptoms: The symptoms of fish pox include white, gray or pink growths on the skin and fins. Fish pox infections appear to be chronic but cyclical; infected fish periodically display the symptoms and then recover within a few months. In severe cases, the viral infection also diminishes the fish's immunity and leaves the lesion-filled (papillomas) area prone to a secondary infection by bacteria.

Pathology: There is elevation of the epidermis with the formation of white to yellow plaques over the body of the fish. Healed lesions usually turn black. Histopathologically, there is epidermal hyperplasia with the epithelial cells occasionally demonstrating intranuclear inclusion bodies.

Diagnosis: Usually external clinical signs are diagnostic. Skin histology will reveal epidermal epithelial cell hyperplasia, and intracytoplasmic and intranuclear inclusions. Either the demonstration of herpes-like particles in the hyperplasticepithelial cells or virus isolation and identification can be attempted by inoculation of tissue cultures, serum neutralisation or *in situ* hybridisation.

Control: The only effective way of control is preventing the introduction of affected fish and to destroy the infected fish. No particular treatment exists, but raising the temperature of the water to above 15°C, liming the ponds, or transferring the fish to ponds supplied with large amounts of clear, oxygenated water help in the recovery. In uncomplicated cases, the lesions are usually replaced by unmarked epidermis. However, in such cases the disease can reappear.

15

Parasitic Diseases of Fish

Parasitic disorders of fish range from microscopic protozoans to grossly visible annelids. There is always a risk of parasitic epizootic in farmed fish which increases with the intensification of the farm system. Many factors in fish culture will favour parasitic diseases. Stocking density, physical trauma due to handling, sub-optimal water quality and quantity, low water-flow rates within the culture system resulting in accumulation of infected stages of parasites, increase in mucus production due to irritation of gills and skin by high levels of ammonia, introduction of new exotic species, poor nutritional status, stress, poor husbandry practices and sudden rise in water temperature are favourable for the presence of different types of parasites on the fish. The major parasites causing diseases in fish vary from protozoa to trematodes, nematodes, cestodes, leaches etc. The important ciliated protozoa include *Ichthyophthirius multifiliis*, Chilodonella, Tetrahymena, Trichodina, Ambiphyra, Apiosoma, Epistylis and Capriniana while the flagellated protozoa comprise Hexamita, Ichthyobodo, Piscinoodinium, Cryptobia, Myxozoa, Microsporidia and Coccidia. Two important trematodes affecting fish are *Dactylogyrous* sp. and *Gyrodactylus* spp.

1. Ichthyobodoosis (Costiasis)

Ichthyobodosis is caused by the parasite Incthyoboda which is worldwide in distribution affecting both freshwater and marine water fishes including aquarium and food fishes.

Etiology: *Ichthyobodo necator* and *I. pyrformis* are the causative agents. These parasites are small, bean-shaped having two flagella, nucleus and contractile vacuoles. The parasite attaches itself to the host epidermis and gills by a disc located at its posterior end. Stress factors like overcrowding, mishandling, poor water quality, malnutrition, starvation and traumatic injuries increase the severity of infection and in causing the outbreaks.

Mode of transmission: The infection spreads through water. The flagella on free swimming stage of this parasite finds a site of attachment on a fish while actual attachment is due to ventral flat disc on the parasite.

Clinical signs: Young age cold water fishes are more commonly affected while the fish in water above 25°C are usually not affected. Light infection is manifested by rolling movement and rubbing against objects and sides of the tank. It is due to skin irritations. Listlessness, anorexia, thickening of mucous causing formation of dull spots on infested parts are common signs in heavy infestation. Respiratory distress due to swollen gills and sometimes covered with mucous and damage to fins make the fish to swim to the water surface. High mortality (40-75%) is associated with heavy infections.

Diagnosis: Case history and clinical signs may help but microscopic examination is important. Skin scrapings from the body surface, fins or gills are examined for the parasite under a microscope.

Treatment and control: Formalin, 250 mg/l for 1 hour by bath method, sodium chloride 10-15 gr/l for 20-30 minutes or 2 gr/l for 10 h or acriflavin 10 mg/l for 10 h by bath method are effective. Rising water temperature above 30°C helps to control the infection. Good environmental and nutritional conditions in the intensive and large scale production, independent water supply and disinfection of equipments assist in prevention and control of infection. Spawning fish must be given a prophylactic bath before stocking in order to prevent infection of the spawn.

2. Hexamitiosis

Hexamitiosis is an important disease caused by excessive parasitism of flagellated protozoa called Hexamita and is manifested by anorexia, emaciation and abdominal distension. Salmonids, trout, ornamental and many other species of fish and other aquatic animals suffer by this disease.

Etiology: *Hexamita salmonis*, *H. truttae* and *H. intestinalis* are three pathogenic species of this protozoa causing this disease. The parasite is pyriform or oval in shape having three pairs of anterior flagella and one pair located at posterior part. They live in the intestine and gall bladder of fish and reproduce by longitudinal binary fission and exist as cysts in fish intestine especially in cecal contents. Malnutrition (especially vitamin B deficiency), overcrowding, improper handling and shipping and physiological disturbance of healthy fish for any reasons are stress factors

Mode of transmission: The parasite may be transmitted by water and route of infection is oral but anal route plays a role in transmission of free-swimming flagellated forms of the parasites. Under stress the reproduction of parasite increases leading to disease. Lesions on skin (especially the head) or at the base of the fins and near the lateral line act as route of infection, especially in tropical aquarium fishes.

Clinical signs: *H. salmonis* has been found in salmonids, *H. truttae* in several species of trout and ornamental fishes while *H. intestinalis* affect several species of fish and other aquatic animals. Young fishes are more susceptible. Anorexia, weakness, emaciation, sunken abdomen, enlarged head, dark skin, pale colouration of gills, red vent, exophthalmia and anaemia are important clinical findings. The morbidity rate is 100% while mortality rate 100% in young fish without therapy.

Pathology: Intestinal contents are yellow and watery or jelly, and contain excess mucus and usually free from food or faeces. Systemic infection may occur that leads to swollen liver with petechial haemorrhages, ascites with blood clots in the visceral cavity. Also enlarged spleen, kidney and gall bladder are reported in infested fishes.

Diagnosis: It is based on the case history and clinical signs. Microscopic examination of intestinal or cecal contents reveals the presence of parasite. Histological preparation of ceca or intestinal tissue can also demonstrate *Hexamita.*

Treatment and control: Metronidazole 5 mg/1 liter for 3 h and repeated every other day for three treatments (25 mg/kg of body weight/day for 5 to 10 days), magnesium sulfate 0.2-0.3% of the diet for 3 days, or carbarsone 0.2% of diet for 3 days are useful. Removal of stress factors, good farm management and disinfection of the bottom of the pond with quick lime and quarantine of newly introduced fish for 14-20 days are helpful.

3. Whirling disease (black tail)

Whirling disease is a chronic, debilitating and highly infectious disease mainly of salmonids, caused by a protozoan parasite, *Myxosoma (Myxobolus) cerebralis.* The disease is characterized by whirling movement of the affected fish, malformations of the skeleton and black colouration of the posterior part of the body.

Etiology: *Myxosoma cerebralis* which exist as spores are nearly circular in shape containing two prominent polar capsules usually pyriform in shape. The spores are destroyed by heating at 60 to 100°C for ten minutes or within 24 h by 0.5 to 2.5% calcium oxide. Spores of *M. cerebralis* remain viable for a long time on the bottom of the pond (up to 12 years).

Transmission: The new host gets the spores orally. After ingestion, the sporeplasm of the spore emerges and migrates to the cartilage through blood and lymph vessels. The sporeplasm, called as trophozoite grows and its nuclei divide repeatedly to form a much larger organism which finally produces spores.

Clinical signs: The incubation period varies from 12 to 60 days depending on water temperature and number of spores involved. The appearance of the clinical signs of the disease depends on the age of the fish and severity of the infection. Young fishes may be more susceptible to the disease than older ones of the same species. Due to disturbed equilibrium, fish swim in circles, then rest on the bottom and again begin to whirl in circles. The posterior third of the body becomes black in colour, which is due to damage of the sympathetic nerve responsible for pigmentation (pigment motor function).Malformations of vertebral column leads it's binding in various directions. The mouth of fish remains open due to retraction and malformation of jawbones Fish cannot feed and die from exhaustion. Morbidity rate among young salmonids will usually reach 100%. Mortality rate among heavily infected young salmonids is 100%.

Diagnosis: Case history and clinical signs are diagnostic. Spores located in cartilage or bone can be demonstrated by staining sections of skull, gill arches and vertebrates with Giemsa stain. Fluorescent antibody techniques help in diagnosis of the disease.

Treatment and control: There is no therapy for treatment of infected fish. Hygienic disposal of dead and infected fish is recommended. Restriction on the movement of infected fish to non-infected farms, drying and disinfection of fish farm with calcium oxide, separation of fry and fingerlings, ensuring water of rearing tanks free of spores and importation of fish free from whirling disease with certification are some of the preventive measures.

4. Proliferative gill (Hamburger gill) disease

It is a protozoan disease that affects the marketability of fish and is characterized by presence of creamy white cyst-like nodules on extra respiratory organs and thickened broken gill filaments. Freshwater fish like catfish, tilapia and carps as well as marine fish are susceptible. The disease is more prevalent in cool temperature.

Etiology: The disease is caused by *H. branchialis* and *H. alexandrines*. Spores of the protozoa are elongated fusiform (spermatozoon-like) having two elongated polar capsule with polar filaments and bi-nucleated sporoplasm and two posterior long whip-like caudal processes. Life cycle of the parasite is not well known but may involve invertebrate intermediate host.

Transmission: Mode of transmission is not well known but infected and dead fishes are the source of infection.

Clinical signs: Creamy white cyst-like nodules filled with parasite spores are found in gill filaments or extra respiratory organ. Cysts attach to gill filaments rendering them nonfunctional (thickened and fuse together). Gill filaments are pale, broken and fused. The fish show respiratory signs and are emaciated and weak. Morbidity and mortality have a wide range. Severe epithelial hyperplasia and fusion of lamellae are some of the histopathological findings.

Diagnosis: Case history of respiratory signs, detection of spores in cyst by wet mount preparation and staining by methylene blue or Giemsa stain and histopathological changes are the diagnostic approaches.

Control: Treatment of infected fish is not possible. Therefore preventive measures like hygienic disposal of dead fish, drying and disinfection of pond with quick lime and water supply free of spores are some of the preventive measures. Any drug causing oxygen debilitation is contraindicated.

5. Dactylogyrosis (Gill fluke)

Dactylogyrosis is a parasitic disease caused by species of genus *Dactylogyrus*, affecting the fresh water and marine water fishes characterized by respiratory manifestation. Most species of freshwater and salt-water fishes are susceptible to take the infection with *Dactylogyrus* sp.

Etiology: The disease is caused by the genus *Doctylogyrus* that belongs to monogenetic trematodes. Several species like *D. vastator, D. extensus, D. anchoratus, D. lamellatus* are known to parasitize on freshwater and marine fish. *D. vastator* and

D. extensus are widely distributed species. All Dactylogyridae have seven pairs of marginal hooks and usually one pair of median hooks and are oviparous with no uterus. They are known as gills flukes because of most are located on the gills of their host.

Transmission: Transmission of these trematodes occurred from fish to other by direct contact or contaminated water.

Clinical signs: Infected fish become restless and collect in large number at water inlet, gasp for air as their respiration is impeded. Gills of infected fish are pale, sometimes mosaic-patterned and covered with mucus. Young fish suffer from inappetence and emaciated. Enlarged head as compared to the body, dark colouration, grayish gills and opercula somewhat opened are some of the signs which can be observed. At the point of attachment of the parasites there is destruction of the epithelium and disruption of tissues, and hyperplasia and necrosis of the gills may occur. Sometimes white to gray-white areas of thickened mucous are seen on the skin, especially behind the fins or anterior to dorsal fin. Secondary infection with bacteria or fungi may also be present.

Diagnosis: Case history and clinical signs and microscopic examination of skin scrapings or a piece of gills for the parasite.

Control: Bath treatment by 2.5% sodium chloride for 1 hour or 1 mg/liter of mebendazole for 24 h or 1 to 2 ml of glacial acetic acid/liter for 1-10 minutes or 250-330 mg/liter of formalin is effective. Besides this, good management and nutrition, restriction on introduction of exotic fish, use of parasite free water and short bath treatment of spawning fish in solution of common salt or formalin help in control of infection.

6. Gyrodactylosis

Gyrodactylosis is a parasitic disease caused by species of genus *Gyrodoactylus*, affecting the most species of freshwater fishes characterized by destruction of the skin or rarely the gills.

Etiology: The genus *Gyrodactylus* has several species like *G. anguillae, G. salmoni, G. ictaluri, G. cyprinid* and *G. salaries* which parasitize very often on the skin, fins and rarely on the gills. They are small in size less than 1 mm and viviparous. The adult parasite has no eyespots but a disk of attachment at the posterior end of the worm with hooks (16 marginal and 2 median). The clinical signs, transmission, treatment and control of the disease are similar to Dactylogyrosis. In addition to these, the skin of the fishes becomes spotted, necrotic, dark and covered with a bluish-gray mucous layer. The fishes also suffer from fin rot, if they are attacked.

7. Digenean trematode infestation

Digenea are common parasites in wild fish. About 1700 species of adult digenea infest fish. Metacercaria are common cause of the disease than adults. The fish are infested when the hosts found to complete the life cycle of the parasite.

Etiology: Adult digenea in definitive host fish lays eggs that hatch to miracidia infecting snails. Miracidium develop into cercaria penetrating the fish to form encysted metacercaria in the infested fish that are eaten by the definitive host.

Clinical signs: Migration of the cercaria causes haemorrhages; necrosis and inflammation along the migration path. In case of heavy infestation, death of the fish may occur, especially small fish. White nodules ranged from 1-4 mm in diameter found in skin, muscles or viscera or other parts of the body and the condition is called as white grub. Nodules may be yellow or black in colour and the conditions are known as yellow grub disease and black spot disease respectively. The variation in nodular colours depends on the colour of worm and/or the host reaction. Blindness to eye infestation and severe gill damage may cause mortality.

Diagnosis: Case history, clinical signs and microscopical examination revealing the presence of the adult or larval stages in the fish tissue.

Control and treatment: There is no therapeutic drug for treatment of the metacercaria stages of trematodes in fish. The interruption of the life cycle is one of the best methods for control of the disease. Eggs of the parasites and snails can be killed by draining, drying, or freezing the ponds. Snails can be destroyed be introducing fish, which feed on them or by chemicals as copper sulphate (5 mg/l).

8. Heart worm disease

It is an internal parasitic disease caused by a nematode, *Amplicaecum* sp. that affects sinus venosus and abdominal cavity of some freshwater fish mainly tilapia and cat fish.

Etiology: *Amplicaecum* sp. which is reddish in colour in anterior part is the etiological agent. Its posterior part is straight in females and curved in males. The larval stage is elongated creamy white. Final hosts are aquatic birds, water snakes, or crocodiles.

Clinical signs: There are no pathognomonic signs except the signs like abdominal distention, paleness of skin and emerging of long creamy-white larvae from sinus venosus.

Diagnosis: Case history, clinical signs and internal examination of fish are useful.

Control: Interruption of the life cycle is the best method. Elimination of intermediate host (molluscs) or addition of molluscophagus fish (snail carp or sea bream) in fish pond are preventive approaches as there is no effective treatment.

16
Fungal Diseases of Fish

Fungi are microorganisms which frequently appear as filamentous growth internally or externally on fish. The tingled white mass frequently seen on the surface of skin is called as mycelium and is made up of single strand of fungus called as hyphae. These hyphae may be non septate (no division) or septate with uninucleate or multinucleate cells. The terminal distended area of hypha is called as sporangia. The spores, called as sporangiospores, are produced within sporangium and are released into the water.

Most of the external fungi are thought to be opportunistic secondary invaders following a primary injury, ulceration or parasitic infestation. These external fungi appear as puff balls or white filaments on the surface of fish. Death is caused by invasion and destruction of internal organs. They can also attack fresh eggs, resulting a widespread infection and death.

Fungal infections in fish can cause damage to multiple body systems, such as the liver, kidney, and brain, and usually occur when the fish is in a weakened state, either due to injury or trauma. It can also develop if a fish is placed in poor living conditions (i.e., substandard water quality or an overstocked fish tank).

1. Icthyophonus infection

Icthyophonus is both an internal and obligate parasite and is well recorded fungal disease of fish.

Etiology: *Icthyophonus hoferi* is primarily responsible for a disease of marine fish but has also been recorded from freshwater fishes like gold fish, cat fish, haddock, herring etc.

Transmission: The transmission and cause of the *Ichthyophonus hoferi* fungus is unknown, but an unclean environment containing dead and decaying organic matter is favourable for infection in fish.

Symptoms: The *Ichthyophonus hoferi* fungus mainly infects older fish which are kept in aquariums. However, it is an uncommon fungal infection that typically occurs due to infected raw fish food. If left untreated, it may prove fatal for the fish. External signs include swimming with sluggish movements as if they were numbed, belly of the fish grows thin and shows a concave instead of convex contour. Fish loses its equilibrium and finally dies without showing the signs of the disease. If the brain is penetrated by fungus, fishes may have tumbling movements. In case of heavy primary infestation, the belly may appear swollen, exopthalmia, fins are torn and folded and whitish in colour. In several species of trouts, irregular black spots may occur on the skin or blackening of the whole body is observed. Occasionally due to involvement of gills, the symptoms of asphyxiation can be observed.

Pathology: The fungi are generally found in internal organs like heart, liver, kidneys, spleen, reproductive organs, stomach, intestine and muscles.

Diagnosis: In living fish, diagnosis is symptomatic but sometimes difficult. Sections of diseased tissues may show cysts of fungus which can easily be recognized. The cysts appear as whitish-grey granules lying between the tissues and having a diameter varying between 10 µm to 50 µm. Under microscope they are seen to be surrounded by thick membrane.

Control: Increased salt levels combined with good electrolyte and calcium levels in the water are good treatment options. Another possible measure is raising the water temperature to 82°F, as the Ichthyophonus fungi are more virulent in colder waters. It is important to thoroughly clean and sanitiz the fish tank, aquarium, or fishpond. If the water temperature is raised to 82°F, the Ichthyophonus infection may not be a problem as colder waters are favourable for their growth. Increased salt levels, combined with good electrolyte and calcium levels in the water are also helpful. Advanced stage of infection is difficult to treat. However, in early stage, treatment can be given. Infected fishes are fed with dried food soaked in a 1% solution of phenoxethol and 10 -20cc of this solution is added per liter of aquarium water. For use, 1 ml of stock solution is mixed in 99 ml of water and then used for water treatment. Penicillin and chloromycetin have also been used but with limited effects.

2. Saprolegnia infection

It is an important fungal infection called as saprolegniasis. Infections are normally restricted to the superficial tissues, resulting in a breakdown of fish's osmoregulatory mechanisms. All freshwater fish species and incubating eggs are susceptible to saprolegniasis.

Etiology: It is caused by *Saprolegnia diclina* type 1 and other *Saprolegnia* sp. which are fresh water fungi. Besides acting as primary pathogen, they frequently occur as secondary infections.

Transmission: The Saprolegnia fungal infection is caused by having an unclean environment containing dead and decaying organic matter. External fungal infections are transmitted through ambient water by infectious biflagellated zoospores released from hyphae sporangia. Systemic infections in cultured fish occur by ingestion of uneaten food that has been colonized by fungal hyphae.

Symptoms: The Saprolegnia fungus infects fish (or its eggs), affecting its internal organs and deeper tissues. Symptoms include light gray, cottony growths on the skin, fins, gills, and eyes. These cotton wool like lesions are normally white in colour but may be discoloured by the accumulation of debris between the fungal hyphae or as a result of a simultaneous bacterial infection. The fungus can colonise almost any area of the external surface of the fish. Frequent occurrence of lesions in the form of a delicate ring of fungus enclosing an apparently uninfected area of the body surface is also common. Saprolegnia may also occur as secondary invaders in various disease conditions like ulcerative dermal necrosis disease, fin rot and other bacterial diseases.

Pathology: The penetration of fungal hypahe is restricted to the epidermis and dermis. Muscular lesions are uncommon.

Diagnosis: Diagnosis is based on typical gross clinical signs where the skin, gills and other surfaces of an infected fish or eggs become covered with white, cottony tufts of fungal hyphae. Wet mounts of fungal mycelium from lesions show large, branching, non-septate hyphae. The fungus can be isolated on potato agar.

Control: Treatment of the Saprolegnia infection is accomplished by medicating the water with potassium permanganate. Topical treatment include the use of strong malachite green solution (100mg/ liter) to clean the lesion and application of a water-proof cream is helpful. Removing dead infected fish and sanitizing the environment are good ways to prevent this fungal infection. Long-term bath treatments include salt 1–5 g / litre indefinitely, malachite green 0.10mg/litre for three treatments at three-day intervals, potassium permanganate at 3-4 ppm every fourth day for four treatments.

3. Gill rot

Gill rot is an aggressive fungal disease that kills fish by adulterating their gill tissue.

Etiology: The causative *Branchiomyces sanguinis* and *Branchiomyces demigrans* fungi have branched hyphae 9-15 µm wide and grow into the veins of gill sheets where they cause complete stoppage of the circulation of the blood through capillaries. *Branchiomyces* sp. grow at temperatures between 13.9-35°C (57-95°F) but grow best between 25-32.2°C (77-90°F) .

Transmission: The fungi infect the gill tissue of fish. As the damaged gill tissue dies and falls off, the spores are released into the water and transmitted to other fish. High mortalities are often associated with this infection.

Symptoms: The course of the disease is very rapid. The fungus attacks the gills of those fishes that have been weakened by lack of oxygen or that have been damaged by other parasites/ mechanical means/ corrosive chemicals/ high water temperature/ high decaying organic matter in water. The infection is mainly confined to summer months, especially following extremely hot weather. The gills appear striated or marbled with the pale areas representing infected and dying tissue. Fish may appear lethargic and may be seen gulping air at the water surface (or piping). Fish will linger at surface and die in three days, sometimes one by one, starting with the smallest fish. The death of fish is due to suffocation.

Pathology: These fungi have branched hyphae 9-15 μm wide and grow into the veins of gill sheets where they cause complete stoppage of the circulation of the blood through capillaries. Large areas of the gills are cut off from the main blood stream. The gills become spotted. The places that are devoid of blood are liable to necrosis and will decay and parts of these fall off.

Diagnosis: Examination of gills is done. Microscopically multinucleated hyphae with globular shaped spores are seen. Hyphae of *B. demigrans* are extended even to the outside at the surface of gills while *B. sanguinis* is confined to the blood vessels only.

Control: Good management practices will create environmental conditions unacceptable for fungi growth. All tanks, raceways, and aquaria must be disinfected and dried. Ponds should be dried and treated with quicklime (calcium oxide). The water should be cooled, which can be accomplished by the frequent water changes. Cool water slows the fungal infection down and saves fish lives. Cool water carries more oxygen and eases the metabolic furnace of the fish. Increasing aeration may be life-saving. Formalin and copper sulphate, especially the former is very effective. However, no formalin treatment should last longer than 2 h.

4. Epizootic ulcerative syndrome

Epizootic ulcerative syndrome (EUS) is an epizootic condition of great importance in wild and farmed freshwater and estuarine fish. *Aphanomyces invadans* causes disease and mortality in farmed and wild fish worldwide. Around 94 species of fish have been confirmed to be naturally affected by *A. invadans* but some fish such as common carp (*Cyprinus capio*), Nile tilapia (*Oreochromis niloticus*) and milk fish (*Chanos chanos*) have been considered to be naturally resistant to infection with A. *invadans*. The disease is also known as mycotic granulomatosis and ulcerative mycosis.

Etiology: It has a complex infectious etiology and is clinically characterized by the presence of invasive *A. invadans*, which is a water mold or oomycetes. This mold grows best at 20–30°C but not in-vitro at 37°C. Parasites and rhabdoviruses have also been associated with outbreaks of this disease and secondary Gram-negative bacteria invariably infect lesions caused by *A. invadans*.

Transmission: The mold *A. invadans* spreads horizontally from one fish to another through water supply. Under unfavourable conditions or in absence susceptible fish species in water, the mold changes to encysted form. This form of mold plays a key role in causing outbreak of this disease when favourable environmental conditions are restored.

Symptoms: The susceptible life stages of the fish are usually juvenile and young adults fishes with no infection in fish fry or fish larvae. The motile spores of causative agent attaches to the skin, germinate under suitable conditions and hyphae invade the fish skin, muscular tissue and reach internal organs. Red spots may be observed on the body surface, head, operculum or caudal peduncle. Large red or grey shallow ulcers, often with a brown necrosis, are observed in the later stages. Large superficial lesions occur on the flank or dorsum. In highly susceptible species, such as snakehead, the lesions are more extensive and can lead to complete erosion of the posterior part of the body, or to necrosis of both soft and hard tissues of the cranium, so that the brain is exposed in the living animal. Important signs include the loss of appetite, dark colouration of body and hyperactivity with jerky pattern of movement. The infected fish float near the surface of the water. Mortality and morbidity may vary greatly depending on the fish species. However, high morbidity (>50%) and high mortality (>50%) might be observed in those years that have a long cold season, with water temperatures between 18 and 22°C.

Pathology: The skeletal muscle is the predilection site which exhibits symptoms and form mycotic granuloma. The lesion due to *A. invadans* hyphae progresses from a mild chronic active dermatitis to a severe locally extensive necrotising granulomatous dermatitis with severe floccular degeneration of the muscle. Lesion scrapes from fish body or ulcers generally show secondary fungal, bacterial and/or parasitic infections.

Diagnosis: For outbreak investigations, diseased fish with ulcerative lesions or red spots on the body should be sampled. Fish specimens should be transported to the laboratory live or in ice-cooled boxes for further diagnosis. Fish collected from remote areas should be anesthetized and can be fixed in normal 10% formalin or 10% phosphate-buffered formalin for at least 1–2 days. The fixed specimens are then transferred to double-layer plastic bags with formalin-moistened tissue paper. The bags containing moist specimens are sealed and sent to the laboratory. Ten diseased fish specimens are sampled from the site affected by infection.

Diagnosis: Diagnosis is achieved using history and clinical signs, histology, isolation of mold on individual fish or a group of a few fish and by serology. Mass mortality of various species of freshwater fish in estuaries, lakes and rivers during periods of low temperatures and after periods of heavy rainfall should be suspected for this infection. Clinical signs including red spots and ulcers, behavioural changes and gross pathology are good indicators of this infection. Fish with minor clinical signs are recommended and the muscle tissue next to or underneath the ulcer is best for oomycete isolation. Severely diseased or dead fish are not suitable for oomycete isolation. Internal tissues and moderate, pale, raised, dermal lesions are most suitable for oomycete isolation using glucose/peptone (GP) agar with penicillin G (100 units ml^{-1}) and streptomycin (100 µg ml^{-1}). Two procedures that can be used to confirm *A. invadans* are bioassay and polymerase chain reaction (PCR) amplification of the rDNA of *A. invadans*. In clinically affected fish, the best tissue for histopathological examination is muscle tissue at the edge of the ulcers. Serological methods for detection and identification of *A. invadans* in diseased specimens are not practical. If necessary, the monoclonal antibody offers a better specificity and sensitivity than polyclonalantibody for serological detection or identification of *A. invadans* in diseased specimens or in pathogen isolates.

Control: There is no effective treatment for infected fish in the wild and in aquaculture ponds. No protective vaccine is available. Water salinity over 2 parts per thousand can stop spread of the agent. Preparing fish ponds by sun-drying and liming are effective disinfection methods for *A. invadans*. To minimise fish losses in infected fish ponds, water exchange should be stopped. Use of ash, lime, and *neem* seeds or branches (*Azadirachta indica*) for treatments in fish ponds have shown variable results

5. Other fungal infections of fish

Penicillium piscium, Nephromyces piscium and *Pullularia* fungi have been found in the internal organs of the fishes but do not show specific external symptoms of the disease. *Penicillium piscium* is found in the ovary and body cavity in various European as well as tropical fishes. *Nephromyces piscium* form whitish foci in kidneys of the carps. *Pullularia* sp. affect the liver of ray fish and cause its death in 28-32 days. For such diseases, feeding minced meat mixed with a specific antifungal drug such as griseofulvin and nystatin is suggested.

17

Diagnosis of Disease in Fish

While the same principles are used in diagnosis of fish as in other animals, greater emphasis is placed on an accurate history, ante mortem signs, fresh necropsy material and direct microscopic examinations of fresh tissue smears and squash preparations. Fish decompose quickly and many saprophytic microorganisms reproduce rapidly in the decaying tissues which complicates isolation of pathogens unless samples are collected immediately after death. Fishes are poikilotherms; hence the environmental impact on fish should also be considered.

Importance of history

Case history information and its scrutiny are very helpful to know the circumstances under which the disease has developed. While sending diseased fish for diagnosis, it should enclose the following details or if a client brings a fish specimen by himself, he should be prepared for providing the following details.

- Owner's name, address and telephone number
- Species, number and age of fish submitted for examination
- Size and design of the system involved, species and numbers of each species in that system, which species are affected, recent additions of fish with species in that system, when was abnormal behaviour or death first noticed, number of sick fish per day and number of mortalities per day, previous disease problems in the system?
- Water quality data: source, temperature, flow rate, dissolved oxygen, hardness, pH and, if possible, levels of ammonia, nitrite and nitrates. When and how much water was changed?

- Behaviour of fish in the pond including flashing, breathing rate, lethargic behaviour etc. Their positions in water and whether they eat or stopped eating.
- When did the disease episode begin, death pattern and treatment administered. Death patterns can give some clue of the cause of the disease. Abrupt onset of deaths, large fish die first, fish die at dawn as well as death of phytoplankton is indicative of oxygen depletion while abrupt onset of deaths, not restricted to morning, young fish die first, death of frogs, snails and turtles etc. reflects intoxication. Continuous mortality over extended period of time raises the doubts of parasites while initial low mortality rate that reaches to high mortality and eventually decline indicates the involvement of viruses and bacteria. Nutritional problem should be doubted when mortality is initially low and reaches to level that constantly maintains.
- Previous treatments: What and when was the last treatment with dosage(s)? Type and size of feed and how often they are fed per day, when purchased and for how long the feed was stored, any change in feeding recently.

Submission of a fish sample

Disease can be diagnosed only in freshly killed fishes and live fishes. If it is late after the death of fish, diagnosis is very difficult. Fish taken for examination should include apparently healthy specimens and those just showing initial signs of disease. A minimum number of ten moribund fish or ten fish exhibiting clinical signs of the diseases in question must be collected: It is highly preferable and recommended to collect organ samples from the fish immediately after they have been selected at the fish production site. An identification label that includes information on the place and time of sampling must be attached to the sample.

Alive fish should be placed into well aerated water in a heavy ply plastic bag or in a bucket with a battery-operated aerator. Sealed bags containing oxygenated water can also be used. Bags with 3 liters of water will hold one large (15-20 cm) fish, 5 to 7 fingerlings or as many as 30 smaller aquarium species.

If the fish are dead or will not make the transport, the fish should be kept moist with wet paper towels in a heavy ply plastic bag. Keep the sample cold packed with ice. Freezing of the sample should be avoided, especially if tissues are to be submitted for histopathology. Always send freshly dead fish.

Submission of a water sample

A good diagnostic laboratory prefers to find any deviation in the quality of water where fish spend their entire life. It is therefore desirable to submit a water sample and it should be separated from fish specimen. Water should be collected in a clean container which is labeled with pertinent information and should be submitted on ice or ice packs. Ideally, dissolved oxygen and temperature should be measured at the pond, and if the pond is large, at multiple depths and locations.

Diagnostic procedures

Once the case history is scrutinized carefully, a general evaluation by the diagnostic laboratory is initiated. Deviation in water quality is determined by water chemistry parameters like total and unionized ammonia, nitrite, pH, total hardness, total alkalinity, and chloride. Measurements of chlorine, dissolved oxygen, hydrogen sulfide, iron, and copper are sometimes warranted. Fish are measured and weighed and abnormal changes to the external body surface are recorded. Grossly fish should be examined very carefully as it can give valuable clues as to what caused the initial problem. Fish's body condition (e.g. thin, bloated), one or both eyes normal, sunken in, or popped out, fins clamped down, frayed, or bloody, gills discoloured, bloody, or frayed, any lesions or growths on the fish or any other abnormality on the fish. Some of the external body changes related to fish diseases are given in Table 17.1. Externally skin scrapings, tip of the tail of small fish, small pieces of fins and pieces of gill lamellae are examined for parasites by placing on the glass slide. Fresh tissue sample of gill filaments, skin, mucous and fins should be collected and prepared as a wet mount and examined under light microscope at 100 and 400x. Tissues should be examined for morphology and for the presence of bacteria. Blood can be collected from caudal vein of fish larger than 25-100 g depending on the species and hematological parameters measured. External slimy layer may also be cultured on suitable media for the growth of bacteria or fungi. The fish are opened to expose the internal organs and examined for lesions and growths (Table 17.2). The kidney is sampled for bacterial culture (brain, liver, spleen, swim bladder, and other organs may also be cultured, as deemed necessary. Tissues may be taken for histological processing and virology. Bacterial and fungal agents and nutritional imbalances can often be suspected microscopically but must be confirmed by other methods.

In general, the laboratory can make an initial diagnosis of water quality and parasitic infection within 24 h of receipt of a sample. However, more time will be needed to determine the causative agents and for histopathological and other detailed procedures.

Table 17.1. External body changes and fish diseases

External signs/changes	Possible disease/infection/condition
Dark colour	Whirling disease of trouts, avitaminosis (broken back syndrome), infectious pancreatic virus infection
Red colour	Shock (circulatory collapse due to abrupt environmental changes
Emaciation	Tuberculosis, nocardiosis
Haemorrhages on the surface	*Aeromonas hydrophila/ A. salmonicida/ Edwardsiella/ Lactobacillus/ Mycobacterium/ Vibrio/ Pseudomonas*
Ulcers	Infestation of fish lice/trematodes, *Aeromonas/Mycobacterium/ Nocardia, Proteus rettgeri/ Renibacterium salmoninarum/ Staphylococcus/ Vibrio*
External abscesses	*A. hydrophila/Edwardsiella tarda/Lactpbacillus* sp./ *Renibacterium salmoninarum*

External signs/changes	Possible disease/infection/condition
Boils (furuncles)	*Aeromonas salmonicida*
Clubbed gills	Bacterial gill disease/fungal infection of gills/nutritional deficiency
Blood filled blisters on the flank	*Renibacterium salmoninarum/Lactobacillus*
Clubbed gills	Bacterial gill disease, fungal infection, nutritional deficiency
Protruded anus (vent)	*Edwardsielle tarda/Plesiomonas* infection
Distended abdomen	*Aeromonas /Edwardsiella/Lactobacillus/Streptococcus/* *Renibacterium salmoninarum/Pseudomonas*
Discrete white spots on the skin	White spot disease
Grey white patches on skin of back or side of fish	Columnaris disease
Yellow golden dust on body as seen by reflected light	Velvet disease
Grey blue areas on skin of large fishes like channel cat fish, trouts etc.	Nutritional deficiency
Frayed fins (necrotic and white)	Fin rot disease
Deformities	Genetic/nutritional/whirling disease
Exophthalmia (Pop-eye)	*A. hydrophila, Edwardsiella ictulari, Mycobacterium, Nocardia, Staphylococcus, Streptococcus, Renibacterium salmoninarum*

Table 17.2. Internal abnormalities of fish and disease conditions

Abnormal condition	Disease condition/infection
Gas filled holes in the muscle	Characteristic of *Edwardsiella tarda*
Petechial haemorrhages in muscles	Aeromonas/ Edwardsiella ictulari/ Lactobacillus/ Peudomonas florescens/ Renibacterium salmoninarum/ Vibrio
Haemorrhages in swim bladder	*Acinetobacter* infection
Swollen kidney	Edwardsiella ictaluri, Renibacterium salmoninarum
False membrane over heart and or kidney	*Renibacterium salmoninarum* (Bacterial kidney disease)
Swollen intestine containing yellow fluid	*Vibrio alginolyticus/ Yersinia ruckeri* (enteric red mouth disease)
Haemorrhages on/in internal organs	Common to most of the bacterial diseases
White nodules on/in internal organs	Pasteurella piscicida/ Edwardsiella tarda/ Mycobacterium sp./ Nocardia
Liver white, gelatinous or having white spots	Nutritional problem, systemic fungal infection, infection with mycobacteria, *Nocardia*
White spots on heart	Systemic fungal infection
Posterior kidney with white nodules	Common site of bacterial or viral infections like nocardiosis, systemic fungal infection, mycobacteriosis
Spleen	Organ of choice for blood parasites like trypanosomes
Swim bladder	Nematodes
Gall bladder	Site for many parasites

Specific diagnostic procedures

These procedures include direct and indirect methods. Direct methods are the ones which detect the particles of agents like bacteria, virus etc. or their components such as their enzymes, proteins, nucleic acid, etc. while indirect methods demonstrate the antibodies induced by the infections. Commonly used direct methods include isolation of bacteria and viruses, electron microscopy, immunofluorescence, immunohistochemistry, antigen enzyme-linked immunosorbant assay (ELISA), nucleic acid hybridization(NAH), the polymerase chain reaction (PCR). As NAH and PCR assays have nucleic acid molecules as targets, they are also termed methods of molecular diagnosis. The most common indirect methods of infectious agent detection are virus neutralisation, antibody detection by ELISA and haemagglutination inhibition tests. Both the direct and the indirect methods can be employed to assure the certainty of a diagnosis. In fish disease diagnosis indirect approach, especially serology has not been adequately developed. The important diagnostic approach is based on isolation of the pathogen followed by its specific identification, or on the demonstration of pathogen-specific antigens using an immunological detection method. Detailed procedures of isolation of specific bacteria and viruses have been described by IOE (2003) in its diagnostic manual.

Isolation of the viruses and bacteria and their identification

Sample material to be used in viral and bacteriological tests depends both on the size of fish as well as clinically diseased fish or carrier fish. Size-wise, the entire fry is the sample, while entire viscera including the kidney and encephalon should be the sample of fish 4-6 cm long and the kidney, spleen and encephalon of fish over 6cm should collected for isolation purposes. In case of brood fish ovarian fluid and other tissues should be made as the samples.

In the case of clinical infection, besides whole alevin or entire viscera, organs to be sampled are anterior kidney, spleen and encephalon for virus screening, and kidney and spleen for bacterial screening. Samples from ten diseased fish will thus be taken and combined to form pools of a maximum of five fish each. The amount of material should be approximately 1.5 g/pool of material from five fish.

For detecting asymptomatic carriers, samples may be combined as pools of no more than five fish/pool, for a total weight of about 1.5 g. Pools of ovarian fluid from five brood fish should not exceed a total volume of 5 ml i.e. 1 ml/brood fish. These ovarian fluid samples are to be taken individually from every sampled female and not collected following the pooling of ova.

Once aseptically removed from fish, the organs and/or ovarian fluid samples are each split into two parts if both bacteriological and virological examinations are to be done.

Virological examination

Samples should be transported and stored at 4°C until processing is performed. It should optimally be carried out within 24 h after fish sampling but never beyond 48 h. The transpotation media include Hanks' balanced salt solution (HBSS) with added antibiotics like gentamycin (1,000 µg/ml) or penicillin (800 IU/ml) and streptomycin (800 µg/ml) or antifungal compounds Mycostatin® or Fungizone®

may also be incorporated into the transport medium at a final concentration of 400 IU/ml. Serum or albumen (5–10%) may be added to stabilise the virus if the transport time will exceed 12 h.

The virus in the sample is allowed to induce CPE in susceptible cell cultures. Fish cell lines recommended for testing fish viruses are Bluegill fry (BF-2), Channel catfish ovary (CCO), Chinook salmon embryo (CHSE-214), Epithelioma papulosum cyprini (EPC), Rainbow trout gonad (RTG-2).

Commonly used culture media for fish virus isolation include Eagle's minimal essential medium (MEM) with Earle's salt supplemented with 10% foetal calf serum (FCS), antibiotics and 2 mM L-glutamine. Stoker's medium, however, which is a modified form of the above medium comprising a double strength concentration of certain amino acids and vitamins, is particularly recommended to enhance cell growth, using the same supplementations as above.

For the production of most of these viruses, the susceptible cell cultures must be inoculated with fairly low multiplicities of infection (m.o.i.) i.e.10^{-2} to 10^{-3} plaque-forming units (PFU) per cell. Virus containing cell culture fluid should be diluted so that it has on an averaging $1\text{–}2\times10^{6}$ PFU/ml and should be freeze and stored at –80°C or liquid nitrogen. Isolated virus can be lyophilized for long term storage.

Bacteriological examination

Internal organs may be used as a source of isolation whenever systemic infections suspected. Due to presence and multiplication of saprophytic microorganisms in fish, live fish are preferred for bacteriological examination.

Besides the use of special media for cultivation of few bacterial pathogens, the peptones like tryptic soya broth, brain heart infusion broth etc. can conveniently be employed for isolation of fish bacterial pathogens. In general there is slow growth of fish bacteria that necessitates the addition of enrichment components like serum or blood. Culturing is generally conducted at temperatures between 20 and 26°C with exceptions of incubation at 15°C as well as at 30 or 37°C.

Bacterial strains can be stored for a short term on ordinary media, placing the slants or broths at 4°C. Freezing is probably the best way to preserve bacterial suspensions of high titer.

Serology

Polyclonal antibodies against fish viruses and different bacteria can be raised in rabbits by employing immunization protocols depending upon the type of the agent and the sera so collected can be frozen at -20°C or lyophilise. Immunoglobulins (Ig) may be extracted from antisera using conventional methods suitable for Ig purification. Selective attachment to protein A constitutes a reliable and effective method.

Mouse monoclonal antibodies to fish viruses and bacteria have been raised and used as biological reagents suitable for the identification of viruses like IPN, VHS, IHN and bacteria like *Renibacterium salmoninarum*.

Virus neutralisation, antibody detection by ELISA and haemagglutination inhibition tests have been employed in fish disease diagnosis.

Molecular techniques for confirmatory testing and diagnosis

Molecular techniques are potentially faster and more sensitive than culture, serology, and histology methods that are traditionally used to identify fish pathogens. During the last 15 years or so, molecular techniques have been increasingly employed to diagnose fish diseases. These techniques include probe hybridization, in situ hybridization, polymerase chain reaction (PCR), restriction enzyme digestion, RFLP, PCR linked to hybridization with specific oligo probes or, non-specific primers used to produce random amplified polymorphic DNA (RAPD). The ability to identification of the presence or absence of a pathogenic organism in fish quickly would have significant economic benefits. An additional benefit would be if the concentration of the infectious organism could be determined in the fish or the environment so that changes in abundance of these organisms could be monitored. Finally, the development of a system that could accurately assess the carrier state of fish within an area containing a disease causative agent would aid in the development of management programs.

Reference

OIE (2003). Manual of Diagnostic Tests for Aquatic Animals. *www.oie.int/doc/ged/D6505.PDF.*

18

Treatment of Disease in Fish

When working with fish, disease prevention is always more rewarding than treatment. However, once disease has appeared in fish, treatment must be administered as early as possible. Accurate identifying the disease problem is important before starting the treatment. Therapy is often based on environmental management followed by the use of targeted therapy to control specific pathogens. There are different methods of disease treatment like adding the drug in water or feed, parenteral injection and topical application. The methods of application and the concentration and duration of application depend on the disease, species, weight and type of aquaculture unit. Generally speaking, bath and topical treatments are most useful for external infections, whereas medicated food and injection are most appropriate for internal infections.

Methods of treatment

1. Adding the drug in water

Drugs may be added to the water in different ways as described below.

i. **Dip method:** In this technique, a concentrated chemical solution is made up in tank. Fishes or eggs are placed in hand net or trays and dipped into solution for few seconds to one minute. This method is used for disinfection of raceways and aquaria for control of the disease.

ii. **Bath method:** The most common method of administration of therapeutic agents to fish is bathing in water soluble compounds. Bath treatment is useful in culture facilities having rapid flow of water. This treatment is essentially of short duration lasting minutes to a maximum of one hour only. This may carried out in ponds or tanks where the water is static during treatment and the fish are left in solution for certain period. Fish suffer from many external diseases (parasitic, fungal and bacterial) that can be treated by this method. There are three types of bath treatments. The difference between these bath treatments is the concentration of the chemical applied and the period of time that the fish are in contract with chemical.

Using a bath treatment requires accurate measurement of the volume of water to be treated. To calculate volume in a rectangular tank, measure length, width, and depth, and multiply the 3 measurements. To calculate volume of a circular tank, multiply 3.14 by the radius squared by the depth. To calculate directly into liters, measure in cm and multiply by 0.001. If the measurements are made in feet, the result will be in cubic feet; to convert cubic feet to gallons multiply by 7.481. If treating an odd-shaped container, volume may be calculated mathematically. Alternatively, the volume of in-flowing water per minute can be measured by determining how long it takes to fill a 1 L graduated cylinder (or 5 gal bucket). Using that information, determining how long it takes to fill a tank or ornamental pond can provide a fairly accurate assessment of volume.

a) **Dip bath**: The fish is dipped into a concentrated chemical bath for a short period of time, often less than one minute. Prolonged exposure to the chemical at the high concentration delivered in a dip would be fatal to the fish because diseased fish are generally intolerant of stressful situations a short period. This method has the advantage of handling large numbers of fish in a short time.

b) **Short bath**: Short bath means that the fish are subjected to a moderate chemical concentration for a period of time ranging from 30 minutes to several hours. This is an excellent method for administering many medications to fish kept in aquaria, tanks, or raceways. The duration of exposure to the chemical will be determined by chemical used, the concentration of chemical used and the facility in which the fish are housed. In most cases, water flow and filtration are shut down while the chemical is in contact with fish. It is widely used in treatment of parasitic diseases.

c) **Prolonged bath**: It means that small concentrations of chemical are applied and left in the water on a permanent basis. This is the only method of administering a bath to pond fish. Because of the low concentrations of chemical applied, a prolonged bath is often the least expensive and safest way of administering a chemical bath. It may last for many hours to days. It is therefore possible only when the therapeutic index of drugs is large.

iii. **Flush method:** Flush is a modification of the bath treatment for flow through system. Water flow is not stopped, but a high concentration of chemical is added at the input and passed through the system as pulse. The introduced dose should be added in 1 to 2 minutes. A measured amount of drugs is added to the system upstream and allowed to flush through. Flush treatment is only suitable for systems that have enough flow to completely flush out the drug within a predetermined time. Here a constant flow siphon or metering pump is used to monitor the drug to give a constant low concentration of therapeutics. This method is more applicable in raceways or recirculatory systems.

2. Adding drugs to the feed

Feed treatment technique is highly popular to administer drugs to fish for systemic infection. Here, the required drugs are mixed with the diet and pellets are prepared. Some medicated feeds can be purchased commercially for aquaculture or pet fish.

3. Administration of drugs to individual fish

Valuable fish can be treated individually by local application or by injection (S/C, I/M and I/P).Injections can be given either intramuscularly, subcutaneously or intraperitoneally. Intramuscular injections ventrally in the lower abdominal region can be administered conveniently. IP injections can be given anterior to the pelvic fins, just off the ventral midline. Parenteral treatment injections are applicable only in the case of valuable brood stock, berried spawners etc. In smaller size shrimps, it is not practicable.

4. Topical treatments

Usually in ointment form, it should be applied directly to the lesion of concern. The fish can be manually restrained, usually without removing the entire animal from the water. The area to which the treatment is applied should be held out of the water for several seconds (<1 min) to allow some absorption before returning the fish to the water. Repeated applications may be necessary. The lesions, ulcers and localized injections of valuable shrimps may be treated with topical application of concentrated chemicals or antibiotics.

Substances used in treatment

1. Chemicals used in treatment

i. **Salt (NaCl):** Salt is commonly used in aquaculture to relieve stress during handling and transport of fish. It can be used in the form of table, rock or meat-curing salt.

ii. **Formalin:** Formalin is effective against parasitic infection but not a preferred treatment for external bacterial and fungal infections. It is used as a bath treatment to control external parasitic infections, protozoans and monogenetic trematodes of fish. It kills parasites on gills, skin, and fins. High concentrations of formalin are used to control fungi on fish eggs. It can be used in ponds by prolonged bath method at a dose of 15 to 25 mg/L (2 drops /gallon) and by short-term baths at 250 mg/L for 30-60 minutes. With the increase in water temperature, concentrations of formalin should be decreased.

iii. **Malachite green:** Used for treatment of many external protozoan and fungal infections. Concentration 0.1 ppm in pond or aquaria at three or four days intervals. It may be administered as bath treatment at 2 ppm for one hour. Treatment of fish eggs for external fungi can be made by giving a 10 sec. dip in 1,500 ppm of malachite green or by the use of 2,000 ppm for 15 min.

iv. Malachite treatment can also be given for indefinite time at 0.1 ppm of water or as bath treatment at 1-3 ppm for 1 h and dip treatment at 66 ppm for 10-30 sec. for external fungal infection on fish.

v. Acriflavin: Used in the treatment of fish affected by protozoa, skin and gills flukes, fin rot and fungal condition. The concentration 0.02 mg/liter for three days and repeated if required. However, it should be remembered its nature to be insoluble in salt water and is phytotoxic.

vi. Potassium permanganate: It is quite effective in controlling many bacterial, parasitic and fungal infections if it is used at an early stage of infection. By a long-term bath method, it can be administered at a concentration of **2** mg/ liter (2 ppm) in fresh water or salt water system.

vii. Copper sulphate: It is effective against external fungal infection on fish. Use of copper sulphate for treatment purposes depend upon the hardness of water. If the water is soft having hardness between 40 and 50 ppm , 0.25 ppm or less copper sulphate should be used while with moderately hard water(between 50 and 90 ppm) the dose is 0.5 ppm and with hard water (between 100 and 200 ppm) it is 1 ppm of copper sulphate. The treatment should be repeated on day 3 using half of original dose.

viii. Iodine and iodophores: These are commonly used as disinfectants in aquaculture and fish eggs.

ix. Mercurochrome: Tincture of mercurochrome can be applied on fungal lesion by a swab.

2. Antibiotics used in treatment against bacteria

Antibiotics are used extensively in fish culture in treatment of problems caused by bacteria. Some of the commonly antibiotics that have been used for treatment of fish diseases are described below.

Chloramphenicol: While using orally with food, the dose is 50 to 75 mg per kg body weight per day for 5 to 10 days while in water it is added at 10-50 ppm for the time as needed. The drug can be injected using single i/p injection in soluble form of 10-30 mg per kg.

Chlortetracycline: Can be used by adding in water or feed at the rate of 10-20 ppm and 10-20 mg per kg food respectively.

Kanamycin: 50 mg per kg of fish or 25-100 mg per kg of food. Feed for 1 weak.

Nalidixic acid: 1 tablet per 50 to 100 litres of water for treatment of 3 to 4 days duration, usually used for infection with Gram-negative bacteria.

Oxytetracycline (Terramycin): 50-75 mg/kg b.wt. /day for 1 day with food. The drug must be discontinued for 21 days before fish are killed for human consumption.

Oxolinic acid: Use for control of *Aeromonas* infections. Use orally 3 mg per kg fish once daily for 5 days; as bath 1ppm for 24 h for columanaris disease.

Potentiated sulfonamide (Sulfadimethoxine potentiated with ormetoprim): Use for control of furunculosis and other systemic infections. Use with food at 50 mg/kg fish/day.

Sulfamerazine: 200 mg/kg b.wt./day with food for 14 days

Sulfamononethoxine: Use with food at a rate of 100 to 200 mg/kg of feed.

Sulfisoxazole: 200 mg/kg b.wt. /day with food

19

Prevention and Control of Diseases in Fishes

Prevention implies all measures taken to exclude a disease from an unaffected (healthy) population while control is a strategy which employs all tactics for reducing the frequency of illness which are already present in population. There are several approaches for disease prevention and control like quarantine, treatment, immunization, early diagnosis etc. In fish culture some of the measures like selection of healthy fish seed, proper density and rational culture, careful management, qualitatively uniform ration and fresh food, good water quality and prevention of fish body from injury are important. Abolishing pathogens and controlling its spreading by using disinfectants, segregation of year class fish population, spot removal of dead fish from the pond, chemoprophylaxis, and immunoprophylaxis are among the important preventive and control measures. In aquaculture environment fish are stressed by high density and unnatural conditions. Therefore, diseases can spread easily and very quickly and have serious effects. The key to prevent constant disease problems in aquaculture operations is to manage the system carefully and to be alert to signs that something is wrong. The fish farm manager should examine the fish on regular bases and immediately investigate any unexpected decreases in population or unfamiliar behaviour or appearances. For example; reduction in feeding, gasping for air, resting on their side or up-side down, or sluggish movement are signs of a problem, as are spots or lesions on the fish surface. Following important considerations should be considered for prevention and control of fish diseases.

General considerations

i. **Good management:** It means seeing that the fish are not excessively stressed, since a weakened fish is more likely to become sick than a strong one. Several basic practices are of key importance in preventing the outbreak of serious diseases. These include; monitoring the quality of water, using foods that supply all the essential nutrients, minimizing over handling, using reasonable stocking densities, isolating and inspecting fish which are suspected of being sick and effective use of antibiotics are the key points.

ii. **Stocking healthy fish:** Disease-free fish should be stocked regardless of whether the fish are to be put into a home aquaria, trout raceways, or catfish production. Purchase fish from reputable sources and quarantine of newly purchased fish for a minimum of four weeks is a good practice.

iii. **Water source:** Excellent water quality should be maintained. It should be free from parasites. Filtration of water, frequent water change and monitoring water quality weekly are some of the important measures to prevent diseases.

iv. **Feed:** A balanced and varied diet consisting of commercially prepared foods (e.g. flake, frozen, freeze dried), supplemented with live foods is good for good health of fish. Overfeeding should be avoided.

v. **Sanitation**: Stocking of fish should be done with particular attention to cleaning and disinfection of the culture system. Equipment shared between aquariums, such as nets, etc., should be soaked in water above 90°F for several minutes or soaked in a weak bleach solution. Use liberal amounts of fresh water to remove any residual chlorine.

vi. **Monitoring of fish health**: Health of fish population must be monitored from time to time. Changes in behaviour or for symptoms of disease must be noted.

vii. **Quarantine:** Fish which are moved from suspected area or infected area to non-infected area must be held in detention for a period of time at least as long as the incubation period of the disease.

viii. **Population density:** Accurate calculation of the number of fish/unit is necessary. Suitable number of fish should be put in suitable unit to ovoid the stress factors. Overstocking increase competition among individual fish (10,000 to 50,000 fry per hectare).

ix. **Genetic manipulation** to produce species that are resistant to disease.

Cleaning of water tanks and equipment

Efforts to maintain as clean an environment as possible including minimal accumulation of organic debris, proper disinfection of nets and equipment, and thorough disinfection of fish-holding units between groups of fish will help minimize disease outbreaks. Dead fish must be removed, aquatic vegetation must be controlled, and wild fish should be controlled. Sanitation of tanks and equipment starts with general cleaning and removal of organic debris. Household bleach (3–6% Sodium hypochlorite) delivered at 35 ml/gal of water creates a concentration of 200 mg/L. A 1 hour contact time at this concentration will destroy most organisms of concern, including most viruses. Bleach should not be used in closed areas containing live fish as the volatile compound may get into solution and kill fish in nearby tanks. Mycobacteria are refractory to bleach disinfection because of their waxy cell wall. Spraying equipment and contact surfaces with alcohol following treatment with bleach should be effective in eliminating mycobacteria. Quaternary ammonium compounds are also excellent disinfectants and can be used at concentrations of 500 mg/L for 1 h.

Disinfection of pails, vats and miscellaneous equipment

- **Chlorine**: 300 PPM, disinfection in 30 to 60 min. Commercial: Chlorex (5.25% hypochlorite)
- HTH (test hypochlorite) contains 65% chlorine concentration
- **Roccal:** One of a group of quaternary ammonium germicidal compound and is excellent for nets. Dosages should be followed as per manufacturer direction.
- **Idophores:** Can be used for net or surface disinfection. It is a good oxidizing agent.
- **Formaline:** Contains 37% body wt. of formaldehyde, which is the active ingredient; 4 ml/gallon of water (about 1,000 ppm) is excellent dip for nets.

Disinfection of ponds

- **Calcium hydroxide (slaked lime):** Dose 5 1b per 100 ft^2 should be used fresh.
- **Calcium hypochlorite (HTH):** Distribute in ponds at the rate of 0.6 1b per 1000 ft^3 of water (10 ppm chlorine). HTH is noxious and gas masks may be required in closed areas.
- **Calcium oxide (quick lime):** Usually added to the bottom and sides of ponds at the rate of about 5 1b to 100 ft^2.

Prevention by Insect Control in Ponds

- **Diesel Fuel:** 2-4 gal per acre. Diesel fuel or kerosene will destroy aquatic beetles and other surface breathing insects. Motor P oil or cotton seed oil is added to the diesel fuel or kerosene to aid dispersion at the surface of water.
- **Baytex:** Organophosphates control predatory insects and are used at a dose of 0.25 ppm.

Prevention by snail control in aquaculture systems

- Periodic drainage to wash down snails to the drain. Other methods include drying, heavy sprinkling of damp spots with quick lime or recently purchased slaked lime. Copper sulphate can also be used at a dose of 0.1 ppm with soft water or 2 ppm with hard water.

Considerations for prophylaxis and treatment

Treatment of fish should be based on an accurate diagnosis of the problems along with an evaluation if the cost of treatment is justified in light of the problem and expected results. A few important considerations as mentioned below should be considered prior to any treatment.

- **Diagnosis**: The choice of a chemical to be added to the water or a drug to be incorporated into the food should be based on an accurate diagnosis.
- **Water quality:** A successful treatment presupposes a knowledge of existing water quality conditions including temperature, total hardness, oxygen levels, pH and organisms load. Dosages of chemicals frequently are dependent on water hardness, as in the case of copper sulphate, pH as in the case of organic phosphate, or relative organic load, as in the case of potassium permanganate.
- **Species of fish:** Some species of ornamental fish are sensitive to dosages of various chemicals easily tolerated by trout or channel catfish. Younger fish may be more sensitive to a particular chemical than young of other species, e.g. the young of many species are more sensitive to malachite green than adults, skinned fish such as eels have an increased sensitivity to malachite green.
- **Laws and regulations:** Chemicals and drugs must be used in accordance with current regulations as promulgated in a country.
- **Preliminary biological tests**: Whenever possible, pretests of chemicals to be added to the water or of drugs to be incorporated into food should be conducted on a small batch basis. Such tests provide toxicity as well as efficacy data.
- **Dosages**: Most chemicals used in treatments of fish diseases will be toxic to the fish if correct dosages are not used or if dosages are not adjusted according to varying water quality conditions. Dosages of chemicals in water are always accompanied by information on the length of treatment, which will vary depending on the concentration of chemical.

Vaccination

Vaccination can be by injection, immersion, bath, spray and the oral route. The efficacy of vaccination is influenced by the quality of the vaccine, the ability of the fish to develop immunity and the conditions under which the fish are vaccinated. Vaccination should not be carried in diseased fish and initially vaccinate a small number of fish for observation for about a week before the rest of the population. It should, be carried under aseptic conditions and ensure to apply the vaccine correctly.

20

Fish as a Food

Fish has been used a food by humans throughout recorded history. Fish is highly nutritious, tasty and easily digested. It is much sought after by a broad cross-section of the world's population, particularly in developing countries. It is estimated that around 60 percent of people in many developing countries depend on fish for over 30 percent of their animal protein supplies, while almost 80 percent in most developed countries obtain less than 20 percent of their animal protein from fish. However, with the increased awareness of the health benefits of eating fish and the ensuing rise in fish prices, these figures are rapidly changing.

A small number of known species fish are commonly eaten. In culinary and fishery contexts, the term fish can also include shellfish which is an exoskeleton-bearing aquatic invertebrate and includes various species of crustaceans, mollusks and echinoderms. *Crustaceans* (shrimp, lobsters, crabs, crayfish) have a segmented body divided in separate parts and have higher quantities of free amino acids in particular and also higher quantities of nitrogenous compounds but low in carbohydrate content (about 0.5%). Mollusks (clams, carpet shells, mussels, oysters, periwinkles, squid, scallops, whelks) have a significant content of carbohydrate and lower quantities of nitrogen in their flesh. They are as good eaten raw as cooked but some of them are only eaten after cooking. They should not be overcooked as they become shriveled and tough or, if they are cooked in a liquid, soft and pasty. Echinoderms are not as frequently harvested for food as mollusks and crustaceans; however sea urchin roe is quite popular in many parts of the world.

Health benefits

Fish is a great addition to the diet, since it is packed with vitamins, minerals, and nutrients that the body needs in order to stay healthy. Fish is rich in most of the vitamins that man requires, it contains a good selection of minerals, and the proteins contain all the essential amino acids in the right proportions.

Fish offers several benefits to consumers like fish oil can help to boost the immune system, and fishes like salmon, tuna, whiting and trout provides omega-3 fatty acids, which are essential for bone and skin health, as well as cell reproduction. Fish has also been reported to reduce the risk of cardiovascular disease in both men and women, especially those with diabetes. Eating fish has also been proven to reduce the risk of strokes for both men and women, since it aids in heart health, and is a food that helps to cleanse the blood so that blood can be transported to and from the heart easier. Not only does eating fish convey those benefits, but eating fish or taking fish oil supplements on a regular basis could help to improve or preserve the vision. Fish contains docosahexaeonic acid (DHA) which is produced in the eye near the light-sensing nerve cells. Since fish provides an extra 'serving' of DHA, people are less likely to experience the muscular degeneration in the eye area that comes with aging.

Composition of fish

The muscular system, the edible part, of fish differs from that of mammals: the long bundles of muscle fibers reaching from bone to bone, attached by strong tendons and connective tissue, are in fish replaced by shorter segments, interconnected by connective tissues and attached to the back bone, which constitutes the complete skeletal system, including the thin side bones and the cranium. Fish have two types of musculature of different colour and with different function: Dark musculature is found utmost on the sides of the most active swimmers (herring, mackerel, sardine etc.). The dark colour is due to the ample blood supply. These muscles are mainly used for slow, persistent swimming for a long time. The dark musculature also contains large amounts of lipids. The white musculature is very sparsely supplied with blood and is mainly used for brief, quick escape or catching maneuvers.

As with many animal products, fish and fishery products contain water, proteins and other nitrogenous compounds, lipids, carbohydrates, minerals and vitamins (Table 20.1). Proteins and lipids are the major components whereas carbohydrates are detected at very limited levels (less than 0.8 percent). Vitamin content is comparable to that of mammals except for vitamins A and D which are found in large amounts in the meat of fatty species, especially in the liver of species such as cod and halibut. Fish meat is a particularly valuable source of several minerals. However, the chemical composition of fish varies greatly from one species and one individual fish to another within the same species depending on age, sex, environment and season. Certain general figures can be given, however, although with wide dispersions.

Table 20.1. Average composition of fish muscle

Component	Content
Water	28-90%
Protein	6-28%
Lipids (fat)	0.2-64%
Ash (minerals)	0.4-1.5%
Glycogen	0.8%

Water: The main constituent of fish flesh is water, which usually accounts for about 80 percent of the weight of a fresh white fish fillet. The average water content of the flesh of fatty fish is about 70 percent that may vary between 28-90 percent in individual specimens of certain species. There is a tight binding of water to proteins and therefore it cannot readily be expelled even under high pressure. After prolonged chilled or frozen storage, some of the water is lost as a drip because the proteins are less able to retain all the water. This loss increases when frozen fish is stored at too high a temperature and affect the quality of fish.

Lipids: The term lipid includes fats, oils and waxes as well as more complex, naturally-occurring compounds of fatty acids. However, for simplicity sometime the term fat is used. The composition of the lipid fraction varies, but it consists mainly of triglycerides with 12-24 carbon atoms in the fatty acids, which often contain 4-5 or 6 double bonds. This special structure with many polyunsaturated fatty acids is very advantageous to the human diet from a nutritional physiology point of view.

Lipid content of fish varies greatly from 0.2 percent to 25 percent. Ratio of the highest and lowest fat values is more than 300 to one which is much wider than the water, protein or mineral content. Depending upon the fat content, fish are classified as lean like cod, saithe and hake which are bottom-dwelling ground fish, semi-fatty like barracuda, mullet and shark or fatty like herring, mackerel and sprat . Semi fatty species store lipids in limited parts of their body tissues only or in smaller quantities. Table 20.2 shows the availability of lipids in different types of fishes.

Table 20.2. Comparative lipid contents in fish and shell fish

Fish type	Water (%)	Protein (%)	Lipid (%)	Ash (%)
Fatty fish	68.6	20.0	10.0	1.4
Semi-fatty	77.2	19.0	2.5	1.3
Lean fish	81.8	16.4	0.5	1.3
Crustaceans	76.0	17.8	2.1	2.1
Molluscs	81.0	13.0	1.5	1.6

The fat content varies as per type of feeding and season. Heavily fed fatty fish may have a fat content of over 20 percent while starved herring may have as little as one half percent. Seasonal fluctuations in fat content are noticed mainly in liver.

The fat is not always uniformly distributed throughout the flesh of a fish body. The highest concentrations are found in the dark musculature and in belly flaps (the muscles surrounding the abdominal cavity) while in lean fish the fat depots are present in the liver.

Proteins: Proteins in fish can be described as structural proteins (actin, myosin, tropormyosin and actomyosin), sarcoplasmic proteins (myoalbumin, globulin and enzymes) and connective tissue proteins (collagen). Similar to proteins in milk, eggs and mammalian meat, fish proteins contain all the essential amino acids and have a very high biological value. Fish proteins are an excellent source of lysine, methionine and cystein which are poor in cereal based diets. The protein content of fish muscle is usually between 15 and 20 percent, but values lower than 15 percent or higher than 28 percent are occasionally found in some species.

The genuine proteins are comparable to those of the domestic animals, but fishes often contain larger amounts of essential amino acids, which makes them comparable to egg protein from nutritional point of view (Table 20.3).

Table 20.3. Amino acids in fish, eggs and beef

Amino acids	Fish	Eggs	Beef
Valine (g/kg)	5.3–5.5	8.3	5.3
Leucine (g/kg)	7.2–7.6	8.6	7.8
Isoleucine (g/kg)	5.0–5.2	7.3	5.0
Methionine + cysteine (g/kg)	4.2–5.0	5.3	3.6
Phenylalanine (g/kg)	3.7–3.8	6.0	3.9
Threonine (g/kg)	4.4–4.5	4.0	4.2
Tryptophane (g/kg)	1.0–1.1	1.3	1.1
Lysine (g/kg)	8.6–9.0	5.4	8.2

Non-protein nitrogen (NPN) compounds: NPN fraction of fish is made of water-soluble, low molecular weight, nitrogen containing compounds of a non-protein nature. These include trimethylamine oxide (TMAO), free amino acids, volatile bases, guanidine, imidazole and purine derivatives. The most important are: trimethylaminoxide (TMAO), which acts as osmotic regulator in salt-water fish while fish species like tuna, bonito and mackerel contain some histidine.

These constitute 9-18% of the total nitrogen content of teleosteans and 34-38% in elasmobranches. They constitute a varied range of substances which are of great importance to the metabolism, the flavour of fish meat, and the course of spoilage.

Carbohydrates: The amount of carbohydrate in white fish muscle is generally much smaller than the other meats. In white fish, the amount is usually less than 1 percent, but in the dark muscle of some fatty species it may occasionally be up to 2 percent. Some mollusks, however, contain up to 5 percent of the carbohydrate glycogen.

Minerals and vitamins: These components are important not only to promote good health but also to maintain life itself. Fish provide a well balanced supply of minerals in a readily usable form. Vitamins can be divided into two groups as fat soluble, such as vitamins A, D, E and K, and those that are soluble in water, such as vitamins B and C. All the vitamins necessary for good health in humans and domestic animals are present to some extent in fish, but the amounts vary widely from species to species. The vitamins are mainly present in skin, liver, gut and flesh of fish. However, liver and gut are richer in oil soluble vitamins than the flesh while more than half of water soluble vitamins are present in the flesh of fish with remaining uniformly present in skin, liver and gut.

As for minerals, fish meat is a particularly valuable source of several minerals like calcium, sodium, potassium and phosphorus as well as magnesium, sulphur, iron, copper, zinc, manganese, selenium and selenium. In addition, saltwater fish contain high levels of iodine. The mineral and vitamin content of fish is not markedly affected by careful processing or by preservation, provided storage is not very prolonged.

Extractives: These are the substances that can be extracted from fish flesh by water or water-based solutions. These are small molecules substances sugars, free amino acids, and nitrogenous bases. These extractives contribute generally to the flavour, odour of fish and are important components to the consumer. They are considered to be indicators of the quality of fish because their quantity varies under storage conditions and their measurement indicate the storage time and hence indirectly the quality.

21

Fish and Shellfish-Borne Diseases

Fish and shellfish can cause infections or intoxication in human beings due to consumption of unhygienic or toxic seafood or by handling these. Many diseases of aquatic food animals bear great public health significance. Certain aquatic organisms accumulate biotoxins in their body which may pose serious threat to the consumers.

Human diseases resulting from consumption of fish and shellfish

Fish-borne diseases are due either to direct contamination of the product with polluted water or to secondary contamination of the product during landing, processing, storage, distribution, or preparation for consumption. Direct contamination of fish and shellfish becomes a problem when the fish food is eaten raw or only lightly processed while secondary contamination of the product is usually more frequent where sanitary conditions are generally poor.

Such public health risks associated with consumption of unhygienic fish include several bacterial infections and intoxications including salmonellosis, typhoid fever, paratyphoid fever, vibriosis, cholera, shigellosis, botulism, staphylococcal gastroenteritis and *Clostridium perfringens* food poisoning. Several parasitic infections like clonorchiasis, paragonimiasis, diphyllobothriasis and anisakiasis also pose threat to the consumers. Among the viral diseases, infectious hepatitis is important. Certain chemical poisons may also accumulate in fish leading to disease in consumers, e.g. chronic mercury poisoning (Minamata disease). Various biotoxins present in some fishes can cause diseases like paralaytic shellfish poisoning, tetradon poisoning and ciguatera poisoning. Apart from these infectious or toxic disease conditions, fish consumption may at times cause allergic reactions in the consumers.

Some of these diseases are briefly discussed below.

Botulism: *Clostridium botulinum* type E is one of commonly associated fish and shellfish borne intoxications. Spores of these bacteria are widely distributed in both fresh and salt water. Since the spores of type E are heat-sensitive, outbreaks have been identified with raw or improperly processed seafood. These organisms are capable of growth at temperatures of 3.3°C and above. C. *botulinum* type E is not proteolytic and therefore growth and toxin production in fish cause no change in its organoleptic characteristics.

***Vibrio parahaemolyticus* food poisoning:** *Vibrio parahaemolyticus* has been isolated from fish and shellfish, marine water and sediment. This type of food poisoning appears to be closely associated with the consumption of raw seafood. These organisms multiply in food materials more rapidly but are usually destroyed by freezing.

Salmonellosis: The infection due to *Salmonella* is more in warmer climate and due to water contamination by animal and human excreta. The risk is enhanced if the fish or shell-fish are washed in polluted water. Under adequate public health control on gathering of fish and shellfish from polluted water and proper fish handling, fish and shellfish may not be important source of salmonellosis.

Cholera: *Vibrio cholera* persists in fish and shellfish at room temperature for 2-5 days and under refrigerated conditions for 1-2 weeks. Contaminated fish have not been identified as cause of infection in man. However, consumption of raw shrimps has been reported to be the cause of an outbreak of cholera.

Parasitic diseases: Trematodes belonging to the genera *Opisthorchis*, *Clonorchis* and *Paragonimus* are important parasites that are widespread and can cause disease in humans by eating raw fishes. Similar other genera are *Metorchis*, *Pseudoamphistomum*, *Metagonimus*, *Clinostomum*, *Nanophyetus*, *Echinochasmus*, *Spelotrema* and *Heterophyes*. They have common epidemiological characteristics like having molluscs as the first intermediate hosts, fishes or crustaceans as second hosts and humans or animals eating raw fish as final hosts. These trematodes parasitize the bile ducts, liver, and intestine. These may invade the lungs, brain and heart.

Diphyllobothrium is an important cestode that may reach man through consumption of raw fish. This parasite involves two types of intermediate hosts: copepods and fish. The larval stage plerocercoids are present in fish, which develop into the adult tapeworm in definitive mammalian host due to consumption of fish and cause debility and anaemia.

Three common fish-borne diseases caused by nematodes include diseases due to genera Anisakis, *Angiostrongylus cantonensis* and *Capillaria philippinensis*. Other similar nematodes include *Ancylostoma*, *Bunostomum*, *Contracaecum*, *Dioctophyme*, *Gnathostoma*, *Phocanema*, *Toxocara*, *Unicineria* etc. Anisakis larvae occur in many marine fishes and man is infected by eating raw or improperly processed fish. The parasite causes an allergic reaction that is responsible for localized enteritis described as eosinophilic phlegmonous enteritis. *Angiostrongylus cantonensis* causes eosinophillic meningitis in man. Its usual intermediate host is a slug or land snail, and occasionally the larva can pass to freshwater prawn, land crab, and possibly fish from which man is infected. *Capillaria philippinensis* causes a syndrome called intestinal capillariasis in man characterized by intractable diarrhea with malabsorption due to atrophic changes in the intestinal epithelium produced by the parasite.

Viral diseases: It has been reported that consumption of clams and oysters taken from seawater grossly contaminated with sewage have caused viral infectious hepatitis.

Allergic reactions: Both crustaceans (shrimp, lobster, crawfish or crab) as well as mollusks (oysters, squid, scallops) can cause allergy in persons eating these foods and are most commonly seen in adults. As crustaceans and mollusks contain the same type of proteins some people may react to both groups of foods. Shellfish allergens are usually found in the flesh and are part of the muscle protein system and cooking does not appear to destroy the allergens. Symptoms range from itching and swelling of the mouth and throat to life threatening reactions. Symptoms most often occur when the seafood is ingested. Seafood handling and inhaling steam while some crustaceans are cooked can become the cause of allergy.

Other diseases of aquatic food animals: Fishes are affected with a number of diseases but not all of them affect man. However, diseases of aquatic food animals impair the food quality thus reducing the available quantity of fish and shellfish fit for consumption as food. Many viral diseases of fish are not transmitted to humans. These include lymphocystis disease, viral haemorrhagic septicaemia, infectious haematopoietic necrosis, spring viraemia of carp, infectious pancreatic necrosis, and channel catfish virus disease. Similarly, mycotic diseases like icthyophorus disease, branchiomycosis, Saprolegnia are not transmitted to man. Bacteria like *Vibrio, Mycobacterium,* and *Aeromonas* are found both in humans and fish. *Vibrio parahaemolyticus* cause health problems after ingestion of raw, improperly cooked, or preserved fish and shellfish from contaminated areas. Fish mycobacteria like *M. fortuitum* can cause infections of wounds in man; *M. marinum* has been isolated from human skin lesions. Among the large number of protozoans, crustaceans, and different types of worms infecting fish and shellfish, only a small number of the worms are of public health significance.

Occupational health risks among fish handlers

These diseases are common among the people engaged in the fish industry. These include dermatological conditions, bites and stings, incidental diseases etc. Bites and stings are known to occur from a variety of commercial and noncommercial species of fish like dogfish, stingrays, catfish etc. during fishing operations.

Infection with streptococci and staphylococci in hands of the workers in the fishing industry are reported. Infection is facilitated by injuries sustained during handling of equipment. The disease erysipeloid is caused by *Erysipelothrix insidiosa*. Dermatitis may be caused by contact with nets, ropes, etc., bearing marine organisms or by repeated handling of the salt and detergents used in processing or by contact with such things as seaweed and invertebrates, including jellyfish and cone shells.

Leptospirosis is caused through skin contact with water contaminated by the urine of infected rodents and other animals. Fish market workers and fishermen may be infected by leptospires due to their occupation and coming in contact with water contaminated by the urine of infected rodents and other animals. Schistosomiasis may also occur in persons fishing in contaminated waters. Conjunctivitis occasionally occurs in workers engaged in processing, probably due to the presence of irritant fluids, splashed during gutting etc. The workers may also suffer allergic reactions by contact with fish, shellfish or fishing gear bearing marine organisms.

Biotoxins in fish and shellfish

A proportion of the species of fish and shellfish taken for human consumption contain biotoxins. Such toxins generally occur in fish from tropical and subtropical waters. These may cause serious local public health problems. Although such toxins are not common in fish taken from cold and temperate water, yet molluscan shellfish from such waters may at times become toxic.

Microscopic planktonic algae are used as a source of food for shellfish. Although proliferation of planktonic algae has a beneficial effect for aquaculture and wild fisheries, these algal blooms may become harmful causing human health impacts. The term "red tide" is used when the algae grow in such abundance that they change the colour of the sea water to red, brown, or green. From the estimated 5000 species of marine phytoplankton, around 40 can produce potent toxins that can enter the food chain through fish and shellfish to humans. Algal blooms due to toxin producing algae are called as "harmful algal blooms" (HABs). Eating shellfish with high levels of certain toxins can lead to serious and potentially fatal illnesses described below.

1. Paralytic shellfish poisoning

Paralytic shellfish poisoning (PSP) is one of the recognized syndromes of shellfish poisoning, which share some common features and are primarily associated with bivalve mollusks (mussels, clams, oysters and scallops). These shellfish are filter feeders and, therefore, accumulate neurotoxins, called saxitoxin, produced by microscopic algae, dinoflagellates, diatoms, and cyanobacteria. Dinoflagellates of the genus *Alexandrium* are the most numerous and widespread saxitoxin producers and are responsible for PSP blooms in subarctic, temperate, and tropical locations. Human toxicity and mortality can occur after ingestion of these animals, but toxicity is also seen in wild animal populations.

Toxins: The principal toxin responsible for PSP is saxitoxin (STX). Additional toxins are found, such as neosaxiton and gonyautoxins I to IV. All of them act primarily on the nervous system. STX and its derivatives are well known for their involvement in this fatal poisoning. The toxins responsible for this type of poisoning are water soluble, heat and acid-stable, and ordinary cooking methods do not eliminate the toxins.

Toxicity: PSP affects those who come into contact with the affected shellfish by ingestion.PSP can be fatal in extreme cases, particularly in immune-compromised individuals. Children are more susceptible. Symptoms can appear ten to 30 minutes after ingestion. Symptoms of PSP can include: a tingling sensation or numbness around the lips that gradually spreads to the face and neck; a prickly sensation in the fingertips and toes; drowsiness; headache and dizziness, and difficult swallowing.

In more severe cases one may also experience: incoherent speech, a prickly sensation in the arms and legs, stiffness and non-coordination of limbs, weakness, and rapid pulse. Respiratory difficulty, dry mouth, salivation, temporary blindness, nausea and vomiting may also occur. In extreme cases, paralysis of respiratory muscles may lead to respiratory arrest and death within two to twelve hours after consumption.

Diagnosis: The most widely applied test method for PSP toxins is the classic mouse bioassay. Detection of STXs is difficult due to their complex chemistry, variations in composition, and their low concentrations

Control: Absolute control or prevention is not possible. Regular inspection of shell fish and analysis for saxitoxin using the mouse bioassay is recommended. Seriously affected people must be hospitalized and placed under respiratory care. There is no known cure for PSP. Consumers should be aware of some potential food safety issues associated with bivalve shellfish (*i.e.* clams, oysters, scallops, mussels, and cockles), other molluscan shellfish (*i.e.* whelks and periwinkles) and the liver of lobster and crab.

2. Ciguatera poisoning

Ciguatera poisoning is the most commonly reported marine toxin disease in the world associated with consumption of contaminated reef fish such as barracuda, grouper, and snapper. A large number of people suffer from Ciguatera worldwide per year especially those who live in or visit tropical and subtropical areas. The dinoflagellate, *Gambierdiscus toxicus* produces ciguatoxin throughout tropical regions of the world.

Toxin: Ciguatoxin and another toxin, maitotoxin, are two most common toxins associated with Ciguatera and are the most lethal natural substances known. Ciguatoxin is synthesized by the dinoflagellates which are eaten by small herbivorous fish which in turn are eaten by larger and older carnivores. It is stable to heat and to high concentration of sodium chloride. Oral intake of as little as 0.1µg ciguatoxin can cause illness in the human adult. Ciguatoxin, a lipid soluble substance affecting the nervous tissue while maitotoxin is water soluble, specifically increases the calcium ion influx through excitable membrane. Scaritoxin, okadaic acid and palytoxin are other toxic substances associated with this toxicity.

Ciguatoxin selectively increases sodium permeability in the nerve cells and striated muscle can be counteracted by calcium ions and tetrodotoxin. The respiratory arrest induced by a lethal dose results mainly from depression of the central respiratory center. It causes biphasic cardiovascular response with hypotension and bradycardia followed by hypertension and tachycardia.

Symptoms: Ciguatera presents primarily as an acute neurologic disease manifested by a constellation of gastrointestinal (diarrhoea, abdominal cramps and vomiting), neurologic (parenthesis, pain in the teeth, pain on urination, blurred vision, temperature reversal) and cardiovascular (arrhythmias, heart block) signs and symptoms within a few hours of contaminated fish ingestion. The pathognomonic symptom of ciguatera intoxication is hot/cold temperature reversal. Acute fatality is usually due to respiratory failure, circulatory collapse or arrhythmias. Lethality is usually seen with ingestion of the Liver is considered as the most toxic part of fish and its ingestion prove to be lethal.

The symptoms of ciguatera poisoning, especially the paresthesias and weakness, can persist in varying severity for weeks to months after the acute illness. Prolonged itching due to chronic Ciguatera can present as a dermatologic disease when it is really due to ciguatera paresthesias. Chronic ciguatera can also present as a psychiatric disorder of general malaise, depression, headaches, muscular aches, and peculiar feelings in extremities for several weeks.

Diagnosis: The mouse bioassay is a simple and standard diagnostic tool that is still be practiced. Radio immune (RIA), counter immunoelectrophoresis or enzyme linked immunosorbant (ELISA) assays have also been developed to investigate ciguatera.

Control and prevention: Control has been to a large extent symptomatic; a variety of agents, including vitamins, antihistamines, anticholinesterases, steroids and tricyclic antidepressants, can be tried. Hypotension and bradycardia can be antagonized with anticholinergicand hypertension and tachycardia can be suppressed by adrenergic blockers. However, opiates and barbiturates be avoided since they may cause hypotension, and opiates may interact with maitotoxin.

Gut emptying and decontamination with charcoal is recommended acutely although often the severe ongoing vomiting and diarrhea prevents this. With apparent considerable success, at least acutely, mannitol infusions have been used. Amitriptyline and similar medications give some success in relieving the symptoms of chronic ciguatera. There is no immunity to these illnesses and recurrences of actual ciguatera in the same individual appear to be worse than the initial illness.

Ciguatera poisoning is difficult to prevent because ciguatoxin in fish is odourless and tasteless, and toxic fish cannot be identified by appearance or behaviour. Ciguatoxin is heat-stable, and therefore, cooking, boiling, freezing, baking or frying does not eliminate or destroy the toxin from the fish tissue. Some protection is offered by avoiding unusually large reef fish and excluding the internal organs and the roe from the deep.

3. Pufferfish poisoning

Pufferfish are generally believed to be the second most poisonous vertebrates in the world. Amazingly, the meat of some pufferfish is considered a delicacy. Called *fugu* in Japan, it is extremely expensive and only prepared by trained, licensed chefs. These are primarily marine and estuarine fish belonging to the family Tetraodontidae and are variously called pufferfish, puffers, balloonfish, blowfish, bubblefish, globefish, swellfish, toadfish, toadies, honey toads, sugar toads, and sea squab. They are morphologically similar in having thin, hidden spines which are only visible when the fish has puffed up. They range in size from the 1 inch long (dwarf puffer) to more than 2 feet (freshwater giant puffer) in length. They are scaleless fish and usually have rough to spiky skin. All have four teeth that are fused together into a beak-like form.

Toxin: Almost all puffer fishes contain tetrodotoxin (TTX), a substance that makes them foul tasting. Poisonous puffers are believed to synthesize their deadly toxin from the bacteria, such as *Pseudoalteromonas tetraodonis*, certain species of *Pseudomonas* and *Vibrio*. To humans, tetrodotoxin is deadly, up to 1,200 times more poisonous than cyanide. TTX is a potent neurotoxin with no known antidote. The toxin can enter the body by ingestion, injection, inhalation and through abraded skin. The mechanism of toxicity is through the blockage of fast voltage-gated sodium channels. The organs (e.g. liver) of the pufferfish can contain levels of tetrodotoxin sufficient to produce paralysis of the diaphragm and, through this mechanism, death due to respiratory failure. Toxicity varies between species and at different seasons and geographic localities, and the flesh of many pufferfish may not be dangerously toxic. It is not always fatal; but at near-lethal doses, it can leave a person in a state of near-death for several days, while the person remains conscious.

Symptoms: Symptoms typically develop within 30 minutes of ingestion, but may be delayed by up to four hours. The first symptom of intoxication is a slight numbness of the lips and tongue, appearing between 20 minutes to three hours after eating poisonous pufferfish. The next symptom is increasing paresthesia in the face and extremities, which may be followed by sensations of lightness or floating. Headache, epigastric pain, nausea, diarrhoea, and/or vomiting may occur. Occasionally, some reeling or difficulty in walking may occur.

The second stage of the intoxication is increasing paralysis. Many victims are unable to move; even sitting may be difficult. There is increasing respiratory distress. Speech is affected, and the victim usually exhibits dyspnoea, cyanosis, and hypotension. Paralysis increases and convulsions, mental impairment, and cardiac arrhythmia may occur. The victim, although completely paralyzed, may be conscious and in some cases completely lucid until shortly before death. Death usually occurs within 4 to 6 h, with a known range of about 20 minutes to 8 h. If the patient survives 24 h, recovery without any residual effects will usually occur over several days.

Diagnosis: The mouse bioassay developed for paralytic shellfish poisoning can be used to monitor tetrodotoxin in puffer fish and is the current method of choice. Tetrodotoxin may be quantified in serum, whole blood or urine to confirm a diagnosis of poisoning in hospitalized patients or to assist in the forensic investigation of a case of fatal over-dosage. Most analytical techniques involve mass spectrometric detection following gas or liquid chromatographic separation.

Control and prevention: Treatment can consist of emptying the stomach, feeding the victim activated charcoal to bind the toxin, and taking standard life-support measures to keep the victim alive until the effect of the poison has worn off. Alpha adrenergic agonists are recommended in addition to intravenous fluids to combat hypotension. Anticholinesterase agents have been used with mixed success. No antidote has been developed and approved for human use.

4. Scombroid food poisoning

Scombroid food poisoning is a foodborne illness that results from eating spoiled fish. It is most commonly associated with Scombroidea fish like large dark meat marine tuna, albacore, mackerel mackerel, tuna, bluefish, mahi-mahi, bonito, sardines, anchovies, and related species of fish that were inadequately refrigerated or preserved after being caught. However, non-scombroid fish like mahi-mahi and amberjack have been reported to cause scombroid poisoning.

Causes: One of the toxic agents implicated in scombroid poisoning is histidine, which exists naturally in many types of fishes especially fish of the *Scombridae* and *Scomberesocidae* families.These fish have large amounts of free histidine that may be converted to histamine during storage via the enzyme histidine decarboxylase produced by enteric bacteria including *Morganella morganii*. Histamine is not destroyed by normal cooking temperatures, so even properly cooked fish can be affected. Histamine is a mediator of allergic reactions, so the symptoms produced are those one would expect to see in severe allergic responses. The presence of high levels of histamine in fish always indicates that decomposition has occurred, even if the decomposition is not obvious. Toxic amounts of histamine can form before a fish smells or tastes bad.

Symptoms: Symptoms usually occur within 10–30 minutes of ingesting the fish and generally are self-limited. Symptoms usually last for approximately ten to fourteen hours and rarely exceed one to two days. Physical signs may include a diffuse blanching erythema, tachycardia, wheezing, and hypotension or hypertension. People with asthma are more vulnerable to respiratory problems such as wheezing or bronchospasms. Initial signs of poisoning are due to allergic reaction with the facial flushing/sweating, burning-peppery taste sensations in the mouth and throat, dizziness, nausea, headache, tachycardia, cold like symptoms As the condition progresses, the additional symptoms include facial and body rash, generalized oedema, short-term diarrhoea and abdominal cramps. In the worst cases, the poisoning may cause blurred vision, respiratory stress, swelling of the tongue.

Control and prevention: Treatment is in the form of supportive care such as fluids and oxygen. Oral antihistamines are very effective, showing improvement within 10–15 minutes. Cooking or other heat treatments (such as canning or smoking) do not destroy histamine. Fish should be kept in refrigerator to avoid the conversion of histidine to histamine by the spoilage bacteria.

5. Amnesic shellfish poisoning

Amnesic shellfish poisoning (ASP) is an illness caused by domoic acid, a naturally occurring acid which is produced by some marine algae. Domoic acid can accumulate in a number of filter-feeding bivalve molluscan shellfish such as clams, mussels, scallops and oysters. The toxins that cause ASP are not destroyed by cooking.

Symptoms: Symptoms usually occur 30 minutes to 6 hours after consumption and include nausea, vomiting and diarrhoea, muscle weakness, disorientation, and memory loss.

Control: If the poisoning is not severe, the symptoms disappear completely within a few days in an otherwise healthy person. However, in extreme cases, death can occur.

6. Neurotoxic shellfish poisoning

Neurotoxic shellfish poisoning (NSP) presents as a milder gastroenteritis with neurologic symptoms compared with paralytic shellfish poisoning.

Toxins: The classic causative organism, *Gymnodinium breve* is relatively fragile and particularly in wave action along beaches, the organism is easily broken open, releasing the toxins. During an active red tide, the aerosol of contaminated salt spray will contain the toxins as well as the organisms. This organism produces 2 types of lipid soluble toxins: haemolytic and neurotoxic. The neurotoxic toxins are known as brevetoxins which are mainly PbTx-2 and lesser amounts of PbTx--1, PbTx-3. The brevetoxins are tasteless, odourless, and heat and acid stable. These toxins cannot be easily detected nor removed by food preparation procedures. Fish, birds and mammals are all susceptible to the brevetoxins.

Symptoms: The two forms of clinical entities are seen. First characterized by an acute gastroenteritis with neurologic symptoms following ingestion of contaminated shellfish (i.e. NSP), and another apparently reversible upper respiratory syndrome following inhalation of aerosols. Aerosolized toxins result in respiratory and conjunctival irritation, copious catarrhal exudates, rhinorrhea, nonproductive cough, and bronchoconstriction. Sometimes dizziness, troubled vision and skin rashes are also seen.

In the normal population, the irritation and bronchoconstriction are usually rapidly reversible by leaving the beach area or entering an air conditioned area. However, asthmatics are apparently particularly susceptible. In elderly people, there may be prolonged lung disease, severe catarrhal rhinitis, pulmonary haemorrhage and oedema, chronic haemolytic anaemia with multi-organ hemosiderosis and evidence of neurotoxicity.

Diagnosis: Based on the clinical scenario of persons becoming ill with gastrointestinal and neurologic symptoms after eating shellfish or with acute respiratory symptoms similar to asthma after inhaling aerosols. There is a mouse bioassay with crude toxic residue extracted with ethyl ether and a mosquito fish bioassay. An FPLC methodology for the identification of the *G. breve* toxins, as well as antibodies to brevetoxin has been employed.

Control and prevention: Affected persons should immediately seek medical attention. In the case of aerosolized toxicity areas, the use of particle filter masks or retreat to air conditioned environment will provide relief from the airborne irritation. Only shellfish harvested from harvest areas and from trusted suppliers should be consumed. Analyse water quality in shellfish harvesting areas and identify waters that do not meet sanitary standards. Monitor biotoxins in shellfish in harvesting areas and in shellfish processing plants.

22
Fish Spoilage

Fresh fish is an extremely perishable food and deteriorates very rapidly at normal temperatures. Reducing the temperature at which the fish is kept lowers the rate of deterioration. Fishery undertaken by very small craft usually lasts only a few hours and fish is consumed or sold on a daily basis. In some of these very small fishing craft, owners are aware of the problems of catch deterioration and often use wet sacking or palm leaves to cover the catch and lower the temperature to reduce spoilage. The use of chilling techniques is however required when the fishing operation is for a longer period of time. Chilling prolongs the shelf-life of fish by slowing the action of enzymes and bacteria, and the chemical and physical processes that can affect quality. The most common means of chilling is by the use of ice. Other means are chilled water, ice slurries (of both seawater and freshwater), and refrigerated seawater (RSW). For the full benefits of chilling to be realized, it is essential to maintain chill temperatures throughout the different fish-handling operations. This method is a short-term storage when compared to freezing, canning, salting or drying, for instance, but relatively cheap and low-tech and low skilled.

Factors affecting spoilage in fish

The most important things to look for the freshness of fish are the general appearance of eyes, gills, surface slime and scales and the firmness or softness of the flesh. The appearance, particularly the presence and absence of discolouration along the underside, of the backbone, the appearance of the belly walls, the odour of the gills and belly cavity, presence or absence of rigor mortis or death stiffening. Fresh fish is, however, an extremely perishable food and deteriorates very rapidly at normal temperatures. The main factors that affect the rate of spoilage in chilled fish are: temperature, physical damage and intrinsic factors.

i. **Temperature:** At low temperature the quality of fish is lost slowly. Also, the faster a lower temperature is attained during fish chilling, the more effectively the spoilage activity is inhibited. Generally, the rate at which fish loses quality when stored in ice (0°C) is used as the baseline when comparisons are made regarding shelf-life at different storage temperatures.

ii. **Physical damage:** Fish is soft and easily damaged; therefore rough handling and bruising result in contamination of fish flesh with bacteria and allow releases of enzymes, speeding up the rate of spoilage. In addition, careless handling can burst the guts and spread the contents into the fish flesh.

iii. **Intrinsic factors:** The intrinsic factors affecting the spoilage rate of chilled fish are shape, size, fat content in the flesh and skin characteristics. Thick skinned, lean species, large and flat fish stored in ice spoil at a slow rate than round, small, fatty and thin skinned fishes. In addition to the above, several other factors contribute to spoilage of fish. These are high fat content, high protein content, weak muscle tissue, extent of bacterial contamination, ambient temperature, high moisture content, unhygienic handling, hastening of rigor mortis due to struggling of fish, lack of oxygen, warm temperature, use of an antibiotic, ice or dip.

Mechanism of fish spoilage

Fish just caught is very fresh and has a sweet, sea weedy and delicate taste. However, it cannot remain in this condition for a long period and spoilage process begins just after it is removed from the water. The spoilage in fish is accompanied by the change in physical characteristic. Changes in colour, texture, odour, colour of eyes, colour of gills, softness of muscle, belly bursting are some of the characteristics of spoiled fish.

The process of spoilage can be divided into four phases. Phase I and II are autolytic changes, caused mainly by enzymes while phase III and IV are due to bacteriological changes by bacteria. Phase I is of short duration of 1 to 2 days or more days after catching and there is very little deterioration, with slight loss of the characteristic odour and flavour. Under phase II of spoilage, there is a significant loss of the natural flavour and odour of fish. The flesh becomes neutral but has no off-flavours, the texture is still pleasant. Bacteriological changes, caused mainly by bacteria begin in phase III and fish shows the signs of spoilage like strong off-flavours and stale to unpleasant smells. There are structural texture changes and flesh becomes either soft and watery or tough and dry. As bacterial changes progresses to phase IV, fish is spoiled and putrid and becomes inedible.

Enzyme action during spoilage

Following the death of fish, the normal circulatory system breaks down and the supply of oxygen is prevented. The enzymes present in the muscle convert glycogen into lactic acid. The pH of the fish muscle falls. The formation of the lactic acid continues till the supply of glycogen is completely used up. There is stiffening of the muscles and the process is called as rigor mortis. After the completion of rigor mortis, muscle stiffness gradually decreases accompanied by increase in pH, ending up in softening of muscle. This is followed by breakdown of proteins by enzymes. This process is called as autolysis that can be described as an internal breakdown of the structure of the protein and fats due to a complex series of reactions by enzymes. Autolysis of protein starts immediately after rigor and creates favourable conditions for the growth of bacteria.

Another important action of the enzymes is that it affects the flavour of fish. The components responsible for the taste and flavour of the fish are changed by the enzymatic action. An example is the progressive, degradation of ATP to AMP and hypoxanthine. Hypoxanthine is a main component of fish muscle nucleotide. The accumulation of hypoxanthine imparts a bitter taste in the fish muscle accompanied by loss of fresh fish flavour. Thus the estimation of hypoxanthine content in fish indicates the degree of freshness.

Enzymatic action also causes decomposition in the fish known as belly bursting. The belly bursting is caused by the action of digestive enzymes present in the gut of the fish. The black spot formation in shrimps is also caused by the action of the enzymes on the amino acid. The black colour is due to the formation of melanin (black pigment) by the action of enzyme tyrosinase on tyrosin present in the shrimps. Black spots present a poor appearance and are, therefore, not acceptable.

Action of bacteria during spoilage

The newly caught healthy fish have sterile tissues and that bacteria can only be found on the skin and gills and in the intestines. Whilst still alive, the fish and the bacteria exist in a state of equilibrium and it is only after death that the bacteria can invade the tissues and spoil the fish and produce undesirable compounds. Invasion of the muscle from the gut is made easier by the autolysis brought about by the gut enzymes. The nature and type of bacteria present in a fish depends upon the water from where it is caught and methods used for handling of the fish after its catch. The numbers of bacteria in the gut are highest when the fish has recently been feeding. It is reasonable to assume that fish caught in polluted waters will be more heavily contaminated than fish from clean areas. Further, bacterial load in fish increases after harvesting due to its contact with other materials like ice, fish boxes, the boat itself and even the handlers. A large number of bacteria are involved in causing spoilage under different atmospheric conditions as noted below.

i. Spoilage at chilling temperature - *Shewanella putrefaciens* and *Pseudomonas* spp. *Achromobacter, Flavobacterium*

ii. Spoilage at normal atmospheric temperature - *Escherichia, Proteus, Serratia, Sarcina* and *Clostridium*

iii. Spoilage at higher temperature - *Micrococcus* and *Bacillus*

iv. Spoilage at modified atmosphere - Stored marine fish from temperate waters are spoiled by the CO_2 resistant *Photobacterium phosphoreum* whereas Gram-positive bacteria are likely spoilers of CO_2 packed fish from fresh or tropical waters.

v. Fish products with high salt contents - These may spoil due to growth of halophilic bacteria (*e.g.* in salted fish) or growth of anaerobic bacteria and yeasts (*e.g.* in barrel salted fish).

The bacteria grow using the fish as food substrte and producing various waste products which accumulate and produce off-odours and bad flavours. It is well known that trimethylamine oxide (TMAO) can be reduced by bacteria to give trimethylamine (TMA) which imparts an off-odour to the fish. The bacterial action of amino acids present in the fish muscle leads to formation of primary amines. Examples are formation of histamine from histidine, arginine from glutamic acid etc. This bacterial action may cause food poisoning in extreme cases. Other bacterial by-products are ammonia and hydrogen sulphide, both of which have objectionable smells. Fermentative microorganisms produce acid, alcohols and gases from carbohydrates while breakdown of fats leads to fatty acids and glycerol, indole and skatole. Normal fish odour changes to sour, gassy, fruity and finally ammonia and faecal odour.

Discolourations of fish due to bacteria are other changes that can be visualized in fish that is undergoing the process of spoilage. Yellow to greenish discolouration due to *Pseudomonas fluorescence*, Micrococcus and others, red or pink due to *Sarcina, Micrococcus, Bacillus* species, molds and yeasts and chocolate-brown by *Asporogenous* yeast are some of the examples.

In the fatty fishes like herring and mackerel, spoilage is oxidative rancidity characterized by bad and unpleasant odour and rancid taste (sour or stale smell or taste). It is because of oxidation unsaturated fatty acid that is easily oxidized at increased temperature and exposure to light. The levels of peroxide value and free fatty acid content both a measure of oxidative rancidity are considered an index of quality of fat fishes.

Methods of detection of fish spoilage

1. **Physical method:** An instrument called Torrymeter is pierced on the skin of about 16 randomly selected fish and 1 of the results is picked as representing the entire lot.
2. **Subjective method**: It involves the use of human sense organs and is called "Sensory test". It however may not be very accurate but represents customer view. Sensory tests use the sense of touch, smell, sight and taste and are considered good for quality assessment of fish. Gill colour, flavour and texture are other characteristics that can be noted in fish.
   (i) Visual examination – general appearance, degree of insect/ mold infestation; in case of cured fish intensity of smoking is noted.
   (ii) Touch - texture of fish is evaluated and is categorized as elastic, firm, soft or flabby.
   (iii) Smell – good and bad flavour, smoke or cooked
   (iv) Taste – sweet, bitter, salt and sour (salty or acidic), fermented
   (v) Flavour – a combination of taste and odour by volatile organic compounds

3. **Physico-chemical methods**

   a) Determination of pH: with digital pH meter, indicator pH strips (just give an indication of pH but not accurate), litmus paper test (gives an idea of range but not actual pH), chemical indicator method (nitrazine yellow, indicates pH range)

   b) Study of chemical indicators of spoilage (late): estimation of trimethylamine, total volatile basic nitrogen, volatile reducing substance, indole, skatole, hydrogen sulphide

   c) Evaluation of spoilage based on lipid markers: Peroxide index, thiobarbitanic acid test, rancidity, texture, refractive index, electrical conductivity

Tests for assessing microbial spoilage

Sample preparation: For bacteriological analysis of fish first place in plastic bags, thaw by immersion in an agitated water bath at about 20°C. Judge the completion of thawing by gently squeezing the bag until no hard core or ice crystal can be left. Render the thawed or wet fish into uniform mass either by double mincing or use of an electrical driven rotary chopper. Store the sample in a air tight container. Analyse as quickly as possible. If storage is necessary keep at a temperature not exceeding 4°C.

All the operations involved in these tests must be carried out in such a way that there is no contamination of the sample by the technician. The sample is weighed out into a sterile bottle from which it is transferred to a blender and homogenised with 450 ml of sterile diluent. The resulting suspension is returned to the bottle. One ml of this suspension is pippetted into each of two petri dishes and 1 ml is transferred to a bottle containing 9 ml of diluent. Two more petri dishes are inoculated in a similar fashion from this bottle; this process is repeated until a suitable dilution has been reached. About 20 ml of nutrient agar, cooled to 45°C, is poured into each dish and after mixing with the sample the agar is allowed to set. The prepared plates are placed in an incubator for a defined period at a set temperature. After incubation, the plates are examined; those for the dilution which has between 30 and 300 colonies growing are counted. By multiplying by the dilution factor, the actual count for the sample can be calculated.

Prevention/reduction of spoilage

Even under ideal conditions, fish will only keep for a defined period with the possible exception of canned fish. The purpose of preservation is to make the storage life of the product suitably long without much increase in its cost of production. Some common methods are noted below.

- If a food is heated to a temperature which is sufficient to kill all vegetative cells but not the resistant spores of *Bacillus* spp. or *Clostridium* spp., then storage in the refrigerator can be quite lengthy since the spores will not germinate unless the temperature rises into the normal mesophilic range.
- Chilling is a means of short term preservation of seafood by reducing the temperature using ice. It involves cooling fish or fish products to a temperature approaching that of melting ice *i.e.* 0°C.

- Freezing (storage temperature well below zero *e.g.* -30°C) is relatively expensive and requires hi-tech operations and high skills. Freezing is the most satisfactory method currently available for a long term preservation of seafood. It is by far the best way of preventing fish from spoilage, since fish continues to remain in almost the same natural conditions even after freezing. It is effective for retaining flavour, colour and nutritive value of seafood. Freezing is a process by which the water in the fish muscle is crystallized into ice. The crystallization will be complete at -40°C. After freezing, the fish must be stored at a temperature maintained constantly at -18°C or below. Fluctuation in this temperature will cause spoilage of products. If there is a wide variation in the temperature recrystallization takes place.
- Reduction in the amount of available water in foodstuff is another effective method of preservation. All the reactions which take place in the cell require an aqueous environment for their proper functioning. Thus, reducing the water availability brings about a slowing or complete cessation of bacterial growth. The available water content (referred to as water activity) can be lowered by removal of water or the addition of a solute which makes the water no longer available to the cells. Sodium chloride is such a solute; it is obvious that although a 22 percent salt solution is too salty for the average palate, it still does not give complete control of spoilage organisms, especially molds and halophilic bacteria. In order to provide the best protection to the food, it is usual to remove some of the water and add salt. The removal of water can be done by the direct application of heat but a more interesting technique is the smoking of foods.
- Dehydration is another important reaction of a physical nature caused by the evaporation of ice due to differences in vapour pressure over the product surface and in the air of the store room. Loss of the moisture by evaporation of ice causes the product surface to dry resulting in dull appearance and even discolouration in some cases.
- Lowering of pH is also useful. Since the pH of fish tissue is 5.6 or more, almost any microorganism can grow on and spoil it. Some bacteria, particularly *Lactobacillus* spp., have the ability to reduce the pH to a level where the normal spoilage flora is inhibited, the usual mechanism being the production of lactic acid from the carbohydrate in the substrate or food.
- Hygienic handling and proper storage are very important aspects. Careful handling of the fish means that, at all stages, it is important to prevent damage to the fish. Careless handling can result in damage.

23

Quality Assessment of Fish

Quality is defined as fitness for purpose. Some of the more important factors that determine quality of fish from the customer's point of view are species; ease of preparation; appearance; odour; flavour; freshness; size; presence or absence of bones, blood and filth; absence of specific microorganisms; condition; packaging; composition. Some aspects of quality are controlled by legislation; for example prohibition of certain chemical additives or colouring materials in fish and fish products or the maximum number of bacteria permitted may be specified.

The methods of quality assessment can broadly be divided into: (1) Organoleptic judgment; (2) Physico-chemical methods; and (3) Bacteriological methods.

1. Organoleptic judgment

It is an important general method of examining fresh fish. In organoleptic judgement, all the changes that can be evaluated by sight, touch and taste in the entire fish are noted with special reference to the eyes, gills, skin and meat. The following chracteristics are examined and evaluated.

a) General appearance: Appearance of the eyes, gills, and outer surfaces

b) Appearance of the flesh, particularly at the cut surface along the backbone and the belly flaps

c) Texture of raw fish under manual pressure, including the reaction to touch of the outer surface of the fish

d) Odour of raw fish, particularly at the gills and body cavity

e) Odour of cooked fish

f) Flavour of cooked fish

g) Texture of cooked fish

The conclusions are drawn on the basis of the following features:

- In the newly caught fish the eyes are clear and convex with a black and clear pupil. During storage the eyes become flatter and finally completely sunken in the center. The translucency disappears gradually and the eyes become opaque, the pupil changes colour from clear black to opaque grey.
- The clear red colour of the gills is bleached, and they gradually become brownish-yellowish. At the same time a layer of slime is formed, which is first clear, then becomes opaque, milky, and muddy.
- The shiny skin becomes dull. During storage, the sheen disappears completely at the same time as the clear slime becomes opaque and milky.
- The fresh meat is bluish and translucent. During storage it becomes more opaque and gradually losses its elasticity, becoming soft and flabby.
- In the newly caught fish the peritoneum adheres so firmly to the flesh that it cannot be pulled off, but it loosens gradually.
- Each species of fish has its characteristic smell, but it is always fresh seaweedy. After a stage of natural odour, a sour and fruity aroma gradually occurs, later becoming a hydrogen-sulphide-like and putrid odour.
- The taste is judged on fish cooked according to a standard procedure. The changes in the taste quality are largely the same as those described for odour.

1.1 Score sheet for evaluation of freshness of fish

For the evaluation of the freshness of fish, organoleptic judgement is performed according to the score sheet as has been followed in the European Economic Community (Table 23.1). On the basis of the scores, the batches of fish are graded into classes of freshness as Extra, A or B. 'Extra' corresponds to a score mark of or above 2.7. The fish must not show marks of pressure, injuries, dirt, or pronounced changes in colour. 'Class A' corresponds to a score mark between 2 and 2.7. It is permitted that a small number of the fish show light marks of pressure or superficial injuries. 'Class B' corresponds to a score mark between 1 and 2. The fish must not be dirty or show great changes in colour, and only a small number may show distinct marks of pressure or light injuries.

Each batch of fish should have a uniform degree of freshness. A batch of a minor number of fish need not be completely uniform; in that case the batch is placed in the class for the lowest quality of fish present in the batch.

Table 23.1. Score sheet of freshness

Object to be judged	**Criteria**			
	Score marks			
	3	**2**	**1**	**0**
	Appearance			
Skin	Intense, shiny pigmentation, no discolouration; Clear slime	Intense pigmentation without lusture; Slightly cloudy slime	Pale, dull; Milky slime	Lusterless pigmentation; Opaque slime
Eyes	Convex, Clear cornea, Black, shiny pupil	Convex and slightly sunken, Slightly shimmering cornea, Black, dull pupil	Flat, Shimmering cornea, Opaque pupil	Sunken in the centre, Milky cornea, Grey pupil
Gills	Clear colour; no slime	Paler colour; slight traces of clear slime	Bleached; opaque slime	Yellowish milky slime
Meat (cuts in the belly)	Bluish, translucent, smooth, shiny; no change of original colour	Waxy, velvety, dull; slight discolouration	Slightly opaque	Opaque
Colour along backbone	No discolouration	Pale rose	rose	red
Organs	Kidneys and rests of other organs, and the blood in aorta red	Kidneys and rests of other organs, and the blood in dull red; slightly bleached blood	Kidneys and rests of other organs pink	Kidneys and rests of other organs and blood brownish
Texture				
Meat	Firm and elastic; smooth surface	Reduced elasticity	Slightly flabby, reduced elasticity surface waxy, velvety and dull	Flabby; scales come off easily; surface rather rough granulated
Backbone	Breaks instead of loosening	Adheres	Can be loosened	Can be loosened easily
Peritoneum	Firmly adherent	Adheres	Can be loosened	Can easily be loosened
Smell				
Skin, gills, belly	**Seaweed like**	**Neutral**	**Slightly acid**	**Sour**

2. Physico-chemical methods

Total volatile basic amines (TVB) are one of the most widely used measurements of seafood quality. It is a general term which includes the measurement of trimethylamine (produced by spoilage bacteria), dimethylamine (produced by autolytic enzymes during frozen storage), ammonia (produced by the deamination of amino acids and nucleotide catabolites) and other volatile basic nitrogenous compounds like VRS (volatile reducing substances) associated with seafood spoilage. These substances have in common that they are mainly formed in the end phase of the course of spoilage, and usually as a consequence of bacterial activity. Therefore, the value of those methods is limited for judgement of the degree of freshness, whereas they may support the evaluation of very bad and already spoiled fish. They are particularly useful for the measurement of quality in cephalopods such as squid, industrial fish for meal and silage, and crustaceans. However, it should be kept in mind that TVB values do not reflect the mode of spoilage (bacterial or autolytic), and results depend to a great extent on the method of analysis.

2.1 Trimethylamine (TMA)

Trimethylamine is a pungent volatile amine often associated with the typical "fishy" odour of spoiling seafood. Its presence in spoiling fish is due to the bacterial reduction of trimethylamine oxide (TMAO) which is naturally present in the living tissue of many marine fish species. Although TMA is believed to be generated by the action of spoilage bacteria, the correlation with bacterial numbers is often not very good. This phenomenon is now thought to be due to the presence of small numbers of "specific spoilage" bacteria like *Photobactetium phosphoreum*, *Shewanella putrefaciens*. The former generates approximately 10 - 100 folds the amount of TMA than that produced from the later. The chief advantages of TMA analysis over the enumeration of bacterial numbers are that TMA determinations can be performed far more quickly and often reflect more accurately the degree of spoilage (as judged organoleptically) than do bacterial counts. The chief disadvantages of TMA analyses are that they do not reflect the earlier stages of spoilage and are only reliable for certain fish species.

2.2 Ammonia

Ammonia is formed by the bacterial degradation/deamination of proteins, peptides and amino- acids. It is also produced in the autolytic breakdown of adenosine monophosphate (AMP) in chilled seafood products. Although ammonia has been identified as a volatile component in a variety of spoiling fish, the quantification of this compound is not practiced since it was impossible to determine its relative contribution to the overall increase in total volatile bases. Test kits for ammonia based on glutamate dehydrogenase are now available and another type of ammonia test kit is available in the form of a test strip which changes colour when placed in contact with aqueous extracts containing ammonia (ammonium ion).Ammonia has been found to be an excellent indicator of squid quality. The ammonia levels increase far more quickly than trimethylamine (TMA) levels which have traditionally been used to reflect the growth of spoilage bacteria on lean demersal fish species. Thus ammonia has potential as an objective quality indicator for fish which degrades autolytically rather than primarily through bacterial spoilage.

2.3 Dimethylarnine (DMA)

Certain types of fish contain an enzyme, TMAO dimethylase (TMAO-ase), which converts TMAO into equimolar quantities of DMA and formaldehyde (FA). Thus for fish in the cod (gadoid) family, DMA is produced along with FA in frozen storage with the accompanying FA-induced toughening of the proteins. The amount of protein denaturation is roughly proportional to the amount of FA/DMA produced, but it is most common to monitor the quality of frozen-stored fish by measuring DMA rather than FA because much of the FA becomes bound to the tissue and is thus not extractable and cannot be measured quantitatively. The most common method for DMA analysis is a colorimetric determination of the DMA in deproteinized fish extracts and the chromatographic methods including gas-liquid chromatography and high performance liquid chromatography. The latter are somewhat more specific, and are not as prone to interferences as the spectrophotometric methods.

2.4 Biogenic amines

Fish muscle has the ability to support the bacterial formation of a wide variety of amine compounds which result from the direct decarboxylation of amino-acids. Most spoilage bacteria possessing decarboxylase activity do so in response to acidic pH, presumably so that the organisms may raise the pH of the growth medium through the production of amines. Histamine, putrescine, cadaverine and tyramine are produced from the decarboxylation of histidine, ornithine, lysine and tyrosine, respectively. Histamine has received most of the attention since it has been associated with incidents of scombroid poisoning in conjunction with the ingestion of tuna, mackerel, mahi-mahi. However, the absence of histamine in scombroid fish (tuna, mackerel, etc.) does not ensure the wholesomeness of the product since spoilage at chill storage temperatures does not always result in the production of histamine.

The biogenic amines are stable to thermal processing, so their presence in finished canned products is a good indication that the raw material was spoiled prior to heating. Some of the methods for biogenic amine analysis include high pressure liquid chromatography,gas chromatography, spectrofluorometric and a rapid enzymatic method for histamine using a micro plate reader

2.5 Nucleotide catabolites

Inosine monophosphate (IMP), inosine (Ino) and hypoxanthine (Rx) are nucleotide catabolites.Breakdown of adenosine triphosphate (ATP) to inosine monophosphate (IMP) are believed to be autolytic whereas the conversion of IMP to inosine (Ino) and then hypoxanthine (Rx) are believed mainly to be due to spoilage bacteria. The factors which have been shown to affect the nucleotide breakdown pattern include species, temperature of storage and physical disruption of the tissue. In addition, since nucleotide breakdown reflects the combined action of autolytic enzymes and bacterial action, the types of spoilage bacteria would no doubt affect the nucleotide patterns.

Quality assessment must never be based upon levels of a single catabolite and a complete nucleotide catabolite profile is always recommended. A complete analysis of nucleotide catabolites may be completed on a fish extract in 12-25 minutes using a high pressure liquid chromatographic (HPLC) system.

2.6 Ethanol

Ethanol has been used for many years as an objective indicator for seafood quality although it is not nearly as common as the analysis of TMA. Since ethanol can be derived from carbohydrates via anaerobic fermentation (glycolysis) and/or deamination and decarboxylation of amino acids such as alanine, it is a common metabolite of a variety of bacteria. It has been used to objectively measure the quality of a variety of fish including canned tuna, canned salmon, raw tuna, redfish, pollock, flounder and cod. One advantage of using ethanol as a spoilage indicator is that it is heat-stable (although volatile) and may be used to assess the quality of canned fish products. The simplest and perhaps most reliable means of measuring ethanol in fish tissue is the use of the commercial enzyme test kits.

2.7 Oxidative rancidity

The highly unsaturated fatty acids found in fish lipids are very susceptible to oxidation and lipid hydroperoxides arethe primary oxidation products. These hydroperoxides have their oxidation potential to oxidize iodide to iodine or to oxidize iron (II) to iron (III). The concentration of the hydroperoxides may be determined by titrimetric or by spectrophotometric methods, giving the peroxide value (PV) as milliequivalents (mEq) peroxide per 1 kg of fat extracted from the fish.

The disadvantage of measuring lipid hydroperoxides is that they are odour- and flavour-less, and thus the PV is not related to the actual sensory quality of the product analyzed. Secondly, lipid hydroperoxides break down with time, and interpretation of its quantity is confusing.

In later stages of oxidation *secondary oxidation products like* aldehydes, ketones, short chain fatty acid and others may be present. Many of these secondary products have very unpleasant odours and flavours, and which in combination yield the fishy and rancid character associated with oxidized fish lipid. The changes in the lipid fraction may be measured by determination of the peroxide index or by means of the thiobarbituric acid test (TBA).Some of the aldehydic secondary oxidation products react with thiobarbituric acid, forming a reddish coloured product that can be determined spectrophotometrically. Using this principle, a measure of thiobarbituric acid-reactive substances (TBA-RS) can be obtained. A good correlation of lipid oxidation products with the organoleptic degree of rancidity is however found only under special conditions

2.8 Texture measurement

Texture is an extremely important property of fish muscle, whether raw or cooked. Fish muscle may become tough as a result of frozen storage or soft and mushy as a result of autolytic degradation. Texture may be monitored organoleptically but there has for many years been a need for the development of a reliable objective rheological test which would accurately reflect the subjective evaluation of a well-trained panel of judges. Some expensive instruments and destructive samplings have been cited in the literature to measure the texture of fish flesh.

2.9 Electrical properties

It has long been known that the electrical properties of skin and tissue change after death, and this has been expected to provide a means of measuring post-mortem changes or degree of spoilage. However, many difficulties have been encountered in developing an instrument to measure such changes because of poor correlation between instrument reading and sensory analysis.

3. Bacteriological methods

Among the bacteriological tests, the total viable count is most common and is used in many variations and modifications. These methods have in common that they cannot be used direct for evaluation of fresh fish, partly because they are time-consuming, and partly because the result has most often no correlation to the storage life. But the methods can be used with advantage in research, in cases of doubtful organoleptic tests, and to determine the degree of freshness and the production hygiene of processed fish.

Direct counting of live and dead cells has been attempted, but the method requires that the bacterial count is above a certain minimum limit, and the results have not a good correlation with the storage life.

Tests involving reduction of dyes are indirect methods of measuring bacterial activity. Methylene blue, resezurin, tetrazolium derivatives and others have been used. But the evaluation of the results of these methods is very varying, and the conclusion is that they are unreliable and not generally applicable.

24
Quality Assurance of Fish

Quality Assurance (QA) is "all those planned and systematic actions necessary to provide adequate confidence that a product or service will satisfy given requirements for quality". In other words, QA is a strategic management function which establishes policies, adapts programmes to meet established goals, and provides confidence that these measures are being effectively applied. The primary function of QA is to provide confidence for both management and the ultimate customer that the company is supplying products with the desired quality which has been specified in trade agreements between the producer and the customer. Quality Control (QC) on the other hand consists of the operational techniques and activities that are used to fulfil requirements for quality. It is a tactical function which carries out the programmes established by QA. Quality control is quite often equated with "inspection" or measurements within a quality assurance programme.

Proper handling of fish between capture and delivery to the consumer is a crucial element in assuring final product quality. Standards of sanitation, method of handling and the time/temperature of holding fish are all significant quality factors. With a few exceptions, fish are considered free of pathogenic bacteria of public health significance when first caught. The presence of bacteria harmful to man generally indicates poor sanitation in handling and processing and the contamination is almost always of human or animal origin.

The quality of fish in the fish industry can be assured by: (1) Microbiological testing to assure that microbiological standards are met; (2) the Hazard Analysis and Critical Control Point (HACCP) system; and (3) certification under an internationally accepted standard (ISO 9000 series).

1. Microbiological testing

A number of microbiological tests on fish and fish products are used to detect pathogenic bacteria (*Salmonella, Staphylococcus aureus, E. coli*) or indicator organisms of faecal pollution (faecal coliforms, faecal streptococci/enterococci) or other types of general contamination or poor handling practices (coliform bacteria, faecal streptococci/enterococci, total viable count). Sampling plan and recommended microbiological limits for seafoods are given in Table 24.1, 24.2 and 24.3.

Table 24.1. Sampling plan and recommended microbiological limits for seafood (FAO)

Product	Test	Case	Plan class	No. of samples	No. of positive results	Limit per gram or per cm² m	M
Fresh and frozen fish	APC	1	3	5	3	5x10^5	10^7
	E. coli	4	3	5	3	11	500
Precooked breaded fish	APC	2	3	5	2	5 x 10^5	10^7
	E. coli	5	3	5	2	11	500
Frozen raw crustaceans	APC	1	3	5	3	10^6	10^7
	E. coli	4	3	5	3	11	500
Frozen cooked crustaceans	APC	2	3	5	2	5x10^5	10^7
	E. coli	5	3	5	2	11	500
	S. aureus	8	2	5	0	10^3	-
Cooked, chilled, and frozen crabmeat	APC	2	3	5	2	10^5	10^6
	E. coli	6	3	5	1	11	500
	S. aureus	9	2	5	0	10^3	-
Fresh and frozen bivalve molluscs	APC	3	2	5	0	5x10^5	-
	E. coli	6	2	5	0	16	-

"M" is indicating the boundary between marginally acceptable counts and unacceptable counts.
"m" divides an acceptable count from an unacceptable.
Source: http://www.fao.org/docrep/X5624E/x5624e08.htm#TopOfPage

Table 24.2. Legal limits for hazardous substances in fish and fishery production

Items	Standards
Mercury (Hg)	0.4 ppm (total Hg)
	0.3 ppm (methyl Hg)
	* Weekly intake is supposed not to be above 170 mg methyl Hg for an average adult weighing 50 kg. Diets of pregnant women and children should be more strictly controlled.
PCB	Offshore fish (edible portion): 0.5 ppm
	Inland sea fish (edible portion): 3 ppm

Items	Standards
Dieldrin (including aldrin), pesticide	0.1 ppm (hard-shelled mussels only)
Paralytic shellfish poison	4 MU*
Diarrhetic shellfish poison, (shellfish poison)	0.005 MU

* 4 Mouse Unit (MU) _ 80 µg/100 g (saxitoxin)

Table 24.3. Guidelines for pathogens

Total viable count	Not to exceed 100,000 per gram
Salmonella	Not to be detected in 25g of meat
E. coli	Less than 10 per gram
S. aureus	Less than 1000 per g
Faecal coliforms	None

Source: http://www.fao.org/docrep/X5624E/x5624e08.htm#TopOfPage

Quality assurance by microbiological testing has several disadvantages like more cost and time and the results are influenced by the number, size and nature of samples. Estimation of bacterial numbers in fish is frequently used to retrospectively assess microbiological quality or to assess the presumptive safety of the product. Therefore, other methods of quality assurance like HACCP should be applied to have assured quality including reasonable degree of protection.

2. Hazard Analysis and Critical Control Point (HACCP) system

Elements of the HACCP System

a) Identify potential hazards. Assess the risk (likelihood) of occurrence.

b) Determine the Critical Control Points (CCPs). Determine steps that can be controlled to eliminate or minimize the hazards. A CCP that can completely control a hazard, is designated CCP-1, while a CCP that minimizes, but not completely controls a hazard is designated a CCP-2.

c) Establish the criteria (tolerances, target level) that must be met to ensure that a CCP is under control.

d) Establish a monitoring system.

e) Establish the corrective action when CCP is not under control.

f) Establish procedures for verification.

g) Establish documentation and record keeping.

Identification of potential hazards: Hazards have been defined as the unacceptable contamination, growth or survival of bacteria in food that may affect food safety or quality (spoilage) or the unacceptable production or persistence in foods of substances such as toxins, enzymes or products of microbial metabolism. In other words, a hazard is a biological, chemical or physical property that may cause food to be unsafe for consumption.

Analysis of hazards constitutes the identification of hazards that could harm the consumer or cause spoilage and also a detailed understanding of how these hazards could arise. In order to be meaningful, hazard analysis must be quantitative. This requires an assessment of both severity and risk. Severity refers to the serious consequences when a hazard occurs, while risk is an estimate of the likelihood of a hazard occurring. It is only the risk that can be controlled.

Determine the CCPs: A CCP is a location, procedure or processing step at which hazards can be controlled. CCP1 is that which will ensure full control of a hazard and CCP2 is that which will minimize but not assure full control. Within the context of HACCP, the meaning of "control" at a CCP means to minimize or prevent the risk of one or more hazards by taking specific preventive measures.

Establish criteria, target levels and tolerances for each CCP: To be effective, a detailed description of all CCPs is necessary. This includes determination of criteria and specified limits or characteristics of a physical, chemical or biological nature which ensure that a product is safe and of acceptable quality.

Establish a monitoring system for each CCP: The monitoring should be able to detect deviations from specifications or criteria for corrective action to be taken. When it is not possible to monitor a critical limit on a continuous basis, it is necessary to establish a monitoring interval that will be reliable enough to indicate whether the hazard is under control. Periodic verification of sanitation controls and random microbiological tests of fish can be very valuable as means of establishing and verifying the effectiveness of control at CCPs.

Corrective actions: The system must allow for corrective action to be taken immediately when monitoring results indicate that a particular CCP is not under control. Action must be taken before the deviation leads to a safety hazard.

Verification and documentation: Verification is the use of supplementary information to check whether the HACCP system is working. Procedures may include review of CCP records, review of deviations, random sample collection and analysis. Inspections should be conducted routinely or unannounced, when the fish originating from the harbor complex is implicated as a vehicle of food-borne disease, or when requested on a consultative basis.

Application of HACCP system for fresh or frozen fish production

A starting point in design and implementation of any quality programme is to achieve a complete and correct definition and description of the product, identification of hazards and the critical limits for them must be stated followed by control of such hazards. A list of possible hazards and Critical Control Points in production and processing of fresh and frozen boneless fillets is given in Table 24.4. After the identification of all hazards, defects and Critical Control Points (CCP), an appropriate monitoring and checking system must be established at each CCP. This includes a detailed description of control measure, frequency of control and nomination of who is responsible; establishment of critical limits for each control measure; records to be kept for all actions and observations and establishment of a corrective action plan.

Table 24.4. Hazards and Critical Control Points (CCP) in production and processing of fresh and frozen boneless fish fillets

Processing flow	Hazard	Preventive Measure	Degree of control
Live fish	Contamination (chemicals, enteric pathogens) biotoxins	Avoid fishing in contaminated areas and areas where biotoxins are prevalent	CCP-2
Catch			
Catch handling	Growth of bacteria	Short handling time Avoid rough handling	CCP-1
	Gaping in fillets		CCP-2
	Discolourations		CCP-2
Chilling	Growth of bacteria	Low temperature	CCP-1
Landing			
Arrival of raw material at factory	Substandard quality entering processing	Ensure reliable source (HACCP-plan onboard or list of approved suppliers) Sensory evaluation	CCP-2
Chilling	Growth of bacteria (deterioration)	Ensure low temperature	CCP-1
Processing De-icing Washing Filleting Skinning Trimming Candling	Pieces of skin, bones and membranes left on fillet	Proper setting of machinery Instructions of personnel	CCP-2
	Visible parasites left on fillet	Ensure light intensity on candling table Frequent change of personnel	CCP-2
Weighing	Short weights/over weights	Ensure accuracy of scales	CCP-1
Packaging	Deterioration during (fresh/ frozen) storage	Ensure adequate packaging material and method (e.g. vacuum)	CCP-2
All processing steps	Growth of bacterial Contamination (enteric bacteria)	Short processing time Factory hygiene/ sanitation water quality	CCP-1 and CCP-2
Chilling/freezing-storage	Deterioration	Ensure correct (low) temperature	CCP-1

Some critical control points in fish industry

Live fish before catching: The hazards include the presence of biotoxins and contamination with chemicals and/or enteric pathogens. Control measures involve monitoring of the environment (fishing areas) for pollution and presence of biotoxins. Critical limits should be set by national governments and the results of surveys should be published at regular intervals. Corrective action includes restricted fishing in grossly polluted areas.

Catch handling: Hazards are growth of bacteria causing histamine formation and/or decomposition, discolouration and gaping in fillets. Control measures include the time from catch to chilling should be as less as possible and it is limited to maximum 3 hours. A detailed log on each haul, proper marking of boxes or containers for identification of lot, time (day and hour) for catch, catch handling time etc. should be mentioned. Corrective actions are check of product (sorting) and rejection of low quality product.

Chilling: The hazard is growth of bacteria. Control measures are continuous recording of temperature (automatic) or visual control of icing of the fish. The critical limit for fish temperature is 1°C, a log on temperature and icing observations must be kept. Corrective action is checking of fish from period out of control, sorting and rejection of low quality fish, identification of reasons for temperature out of control.

Arrival of raw material at factory: The hazard is risk of substandard quality entering processing. Control measures are check of identity of raw material, sensory assessment (visual) and control of fish temperature of all arriving raw material. No low quality fish should be accepted. Rejection of low quality fish should be done. Identify reason for low quality and the supplier of low quality fish should be changed.

Chilling/Freezing : The hazard is growth of bacteria deterioration. Control measures are continuous recording (automatic) of temperatures in chill room and check on icing of fish. Accuracy of thermometer must be checked regularly against an accurate mercury-thermometer. Critical limits are +1°C for chilled fish and -18°C for frozen fish. Chill room temperature must be about 5°C. If temperatures are out of control, all products must be inspected, sorted and low quality products should be rejected

Processing like filleting, skinning and trimming: The hazards are pieces of skin, bones and membranes left on fillet. Control measures are daily check of machinery for correct setting and daily careful visual examination. Critical limits must be specified in product specification, recording on all actions and observations, sorting and reprocessing fillets with defects.

Candling: The hazard is visible parasites on fillet. Control measures are continuous candling of all fillets and to observe for parasites. Critical limits must be set by buyer or by company policy. Fillets with visible parasites are reprocessed or rejected.

Weighing: The hazards are short weight or over weight. Control measures are frequent (1-2-3 times daily) check of weighing procedures, control weighing of samples and daily check of accuracy of scales. Reweighing of products processed when out of control. Identification of reason for deviation should be done.

Packaging: The hazard is spoilage in frozen storage if packaging (packaging material, vacuum) is inadequate. Packaging is in agreement with product specification.

All processing steps: The hazards are growth of bacteria and gross contamination by enteric pathogens. Control measure includes establishment of short processing time - which must be checked on a daily basis, control of contamination by the personal hygiene must be supervised continuously and prescribed procedures must be followed (medical certificate, report on illness, dress, etc.). Microbiological control of water quality must be carried out on a regular basis and if chlorination of water is applied, the level of free chlorine must be determined on a daily basis. Critical limits for water quality are standards for drinking water. Limit for chlorine is 0.5 mg/l. No person with gastrointestinal disorders must work in direct contact with unwrapped fish. Corrective action is microbiological testing of products and rejection of all contaminated products.

In order to be effective, the HACCP system needs to be applied from origin of food (catch) to consumption. In the case of fresh fish, the situation is most often that the fish change owner at the time of landing. Here, the new owner (the processor) must ensure that the fish are supplied from a reliable source (fisherman) who also applies the HACCP principles. If this is possible, the processor has the situation under control and needs only occasionally to verify the quality on arrival to the factory by checking quality (sensory evaluation) and temperature of fish on arrival. In this case it is not a critical situation and this step can be designated a Control Point (CP) only.

The situation is very different if the processor needs to buy fish from a number of unknown fishermen (auction system). This will require constant checking of fish quality on arrival to the factory in order to ensure compliance with all the requirements of the product. In this case, it is therefore a critical Control Point, and since there is still a risk of substandard quality entering the processing line, it is a CCP-2.

Most on-line control (continuous control of temperatures, quality of work, and sensory quality of product) should be the responsibility of the processing manager.

Application of HACCP system in fishery harbours

In most fishery harbours where there is no seafood processing other than handling of fresh fish, all that is needed may be temperature and water quality controls besides encouraging a cleanliness ethics. To ensure safety, following measures are advisable.

- Avoid exposure of landed fish to the sun and should immediately be iced.
- Appearance and odour should be inspected and fish of unacceptable quality must be rejected.
- Bacteriological testing of representative samples periodically.
- Follow a cleaning schedule for all work areas and surfaces should be cleaned as per a cleaning schedule using water containing 5 to 10 ppm of free chlorine.

- Fishes should be washed with chlorinated water followed by rinsing with clean water having 5 ppm chlorine. Ensure that slime and blood on the body surfaces are removed.
- Apply personal hygiene like exclusion of smoking and spitting in work areas and washing of hands with bactericidal soaps after fish handling or after a visit to the toilet.
- Check that water supply and treatment systems are in order.
- The harbour should be free from animals, birds and bird nests, rodents, pests, litter and other wastes. All drainage systems should be in good working order.
- Right temperature is being maintained in cold storage equipment.
- Ensure that all precaution and warning signs are readable.

Advantages of the HACCP system

The HACCP system is an ideal tool and has several advantages to assure fish safety. It is cost effective and proactive in that remedial action can be taken before a problem occurs. Control is through features that are easy to monitor such as time, temperature and appearance and the operation is controlled by persons directly involved with the fish product.

3. Certification of the International Standards Organization

For seafood processing establishments, the most relevant standards of the ISO 9000 series are the ISO 9001 and 9002. The former is a quality system standard that lays down requirements for product development, production, delivery and after sales functions. The latter concerns only production and delivery. The ISO 9003 deals with quality system requirements for final inspection and testing. ISO 9000 standards comprise:

- Management responsibility and commitment
- The presence of a documented quality system comprising the Quality Manual, Procedures and Instructions.
- Process control
- The schedule of testing and inspection and the test equipment used as per the defined specifications.
- A corrective action system to try and eliminate the causes of failure.
- Maintenance of quality records including inspection reports, analytical results and corrective action reports
- Internal quality audits on a regular basis
- Training of staff, personal hygiene, cleaning and disinfection

Marketing merits, reduced quality costs and higher efficiency are the main advantages of the quality system that contribute to a higher profitability. Quality systems such as the ISO 9000 series serve to establish confidence in the customer.

25

Fish and Fishery Products and their Bacteriological Examination

Fish and Fishery Products

Fish: Any of the cold-blooded (ectothermic) aquatic vertebrates. Amphibians and aquatic reptiles are not included.

Shellfish: Those species of aquatic mollusks and crustaceans that are commonly used for food.

Whole fish (or round fish): Fish as captured, ungutted.

Lean fish (white fish): Fish in which the main reserves of fat are in the liver and less than 2 percent fat in the body tissue.

Fatty fish: Fish in which the main reserves of fat are in the body tissue and the fat content is more than 2 percent.

Fresh fish: Fish or fishery products that have received no preserving treatment other than chilling.

Frozen fish: Fish that have been subjected to a freezing process sufficient to reduce the temperature of the whole product to a level low enough to preserve the inherent quality of the fish and that have been maintained at this low temperature (–18°C), uneviscerated and eviscerated during transportation, storage and distribution up to and including the time of final sale.

Frozen surimi: The fish protein product for further processing that has been processed by heading, gutting and cleaning fresh fish, and mechanically separating the edible muscle from the skin and bone. The minced fish muscle is then washed, refined, dewatered, mixed with cryoprotective food ingredients and frozen.

Quick-frozen fish products

Batter: Liquid preparation from ground cereals, spices, salt, sugar and other ingredients and/or additives for coating. Typical batter types are non-leavened batter and leavened batter.

Breading: Dry breadcrumbs or other dry preparations, mainly from cereals with colourants and other ingredients, used for the final coating of fishery products. Typical breading types are: free-flowing breading, coarse breading, and flour-type breading.

Coating: Covering the surface of a fishery product with batter and/or breading.

Pre-frying: Frying of breaded and battered fishery products in an oil bath in a way so that the core remains frozen.

Sawing: Cutting (by hand or fully mechanized) of regular shapes of fish blocks into pieces suitable for later coating.

Fillet: A slice of fish of irregular size and shape removed from the carcass by cuts made parallel to the backbone.

Steak: A section of fish removed by cutting approximately at right angles to the backbone.

Minced fish: Comminuted flesh produced by separation from skin and bones.

Canned fish: Commercially sterile fish/shellfish in hermetically sealed containers. Hermetically sealed containers are the containers that are sealed to protect the content against the entry of micro-organisms during and after heat treatment. Commercial sterility of thermally processed fish food is achieved by application of heat, sufficient, alone or in combination with other appropriate treatments, to render the food free from micro-organisms capable of growing in the food under normal non-refrigerated conditions at which the food is likely to be held during distribution and storage.

Salted and dried salted fish: Salting is mainly caused by a decrease in the water activity. The fish is placed in brine solution for a period of sufficient length for the fish tissue to absorb a specific quantity of salt. The process for injecting brine directly into the fish flesh is sometimes practiced. Dry-salting is another process of mixing fish with suitable food-grade salt and stacking the fish in such a manner that the resulting brine drains away.

Dried fish: Dried fish is in nearly the same situation as salted fish. In this case it is also a reduction of the water activity that has the preserving effect. Often the two methods are combined in salted-dried fish products.

Smoked fish, smoked-flavoured fish and smoke-dried fish

Smoking: It is a process of treating fish by exposing it to smoke from smouldering wood or plant materials. The process of smoking is usually characterized by an integrated combination of salting, drying, heating and smoking steps in a smoking chamber.

Smoking by regenerated smoke: It is a process of treating fish by exposing it to smoke which is regenerated by atomizing smoke condensate in a smoking chamber under the time and temperature conditions similar to those for hot or cold smoking. Smoke condensates are products obtained by controlled thermal degradation of wood in a limited supply of oxygen (pyrolysis), subsequent condensation of the resultant smoke vapours, and fractionation of the resulting liquid products.

Smoke drying: It is a process in which fish is treated by combined smoking and drying steps to such an extent that the final product can be stored and transported without refrigeration and to achieve a water activity of 0.75 or less (10% of moisture or less), as necessary to control bacteria pathogen or fungal spoilage.

Drying: It is a process in which the moisture content in the fish is decreased to appropriate required characteristics under controlled hygienic conditions.

Hot smoking: It is a process in which fish is smoked at an appropriate combination of temperature and time sufficient to cause the complete coagulation of the proteins in the fish flesh. Hot smoking is generally sufficient to kill parasites, to destroy non-sporulated bacterial pathogens and to injure spores of human health concern.

Cold smoking: It is a process of treating fish with smoke using a time/temperature combination that will not cause significant coagulation of the proteins in the fish flesh but that will cause some reduction of the water activity.

Smoke flavours: These are either smoke condensates or artificial flavour blends prepared by mixing chemically defined substances in known amounts or any combination of both (smoke preparations).

Smoke flavouring: It is a process in which fish or fish preparations are treated with smoke flavour. The smoke flavour can be applied by any technology (*e.g.* dipping, spraying, injecting, soaking).

Shrimps and prawns

Fresh shrimps: Freshly caught shrimps that have received no preserving treatment or that have been preserved only by chilling. It does not include freshly cooked shrimps.

Raw headless shrimps: Raw shrimps with heads removed and the shell on.

Peeled shrimps: Shrimps with heads and all shell removed.

Deveined shrimps: All the shrimps that have been peeled, the back of the peeled segments of the shrimps have been opened out and the gut ("vein") removed.

Live and raw bivalve molluscs: These are conditioned by placing live bivalve mollusks in tanks, floats or natural sites to remove sand, mud or slime and improve product acceptability. After conditioning, they are washed, cleaned, graded and packaged as live bivalve mollusks fit for human consumption.

The process of subjecting bivalve molluscs in the shell to any form of heat treatment, such as steam, hot water or dry heat, for a short period to facilitate rapid removal of meat from the shell for the purpose of shucking is called as 'heat shocking'.

The reduction of microorganisms to a level acceptable for direct consumption by the process of holding live bivalve mollusks for a period of time under approved, controlled conditions in natural or artificial seawater suitable for the process, which may be treated or untreated is called 'depuration'.

Bacteriological examination

The aim of microbiological examinations of fish products is to evaluate the possible presence of bacteria or organisms of public health significance and to give an impression of the hygienic quality of the fish including temperature abuse and hygiene during handling and processing. Microbiological data will in general not give any information about eating quality and freshness.

Bacteriological examination can be done by different methods and for different types of organisms depending upon the type of fishery product. The examination is done for spoilage organisms, pathogens and for other types of organisms as explained below.

Bacterial types

Spoilage bacteria: The total number of bacteria on fish rarely indicates sensoric quality or expected storage characteristics. However, it is recognized that certain bacteria are the main cause of spoilage. Different peptone rich substrates containing ferric citrate have been used for detection of H_2S-producing bacteria such as *Shewanella putrefaciens,* which can be seen as black colonies due to precipitation of iron sulphide. Ambient spoilage is often caused by members of Vibrionaceae that also will form black colonies on an iron agar to which an organic sulphur source is added (e.g. Iron Agar). No selective or indicative medium exists for the *Pseudomonas* spp. that spoils some tropical and freshwater fish or for *Photobacterium phosphoreum* that spoil packed fresh fish.

Pathogenic bacteria: Several pathogenic bacteria may either be present in the environment or contaminate the fish during handling. The presence or absence of pathogenic bacteria is now often evaluated by methods based on immuno- or molecular biology techniques. Culture methods can also be employed but they are time consuming.

Bacteria in salted fish: In salted fish, all common microorganisms will grow at a salt concentration below 10%, though the growth of most organisms is much delayed in the upper part of concentration area, except for some halophilic and salt tolerant organisms. *Clostridium* can cause spoilage in meat and produce toxins at concentrations under 6.3%. Between 6.3 and 7.2% toxin production may take place without apparent spoilage, but above 7.2% nothing will happen. *Salmonella* is restrained at 5, *E. coli* at 6-7 and faecal streptococci at 10-11g sodium chloride per 100 ml of water. At concentrations between 10 and 20%, common microorganisms will grow, but no food poisoning bacteria, except Staphylococcus and growth of salt-tolerant and halophiles.

Salt-tolerant organisms can grow at low salt concentrations (about 0.5) as well as at very high concentrations. Important salt tolerant species are *Micrococcus* and

Bacillus. Halophilic organisms can grow only at high concentrations of salt. They include *Pseudomonas, Sarcina, Halobacterium, Micrococcus* that produce red pigment and spoil the fish. The extremely halophilic bacteria are able to grow in saturated brines, but are killed nearly momentarily if they are suspended in fresh water.

In the contents of salt and water in salted fish are correct, the microbiological test should find halophilic and salt-tolerant bacteria, as the contents of these will determine the shelf life of the product. Staphylococci may also cause trouble and should be examined for this pathogen.

Bacteria in dried fish: From a microbiological point of view, dried fish is in nearly the same situation as salted fish. Drying alone inhibits the bacteria, but does not always kill them. There is a possibility of the development of toxins or pathogenic organisms if the unwanted bacteria have been introduced through poor hygienic treatment, if the processing time has been too long, if the storage has been inadequate, and/or the consumers do not treat the fish carefully. It is more effective and safer to keep a strict control on the processing and storage practice rather than bacteriological examination of dried fish products.

Bacteria in smoked fish: In smoked fish products, the microorganisms are inhibited due to drying and chemical treatment and may be killed by heat. Smoking is often done to give a special flavour and also as a direct preserving treatment. Hence, the types of bacteria depend on the processing method. If the product is given a short time exposure to high temperature, spores of certain organism may survive and in such cases examination should be for these spores like that of Clostridium botulinum.

Bacteria in canned product: Canning has the specific purpose to kill present microorganisms and to avoid secondary contamination by enclosing the product in tight containers. Examination of such products is done to determine if any organisms have survived. In practice, complete sterility is not attempted, but only the so-called commercial sterility, which means that very few spores are allowed to survive that, cannot develop during normal handling and storage of the product.

Examination of canned fish products is made to make surviving organisms grow by preincubating at 30°C and sometimes also to 50°-55°C for some time. If any organisms are found by following examination techniques, the product should highly suspected of not being sufficiently sterile. Secondly spore forming organisms have the best possibility of surviving as the spores are highly heat-resistant. Among the spore forming groups *Clostridium botulinum* is important from health aspect while hemophilic spore forming bacteria are also important as they inhabit canneries around leaking steam pipelines of the like.

Bacteriological media

In the selection of media for bacteriological examinations the composition of the microflora and the special composition of the fish should be taken into consideration, as these factors have the effect that some very commonly used media are not the most ideal for the examination of fish products.

For total viable count, plate count agar is most often used, as it is a good nutrient medium for practically all types of bacteria. But it has been found that the addition of gelatin in amounts of 1% or up to 4% has favourable effect on growth, since both the number of colonies and the rate of their occurrence are increased. Similarly Iron agar is considered as a more enriched nutrient agar as it gives significantly higher counts than PCA. Furthermore, the iron agar yields also the number of hydrogen sulphide producing bacteria, which in some fish products are the specific spoilage bacteria.

The violet red bile agar medium, commonly used for coliform bacteria, is not suitable for the examination of fish products. A large number of Gram-negative bacteria (other than coliforms) are able to grow in the medium where they cause precipitation through acid production from the content of lower carbohydrates in the fish, hence giving false positive reactions of coliforms. A more suitable medium is lauryl sulphate tryptose broth, which may be used with Durham tubes according to a most probable number method. For demonstration of thermo-tolerant *E. coli* type I (44°C) EC broth (Eijkman's lactose broth) combined with an IMViC test may be used. MacConkey broth may be used for both types of *E. coli*.

Faecal streptococci/enterococci can be determined by surface spreading on Slanetz agar. For staphylococci, polymyxcin blood agar may be used possibly combined with other medium like Carter's agar medium. *Vibrio parahaemolyticus* is of special interest in case of cross contamination as they are able to multiply very rapidly at a suitable temperature. The organism can be cultivated on ordinary media to which ½ to 1% sodium chloride has been added.

Bacteriological methods

Traditional bacteriological examinations are laborious, time consuming, and costly and require skill in execution and interpretation of the results. It is recommended that such analyses be limited in number and extent. Various rapid microbiological methods are now available and some of these automated procedures may be of use when large numbers of samples are to be analyzed (Table 25.1).

Total aerobic count (TAC) is synonymous with standard plate count (SPC). Common plate count agar (PCA) is still the substrate most widely used for determination of SPC. However, when examining several types of seafood a more nutrient rich agar (Iron Agar) gives significantly higher counts than PCA. Incubation temperature at and above 30°C are inappropriate when examining seafood products held at chill temperatures. Pour plating and 3-4 days incubation at 25°C is relevant when examining products where psychrotrophs are the most important organisms, whereas the products carrying psychrophilic *Photobacterium phosphoreum* should be examined by surface plating and incubation at maximum 15°C.

Microscopic examination of foods is a rapid way of estimating bacterial levels. By phase contrast microscopy the level of bacteria in a sample can be determined within one log-unit. The staining of cells with acridine orange and detection by fluorescence microscopy has earned widespread acceptance as the direct epifluorescence filter technique (DEFT). Whilst microscopic methods are very rapid, the low sensitivity must be considered their major drawback.

Bacterial numbers have been estimated in foods by measuring the amount of bacterial adenosine triphosphate (ATP) or by measuring the amount of endotoxin (Gram-negative bacteria) by the Limulus amoebocytes lysate (LAL) test. The former is very rapid but difficulties exist in separating bacterial and somatic ATP.

Several methods (microcalorimetry, dye reduction, conductance and capacitance) used for rapid estimation of bacterial numbers are based on the withdrawal of a sample, incubation at high temperature (20-25°C) and detection of a given signal. Heat generated by the sample and conductance and capacitance measurements of the change in electrical properties of the sample, as compared to a sterile control, is registered in microcalorimetery and conductance and capacitance tests respectively. The time taken before a significant change occurs in the measured parameter (heat, conductance, etc.) is called the Detection Time (DT). The DT is inversely related to the initial number of bacteria, i.e., early reaction indicates a high bacterial count in the sample. The disadvantage of these methods is that only a small fraction of the microflora gives rise to the signal and care must be taken in selection of incubation temperature and substrate.

Table 25.1. Methods for determination of bacterial content in seafood

Method	Temperature, °C	Incubation	Sensitivity, cfu/g
Plate count or Iron agar	15–25	3–5 days	10
Micro-colony-DEFT	15–30	3–4 hours	10^4–10^5
DEFT	–	30 min.	10^4–10^5
ATP	–	1 hour	10^4–10^5
Limulus lysate test	–	2–3 hours	10^3–10^4
Micro-calorimetry/ dye reduction/ conductance/ capacitance	15–25	4–40 hours	10

Standards

It is more reasonable and often psychologically convenient to construct standards which work as guidelines and which are not strictly enforced. The guidelines should work in such a way that if the fish product is passed (if the eating quality is not bad, and if no health risks are involved), the product should not be rejected, but the reason for the fault should be found and corrected. Codex Committee on Fish and Fishery Products (CCFFP) has issued several guidelines on fish and fishery products that may be referred by the readers.

26

Quality Control in Fish Industry

Quality control (QC) can be defined simply as 'maintenance of quality at a level that satisfies the customer and that is economical to the producer or seller'. QC minimizes customer complaints about quality, and hence avoids loss in business. Since fish is more variable than most other foods, the need to apply QC is correspondingly greater. Inspection and Process Control are parts of quality control. Inspection means examination of raw material or finished product to make sure it meets the specification while Process Control means checking the process to ensure that all operations on the fish are done correctly and consistently to a set standard that is usually described in the process specification. Process specification is a written description, mainly for the benefit of the producer, of how the product is to be made.

The cost of mandatory inspection or QC is inescapable but this cost must be not more and preferably much less than the benefit that accrues from its operation. The cost should not be more than about 1 percent of sale value, and may well be only a fraction of this.

Stages of application of Quality Control

1. Drawing up a product specification

This is the first stage and is primarily be determined by the customer. However, QC staff can advise to determine it. A product specification includes at least a description of the product and of the quality factors the product should possess. Important quality factors include appearance, odour and flavour, texture, ingredients and composition, packaging, defects and blemishes, size and weight. In the canned fish, heat processing while in fish meal, composition is a product specification.

2. Inspecting or testing raw material

This is the stage 2 and is the job of quality controller. The processing factors that most affect quality in the fish industry are time, temperature, contamination, damage or deterioration, hygiene and sanitation, equipment and methods, packing for product appeal, correctness of fill. Raw material and packaging specifications should be included in the process specification if they are not described elsewhere.

Time: It is desirable to process the fish quickly because of its perishable nature. The time the fish has taken to pass through the processing like chilling and freezing should be checked. Freezing times can be important to quality maintenance, and in the same way maximum cold storage times for raw material or finished product may be stated.

Contamination: Contamination by materials like dirt, scales, bones, blood, water, lubricating oil, unpleasant odours and flavours, and hair should be noted and the main methods of avoiding contamination should be emphasized.

Damage or deterioration: Damage or deterioration like fish being trodden on, knocked, bruised, pierced with hooks, bent while stiff in rigor, or squashed, drying or freezer burn, glazing or suitable packaging may be specified. Permitted additives and their manner of use might be specified and checked, and conditions of storage of raw material or product may also be controlled under this head.

Hygiene and sanitation: Being food, fish should be handled hygienically.

Equipment and methods: The equipment to do a specific job should be specified; for example a deboning machine that produces material of the required quality, or a labeling machine that affixes labels of the right type, may be specified and evaluated.

Packing for product appeal: Process specifications that make the product attractive and appeal to the eye should be described. This includes neat cutting and trimming, arranging the fish attractively in the pack, filling the pack with the right number, size and weight of fish, and the manner of labelling and stapling can be described.

Yield and efficiency: Maximum yield and high efficiency depend on close supervision of such things as skill of filleters and other hand workers, machine settings, and weight changes during processing due to drying, drip loss, water absorption, and uptake of salt, polyphosphate and cooking oil.

3. Processing

Stage 3 involves monitoring the process at points where the quality controller or fish technologist knows quality may be affected. There are two kinds of operations that should be checked, the work of operatives and the settings on equipment. Operation checks can sometimes be combined with product checks; for example where both the way in which a fish is to be trimmed and the form of the trimmed fish are specified, the two can be checked together. On the other hand, checking a temperature recorder on a cold store is solely an operation check.

4. Inspecting or testing finished products

Stage 4 involves checking the product to make sure it meets the product specification. Methods of inspecting and testing quality are of two main types, sensory or organoleptic tests, and instrumental and chemical tests. The sensory type employs only the human senses of sight, smell, taste and touch, whereas the second employs instruments like thermometers and chemical apparatus etc. In the fish industry sensory methods are used most widely because they need less time to assess the quality of fish. However, sensory methods have disadvantages; for example the results can be variable, and the operator may be subject to outside influences and fatigue. Chemical methods of measuring freshness are available that can largely replace the sensory methods. However, these are generally too elaborate and expensive for use in routine. These may therefore be employed in the instances of doubt or dispute about the sensory measurements where these can serve as reference methods.

Sensory methods are of two types, subjective and objective. With a subjective method, a personal assessment is made; for example the inspector may say whether he likes the sample of fish or not, how much he likes or dislikes it etc. With an objective sensory method, the inspector attempts to assess the fish without prejudice by concentrating his attention on specific quality factors, for example degree of saltiness. To reduce personal bias further, it is often advisable to have a group of experts examining the fish; the independent assessments of the members are then averaged statistically. Such a group is loosely called a taste panel. The number of objective tests, whether sensory or instrumental, available for the assessment of fish is still small; thus subjective methods, despite their disadvantages, are commonly used in QC. Some of them are described below.

Freshness: Freshness is a most important quality factor to the consumer; thus assessment of freshness is vital in QC. In general the sensory method of assessing freshness is the best at present for QC purposes. As fish spoils, its smell, taste, appearance and feel go through characteristic and well defined stages that trained experts or experienced staff can consistently recognize. Freshness is now expressed in numbers for product specifications and standards.

Chemical methods can assess freshness sufficiently well for QC purposes and they measure the concentration of certain chemical substances in the flesh and, since the sample is destroyed in the process, they cannot be used to test every fish in a batch. The concentration of the chemicals changes in a regular manner as the fish spoils, so that the level of concentration indicates the freshness. All the methods require the use of a laboratory or fairly elaborate facilities. The main methods used are the measurement of trimethylamine, TMA, hypoxanthine, volatile reducing substances, and total volatile bases, TVB. The methods do not apply to all species and products alike, but the method used widely is TMA. The maximum TMA value and occasionally the maximum TVB value are currently mentioned in some specifications.

Species: The distinguishing features of whole fish of different species make identifications and control of supply fairly straightforward, but identification of skinless fillets, canned fish and fish in products like fish cakes is more of a problem. A chemical method, known as electrophoretic method, is now available which can be used to identify with certainty the species in an unknown sample. The method is applicable to frozen, cooked and canned products as well as to wet fish.

Condition and texture: This category includes factors like plumpness, thinness, toughness, softness, oiliness, greasiness, wateriness, presence of roe or milt. Most of these can only be assessed subjectively, and this is all that is necessary. The fat content of the flesh or of the whole fish for species like herring and sprat can be measured, and there are sensory scoring schemes for measuring degree of toughness of flesh, particularly for frozen fish.

Blemishes: Blemishes here mean mainly intrinsic defects, ones found in the raw material, but a few arise from defects in handling; all are assessed by eye.The presence of dirt or gross filth,bruises and blood marks, chalky or gaping flesh, parasites, and crystals should be checked.

Skin, bones and belly membrane: Inspection is made in the same manner as for blemishes. The presence of bones after filleting or trimming is detected by sight and touch.

Off odours and flavours: Fish with strong objectionable odours are normally detected and discarded during processing. Otherwise two kinds of unpleasant odour and flavour can be described; these are the so-called cold storage odour or flavour of white fish, and rancidity in fatty fish. Sensory scoring systems are available and may be specified for the assessment of these and similar defects. In addition it is always good practice to taste the product from time to time to reduce the chance of off flavours escaping detection. Cold storage odour and flavour can be assessed indirectly by chemical tests, for example by measuring the concentration of formaldehyde in frozen cod, or by measuring the peroxide value in frozen herring.

Bacterial count: Bacterial counts are necessary in QC for two reasons. First, the presence of harmful microorganisms in fish products that may cause illness, and secondly the presence of large numbers of organisms indicating either gross contamination or spoilage. Thus a low or moderate incidence of microorganisms is one indicator of good quality.Bacterial testing can be time consuming and expensive and need laboratories. Representative samples are taken and interpretations are made according to the standards/limits available to assess the quality.

Salt content: The acceptable amount of salt in fish products is usually 1-4 percent, but for some products it may be 1.8-2.5 percent. Process control may involve either sensory or chemical tests. A group of people independently assess the degree of saltiness; a trained panel is not normally necessary. Chemical or physical tests can be used when the salt content is closely specified.

Additives and colouring materials: The use of additives and colouring materials is governed by legislation Examples of the use of additives to improve the product include the use of polyphosphates to prevent drip loss, antioxidants to control rancidity, and flavourings. Most foreign countries have their own legislation, and exporters should be aware of the relevant laws.

Colour and gloss: These factors greatly influence the appeal of the product to the consumer. Usually these are assessed by eye. Descriptive scales can be used for shades of colour and degree of gloss. Standard shade cards can be used for matching.

Shape and size: The shape and size of frozen blocks of fillets and of fish fingers and portions have to be controlled within specified limits; in particular the edges of blocks, fingers or portions need to be at right angles to the faces. Defects are assessed by eye or by measurement.

Minced fish content: The amount of minced or fragmented fish allowable in a frozen fish block is sometimes specified. A representative sample of blocks has to be thawed, the fillets separated from the mince or fragments, and the two lots weighed.

Fish content: The amount of fish in a fish product may sometimes be specified. The fish content can be controlled straightforwardly during processing. Occasional checking may be necessary on samples of the product; this is done by analysing the fish protein content.

Composition: The exact chemical or nutritional composition of fish and fish products is not normally an important quality factor, but for herring products and for fish meal the composition may be specified. For herring products, and particularly kippers, the raw material should have a specified minimum fat content to ensure a good product. Protein and fat content of fish meal are important in determining the nutritive value to animals, and the composition thus determines the selling price to some extent. Composition is always assessed by destructive chemical methods.

5. Recording, reporting and action

Decisions taken as a result of QC can be important and occasionally may be vital; it is therefore important to keep adequate records. Records should be sent quickly in understandable form to those who will make the decisions.

Bibliography

Abera L, Getahun A and Lemma B (2014). Composition of commercially important fish species and some perspectives into the biology of the African Catfish *Clarias gariepinus* (Burchell), Lake Ziway, Ethiopia. Int. J. Adv. Res. 2: 864-871.

Abowei JFN and Briyai OF (2011). A review of some bacteria diseases in Africa culture fisheries. Asian J. Med. Sci. 3: 206-217.

Ahne W, Bjorklund HV, Essbauer S, Fijan N, Kurath G and Winton JR (2002). Spring viremia of carp (SVC). Dis. Aquat. Organ. 52: 261-272.

Akinsanya B, Hassan AA and Adeogun AO (2008). Gastrointestinal helminth parasites of the fish *Synodontis clarias* (Siluriformes: Mochokidae) from Lekki lagoon, Lagos, Nigeria. Int. J. Trop. Biol. 56: 2021-2026.

Allumma MI and Idowu RT (2011). Prevalence of gills helminth of *Clarias gariepinus* in Baga side of Lake Chad. J. Appl. Sci. Environ. Manage. 15: 47-50.

Amare A, Alemayehu A and Aylate A (2014). Prevalence of internal parasitic helminthes infected *Oreochromis niloticus* (Nile Tilapia), *Clarias gariepinus* (African Catfish) and *Cyprinus carpio* (Common Carp) in Lake Lugo (Hayke), Northeast Ethiopia. J. Aquac. Res. Development 5: 233. doi: 10.4172/2155-9546.1000233.

Anantaphruti MT (2001). Parasitic contaminants in food. Southeast Asian J. Trop. Med. Public Health 2: 218-228.

Anonymous (2011). Common tropical fish diseases: The symptoms, diseases, and remedies for the most common fish maladies. http://www.fishchannel.com/fish-health/disease-prevention/common-freshwater-fish-diseases.aspx.

Bagnis R, Berglund F, Elias PS, van Esch GJ, Halstead BW and Kojima K (1970). Problems of toxicants in marine food products. 1. Marine biotoxins. Bull. Wld. Hlth. Org. 42: 69-88.

Borgstrom G (ed) (1961-1965). Fish as food. Vol.I-IV. Academic Press, London.

Bullock GL (1972). Studies on selected myxobacteria pathogenic for fishes and on bacterial gill disease in hatchery reared salmonids. Technical Paper 60, U.S. Fish and Wildlife Service, Washington, DC.

Bullock GL, Cipriano RC and Snieszko SF (1983). Furunculosis and other diseases caused by *Aeromonas salmonicida*. Paper 133, US Fish and Wildlife Service.http://digitalcommons.unl.edu/usfwspubs/133.

Bullock GL and Herman RL (1988). Bacterial kidney disease of salmonid fishes caused by *Renibacterium salmoninarum*. Fish Disease Leaflet No. 78. U.S. Fish and Wildlife Service, Washington, DC.

Camus A (2014). Fish pox (Cyprinid Herpesvirus I). http://www.petplace.com/article/fish/general/when-your-fish-is-sick/fish-pox-cyprinid-herpesvirus-i.

Cervinka S, Vitovec J, Lom J, Hoska J and Kubu F (1974). Dermocystidiosis - a gill disease of the carp due to *Dermocystidium cyprini* n. sp. J. Fish Biol. 6: 689–699.

Chichester CO and Graham HD (eds) (1973). Microbial safety of fishery products. Academic Press, New York.

Cipriano RC and Bullock GL (2001). Furunculosis and other diseases caused by *Aeromonas salmonicida*. Fish Disease Leaflet 66, US Fish and Wildlife Service, Washington, DC. https://articles.extension.org/sites/default/files/w/b/b7/Furunculosis.pdf.

Codex Alimantarius Commission (2012). Code of practice for fish and fishery products, 2nd edition. Joint WHO/FAO Codex Alimantarius Commission.World Health Organization, Geneva.

Colorni A (1992). A systemic mycobacteriosis in the European sea bass, *Dicentrarchus labrax*, cultured in Eilat (red sea). Isr. J Aquacult. 44: 75-81.

Connell JJ (2001). Quality control in the fish industry. Torry Advisory Note No. 58. Ministry of Agriculture, Fisheries and Food, Torry Research Station. http://www.fao.org/wairdocs/tan/x5934E/x5934e00.htm.

Edema CU, Okaka CE, Oboh IP and Okogub BO (2008). A preliminary study of parasitic infections of some fishes from Okhuo River, Benin City, Nigeria. Int. J. Biomed. Hlth. Sci. 4: 107-112.

Evensen O and Santi N (2008). Infectious pancreatic necrosis virus. In: Mahy BWJ and Van Regenmortel MHV (eds) Encyclopaedia of virology. Elsevier, Oxford, UK, 83–89.

Ewing EW, Ross AJ, Brenner DJ and Fanning GR (1978). *Yersinia ruckeri* sp. nov., the redmouth (RM) bacterium. Int. J. Syst. Bacteriol. 28:37-44.

FAO (1997). Fish disease prevention and treatment. ftp://ftp.fao.org/fi/cdrom//FAO_Training/General/x6709e/x6709e15.htm.

FAO (1997). Principles for the establishment and application of microbiological criteria for foods. http://www.fao.org/docrep/w6419e/w6419e04.htm.

FAO (2009). Epizootic ulcerative syndrome (EUS). Food and Agriculture Organization of the United Nations, Rome. http://www.fao.org/docrep/016/i0777e/i0777e.pdf.

FAO (2010). The state of the world fisheries and aquaculture 2010. FAO Fisheries and Aquaculture Department, Food and Agriculture Organization of the United Nations, Rome. http://www.fao.org/3/a-i1820e.pdf.

FAO (2014). FAO Yearbook 2012. Fishery and Aquaculture Statistics 2012. Food and Agriculture Organization of the United Nations, Rome. http://www.fao.org/3/a-i3740t.pdf.

FAO (2016). Fisheries and aquaculture topics. Quality and safety of fish and fish products. Fact Sheets. FAO Fisheries and Aquaculture Department, Food and Agriculture Organization of the United Nations, Rome.http://www.fao.org/fishery/quality_safety/en#container.

Fryer JL and Sanders JE (1981). Bacterial kidney disease of salmonid fish. Ann. Rev. Microbial. 35: 273-298.

FWC (2016). Fish Anatomy. Florida Fish and Wildlife Conservation Commission, Florida. http://myfwc.com/fishing/freshwater/fishing-tips/anatomy.

Haenen OLM, Way K, Bergmann SM and Ariel E (2004). The emergence of koi herpesvirus and its significance to European aquaculture. Bull. Eur. Assoc. Fish Pathol. 24: 293–307.

Haenen OL, Evans JJ and Berthe F (2013). Bacterial infections from aquatic species: potential for and prevention of contact zoonoses. Rev. Sci. Tech. 32: 497-507.

Hanson L, Dishon A and Kotler M (2011). Herpesviruses that infect fish. Viruses 3: 2160–2191. doi: 10.3390/v3112160.

Healy GR (1970). Trematodes transmitted to man by fish, frogs, and crustacea. J. Wildl. Dis. 6(4): 255-261.

Hoffman GL (1970). Control and treatment of parasitic diseases of freshwater fishes. Fish Disease Leaflet 28. U.S. Fish and Wildlife Service. https://pubs.er.usgs.gov/publication/fdl28.

Hussain MM and Uddin MH (1997). Quality control and marketing of fish and fish products: Needs for infrastructure and legal support. http://www.fao.org/docrep/X5625E/x5625e0f.htm.

Janko AM (2014). Fish production, consumption and management in Ethiopia. Res. J. Agric. Environ. Manage. 3: 460-466.

Kreuzer R (ed)(1971). Fish inspection and quality control, microbial safety of fishery products. Academic Press, New York.

Kumar G, Menanteau-Ledouble S, Mona S and El-Matbouli M (2015). *Yersinia ruckeri*, the causative agent of enteric redmouth disease in fish. Vet. Res. 46: 103. DOI: 10.1186/s13567-015-0238-4.

Langdon JS and Humphrey JD (1987). Epizootic haematopoietic necrosis a new viral disease in redfin perch, *Percafluviatilis* L., in Australia. J. Fish Dis. 10: 289–298.

Leatherland J and Woo PTK (eds) (2010). Fish diseases and disorders. Vol. 2: Non-infectious disorders. CAB International, Oxfordshire.

Lehane L and Rawlin GT (2000). Topically acquired zoonoses from fish: A review. Med. J. Aust. 173: 256-259.

Lom J and Dykova I (1992). Protozoan parasites of fishes. Elsevier, Amsterdam.

Lowry T and Smith SA (2007). Aquatic zoonoses associated with food, bait, ornamental, and tropical fish. J. Am. Vet. Med. Assoc. 231: 876-880.

Maria Declercq AM, Haesebrouck F, van den Broeck W, Bossier P and Decostere A (2013). Columnaris disease in fish: A review with emphasis on bacterium-host interactions.Vet. Res. 44: 27. https://doi.org/10.1186/1297-9716-44-27.

McDaniel D (1979). Procedures for the detectionand identification of certain fish pathogens. American Fisheries Society, Fish Health Section, Bethesda, MD.

Mohanty BR and Sahoo PK (2007). Edwardsiellosis in fish: A brief review. J. Biosci. 32: 1331-1344.

Myers BJ (1970). Nematodes transmitted to man by fish and aquatic mammals. J. Wildl. Dis. 6: 266-271.

Noga EJ (2010). Fish disease: Diagnosis and treatment. 2nd edition. Wiley-Blackwell. Ames, Iowa.

OIE (2017). Manual of diagnostic tests for aquatic animals. World Organization for Animal Health, Paris, France. http://www.oie.int/international-standard-setting/aquatic-manual/access-online/.

Shotts EB Jr (1987). Bacterial diseases of fish associated with human health. Vet. Clin. North. Am. Small Anim. Pract.17: 241-247.

Snieszko SF and Axelrod HR (eds) (1971). Diseases of fishes. TFH Publications, Inc.

Spliethoff PC, Wudneh T, Tariku E and Senbeta G (2009). Past, current and potential production of fish in lake Ziway. Capacity Development and Institutional Change Programme, Wageningen International, Netherlands.

Swift DR (1993). Aquaculture training manual, 2nd edition. Wiley-Blackwell.

Thomas LE (1972). Diseases of fish. Academic Press, London.

Tobback E, Decostere A, Hermans K, Haesebrouck F and Chiers K (2007). *Yersinia ruckeri* infections in salmonid fish. J. Fish Dis. 30: 257–268.

Tucker CS (1985). Channel catfish culture. Elsevier Science Publishers, Amsterdam.

Untergasser G, Untergasser Dieter, Herbert R, Axelrod and Herbert R (1992). Handbook of fish diseases, TFH Publications, Inc.

van Rensburg CJ, van As JG and King PH (2013). New records of digenean parasites of *Clarias gariepinus* (Pisces: Clariidae) from the Okavango Delta, Botswana, with description of *Thaparotrema botswanensis* sp. n. (Plathelminthes: Trematoda). Afr. Invertebr. 54: 431–446.

Weir M, Rajic A, Dutil L, Cernicchiaro N, Uhland FC, Mercier B and Tusevljak NB (2012). Zoonotic bacteria, antimicrobial use and antimicrobial resistance in ornamental fish: A systematic review of the existing research and survey of aquaculture-allied professionals. Epidemiol. Infect. 140: 192-206.

Wetzel RG and Gopal B (eds) (1999). Limnology in developing countries. Vol. 2. International Scientific Publications, New Delhi.

Willoughby LG (1978). Saprolegniasis of salmonid fish in Windermere. J. Fish Dis. 1: 51–57.

Wolf K (1988). Fish viruses and fish viral diseases. Cornell University Press, Ithaca, New York.

Woo PTK (2006). Fish diseases and disorders. Vol. 1: Protozoan and metazoan infections. CAB International, Oxfordshire.

Woo PTK and Bruno DW (eds) (2011). Fish diseases and disorders. Vol. 3: Viral, bacterial and fungal infections. CAB International, Oxfordshire.

www.ingramcontent.com/pod-product-compliance
Ingram Content Group UK Ltd.
Pitfield, Milton Keynes, MK11 3LW, UK
UKHW020816290926
15470UKWH00003B/1188

9 789387 057289